PICTORIAL GUIDE TO

POTTERY & PORCELAIN MARKS

Chad
Lage

COLLECTOR BOOKS
A Division of Schroeder Publishing Co., Inc.

ON THE COVER:

Front:
1. Unknown Maker (late 1800s) 2. Clew, James and Ralph (1818 – 1834) 3. Laughlin, Homer (1940 – 1965)
4. University of North Dakota (1892 – 1963) 5. Schiller, W. and Sons (1895+)

Back:
1. Meakin, Alfred (1897+) 2. Pillivuyt, Charles (1920s+) 3. Ridgway Pottery (1912+) 4. McCoy (1940 – 1966)
5. Buffalo China (1923) 6. Limoges; Gerard, Dufraisseix, and Abbot (1937 – 1976)
7. Desert Sands Pottery (1940 – 1978) 8. Davenport (1793 – 1810)

Cover design:
Beth Summers

Book design:
Allan Ramsey

COLLECTOR BOOKS
P.O. Box 3009
Paducah, Kentucky 42002-3009
www.collectorbooks.com

Copyright © 2004 Chad Lage

Searching For A Publisher?

We are always looking for people knowledgeable within their
fields. If you feel that there is a real need for a book on your collectible subject and have a large comprehensive collection, contact
Collector Books.

This book is dedicated to:

Tanya

&

In memory of:

Harriett Kretsinger

Acknowledgments

I wanted to say thank you to all those individuals that helped make this book a reality by thought, word, deed or inspiration. Please consider this an all-encompasing (like my Christmas cards that are good for not only Christmas, but birthdays, St. Patrick's Day, Valentines Day, and other holidays) but very sincere thank you. You are always in my thoughts. There are a few names I want to mention for highest honors: Gail Ashburn, Amy Sullivan, Tanya Lage, Mason Lage, Jerry Lage, Char Lage, Marc Schmidt, Pat Giese, Gary Giese, Jason Lage, Heather Fedt, Jennifer Lage, Doug Fedt, Chad Emsweller, William and Robyne Fraize, Chuck Emsweller, Jodie Puckett, Fred Puckett, Ashley Emsweller, Mark Short, John W. Streetman III, Mary Bower, John Buxton, Dave Maloney, Don Sohn, Ken Drew, Forrest Poston, and finally, all the brilliant collectors trading on eBay. Once again, thank you.

INTRODUCTION

Collectors of anything, at any level, all have one thing in common: the desire to have the quickest and most efficient route to the information they need for any particular piece they may be researching. Pottery and porcelain marks represent an enormous amount of information. There are literally thousands of different marks. The goal of this guide is to make the first step of information gathering for the collector a fast and pleasurable experience. The use of color photographs of not only the mark itself, but also of an example of the type of piece that the mark identifies, simplifies the process of identification by eliminating any doubt as to the actual appearance of the mark in its true state.

I am a collector. I collect everything, including information, which is kind of how this book got started in the first place. What I found out through the process of writing this book is, I am not a photographer. So, my apologizes for the worst of the photos, but the marks in them were of merit and worth noting. Most of the photos were taken with a Kodak DC210 (of course, predating the mega-pixel) Digital Camera. I liked the convenience of being able to instantly see what I had just snapped a picture of.

The pieces in the book were chosen because I wanted to show all kinds of pieces (along with their dates of manufacture) from every category of pottery and porcelain. Unfortunately, because of space considerations, the lists of examples are not comprehensive. For the most part, I did not list artist or decorator marks, but if they were in the picture of the piece I left them alone in order to help show what the piece would actually look like. I have included pictures of different pieces with slightly varied marks. Sometimes, variances can help date the piece. A potter who is best known for work of a particular range may have produced apparently uncharacteristic pieces at some time or another.

There are other things I must mention: A mark is one of many identifying characteristics used to ascertain a porcelain manufacturer or the origin of a piece of pottery. No attempt has been made to reproduce the exact size of the individual marks, because of the constant variations in size and form of the same mark on different pieces. Also, the caption describing the picture, or the location of the mark in the book, should not be taken as an indication of a subject's importance.

The dates provided for the pieces derive from research, the actual date on the piece, and outstanding references such as *Kovel's*, *Lehner's*, and so on. To further explain the dates given:

(1930s – 1940s) This means the piece was made sometime in this time period, including and up to the year 1949.

(1930s – 1940s+) This means the piece was made sometime in this time period; including, up to, and a little beyond the year 1949 — perhaps up to 1952 or so.

(1881+) This means that it is known for sure the mark existed in 1881, we are but unable to know how long it was used.

(A single date) This is the exact date of the piece in the picture.

I have to use a quote from Lehner's book on *American Marks*: "This book is dependent on the work of others and may sometimes be a compounding of other people's errors. I apologize for any errors. They were unintentional."

Also, all copyrighted material, any designated trademark, and any brand information is the property of its respective owner. This information is made available for reference.

In the alphabetical arrangement of the book the last name appears first, including names that contain a surname the exception being names that are commonly known together and would be out of context if separated, like *Van Briggle*. Also, a very few companies are listed alphabetically within a more widely-known regional category. For instance, Bawo and Dotter will not be found in the *B*s. Instead, it will be found in the *L*s, for Limoges, and it will fall alphabetically between Limoges, A. Laternier and Limoges, Beaux-Arts.

There are three indexes: alphabetical, sight, and date range.

The author of this book would like to complete a series of pictures of every impressed Minton date cipher and the piece the mark represents. If you have a mark you would like to share with the author, or can help the author complete the series, please contact the publisher or write to me at PO Box 14422, Evansville, IN 47728.

This book will cater to every collector of pottery and porcelain, from the expert to the most casual of antique lovers. It is hoped that this guide can and will, when used in conjunction with the myriad of specific guides, enhance the enjoyment of collecting for every reader, not only by being a great tool, but also by being a work of art worthy of any coffee table.

I hope you enjoy the book.
Chad Lage

Marks

Abbeydale (1962+)

Adams, William (1804+)

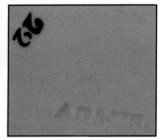

Abington (1934 – 1950)

Adams, William
(1819 – 1864)

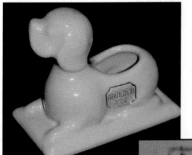

Abington (1940+)

Adams, William
(1829 – 1861)

Adams, William
(1804 – 1840)

Adams, William
(1836 – 1864)

Adams, William
(1836 – 1864)

Adams, William
(1836 – 1864)

Adams, William
(1836 – 1864)

Adams, William
(1839 – 1855)

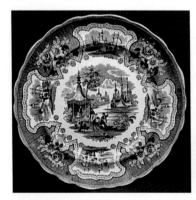

Adams, William
(1836 – 1864)

Adams, William
(1839 – 1855)

Adams, William
(1836 – 1864)

Adams, William
(1850 – 1900)

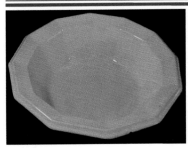

Adams, William
(1860 – 1880)

Adams, William
(1879 – 1891)

Adams, William
(1870 – 1890)

Adams, William
(1879 – 1900)

Adams, William
(1870s – 1880s)

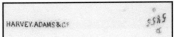

HARVEY. ADAMS & Cᵒ

Adams, William
(1880 – 1900)

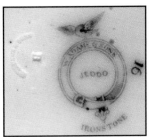

Adams, William
(1879 – 1891)

Adams, William (1891+)

Adams, William
(1893 – 1917)

Adams, William
(late 1800s)

Adams, William (1896+)

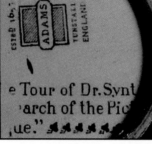

Adams, William
(1914 – 1940)

Adams, William (1896+)

Adams, William (1950+)

Adams, William
(1896+)

Adams, William
(1950 – 1966)

Adams, William (1950+)

Adderleys
(1876 – 1905)

Adams, William (1962+)

Adderleys
(1876 – 1905)

Adams, William (1972)

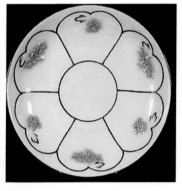

Adderleys
(1912 – 1926)

Adams, William (current)

Adderleys
(1912 – 1926)

Adderleys
(1947 – 1950)

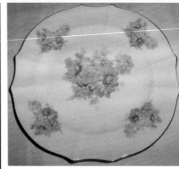

Alboth & Kaiser
(1953 – 1970)

Adderleys (1950 – 1972)

Alboth & Kaiser
(1960s – 1980s)

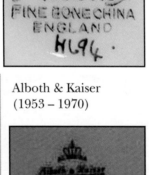

Alboth & Kaiser
(1953 – 1970)

Alcock, Henry
(1880 – 1910)

Alboth & Kaiser
(1953 – 1970)

Alcock, John (1855)

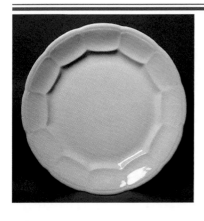

Alcock, John (1857)

Allertons Ltd. (1912+)

Alcock, Samuel (1828)

Allertons Ltd.
(1915 – 1929)

Allerton, Charles
(1870 – 1890)

Allertons Ltd.
(1929 – 1942)

Allerton, Charles
(1891 – 1912)

Altenburg (1900 – 1915)

11

Altenkunstadt
(1933 – 1960)

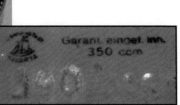

Altenkunstadt (1960 – present)

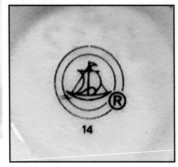

1

Altenkunstadt
(1960 – present)

14

Altrohlau Porcelain
(1918 – 1939)

American Bisque (1950 – 1960)

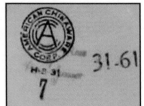

American China
(1894 – 1910)

American Chinaware
(1929 – 1931)

31-61

American Encaustic
Tile Co. (1875 – 1935)

American Encaustic
Tile Co. (1893)

American Limoges
China (1910 – 1930)

American Encaustic
Tile Co. (1926)

American Limoges
China (1927 – 1932)

Ivory Ware
by
Limoges
Sebring, Ohio
Bel Glare
3M133

American Limoges
China (1900+)

IVORY
THE LIMOGES CHINA CO.
MADE IN
U.S.A.
SEBRING, OHIO.
CARNATION
10133

American Limoges
China (1927 – 1932)

peach-blo
by
Limoges
Goldenrod
1M198

American Limoges
China (1910 – 1930)

LIMOGES CHINA CO.
U.S.A.
SEBRING, OHIO.
GOLDEN GLOW
PAT. APPLIED FOR

American Limoges
China (1933 – 1936)

AMERICAN
LIMOGES
SEBRING·OHIO

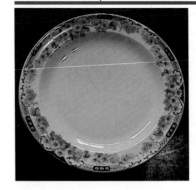

American Limoges China (1935 – 1936)

American Limoges China (1936 – 1950)

American Limoges China (1936 – 1950)

American Limoges China (1939 – 1950)

American Limoges China (1939)

American Terra Cotta & Ceramic (1888 – 1929)

American Terra Cotta & Ceramic (1895 – 1930)

American Terra Cotta & Ceramic (1895 – 1930)

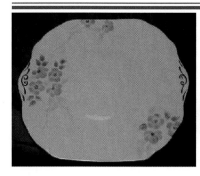

Amison, Charles
(1930 – 1941)

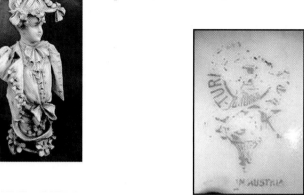

Amphora (1892 – 1905)

Amison, Charles
(1953 – 1962)

Amphora (1903 – 1918)

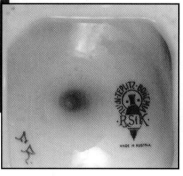

Amphora (1892 – 1905)

Amphora (1903 – 1918)

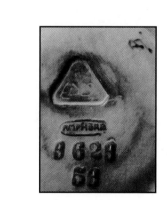

Amphora (1892 – 1905)

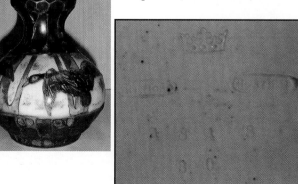

Amphora (1905 – 1910)

Amphora (1905 – 1910)

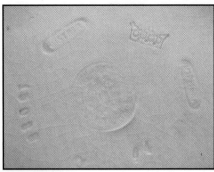

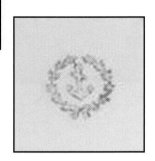

Anchor Pottery
(1893 – 1927)

Amphora (1905 – 1910)

Anchor Pottery
(1894 – 1898)

Amphora(1905 – 1910)

Anchor Pottery
(1894 – 1910)

ROYAL IRONSTONE
CHINA
ANCHOR POTTERY

Amphora(1918 – 1939)

Anchor Pottery
(1908 – 1927)

Anna Perenna
(1977 – present)

Anna Perenna
(1977 – present)

Arabia Porcelain (1928 – 1932)

Arabia Porcelain (1930+)

Arabia Porcelain (1930+)

Arabia Porcelain
(1932 – 1949)

Arabia Porcelain
(1949 – present)

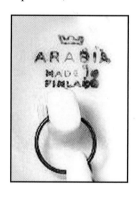

Arcadian China (1920s)

17

Arcadian China (1950s)

Arequipa Pottery
(1911 – 1918)

Arcadian China (1950s)

Arequipa Pottery
(1911 – 1918)

Arequipa Pottery (1911 – 1918)

Arkinstall & Sons (1904 – 1924)

MODEL OF ROMAN VASE
FOUND NEAR
CANTERBURY ORIGINAL
IN CANTERBURY
MUSEUM

Arequipa Pottery (1911 – 1918)

Arkinstall & Sons
(1905 – 1930)

18

Arkinstall & Sons
(1905 – 1930)

Arklow Pottery (1959)

Arklow Pottery
(1934 – 1950)

Arklow Pottery (1978+)

Arklow
HONEY STONE
MADE IN IRELAND
BONNIE BLOOM
No. 8169
OVEN TO TABLE
TO DISHWASHER

Arklow Pottery (1950+)

Arklow Pottery (current)

brendan
ERIN STONE
MADE IN ARKLOW IRELAND
F

Arklow Pottery (1950+)

Arnart Imports
(1957 – 1981)

Arnart Imports (1982)

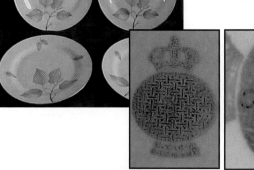

Arzberg Porcelain
(1974 – present)

Artists of the World
(1977 – present)

Ashtead Potters
(1926 – 1936)

Arzberg Porcelain (1927 – 1981)

Ashworth, G. L. & Bros.
(1860 – 1880)

Arzberg Porcelain
(1970 – present)

Ashworth, G. L. & Bros.
(1862 – 1880)

Ashworth, G. L. & Bros.
(1862 – 1880)

Ashworth, G. L. & Bros.
(1862 – 1890)

Ashworth, G. L. & Bros.
(1862 – 1890)

Ashworth, G. L. & Bros.
(1862 – 1890)

Ashworth, G. L. & Bros.
(1862 – 1890)

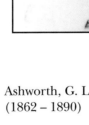

Ashworth, G. L. & Bros.
(1870)

Ashworth, G. L. & Bros.
(1862 – 1890)

Ashworth, G. L. & Bros.
(1910 – 1920)

Ashworth, G. L. & Bros. (1932+)

Augarten Porcelain (1923 – present)

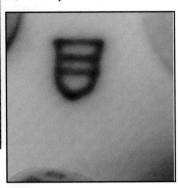

Ashworth, G. L. & Bros. (1957 – 1964)

Ault (1887 – 1923, 1937 – 1964)

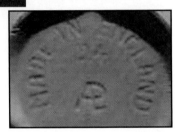

Ashworth, G. L. & Bros. (1957+)

Ault (1887 – 1923)

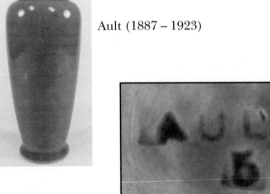

Augarten Porcelain (1923 – present)

Ault (1887 – 1923)

Ault (1887 – 1923)

Avon Art Pottery
(1939 – 1947)

Aultcliff (1923 – 1937)

Avon Art Pottery
(1947 – 1964)

Avon Art Pottery
(1930 – 1939)

Avon Faience
(1902 – 1905)

Avon Art Pottery
(1930 – 1939)

Axe Vale Pottery
(1959 – present)

Aynsley (1891+)

Baker & Chetwynd
(1882 – 1901)

Aynsley (1940 – 1960)

Baker & Co. (1880 – 1920)

Aynsley (1955+)

Baker & Co.
(1893 – 1932)

Baggaley, E.
(1947 – present)

Balleroy, Jullien (1914+)

Balleroy, Jullien (1914+)

Bareuther (1931 – 1950)

Balsham, Leah (1933)

Bareuther
(1966 – 1981+)

Banko Pottery (1930s – 1940s)

Bareuther (1966 – 1981+)

Banko Pottery
(1930s – 1960s)

Barker Bros. (1912 – 1930)

Barker Bros.
(1912 – 1930)

Barker Bros. (1960+)

Barker Bros. (1937+)

Barker Bros. (1960+)

Barker Bros. (1937+)

Barker Bros. (1960+)

Barker Bros. (1960+)

Barluet & Cie (1880)

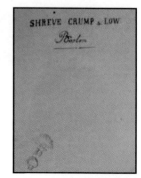

Barons Pottery (1905 – 1938)

Bauer Pottery
(1905 – 1958)

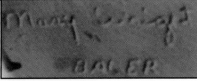

Barratts (1945+)

Bauer Pottery
(1930 – 1950)

Batchelder, Ernest
(1900 – 1920)

Bauer Pottery (1932+)

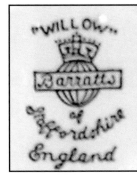

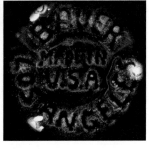

Batchelder, Ernest
(1900 – 1920)

Bauer Pottery (1934 – 1942)

Bauer Pottery (1945)

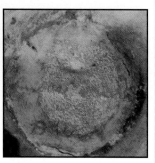

Bauer Pottery (1945)

Bauscher Bros. (1910 – 1939)

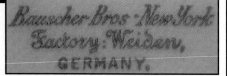

Bauscher Bros.
(1915 – 1939)

Bauscher Bros.
(1921 – 1939)

Bawo & Dotter (1884 – 1914)

Beadmore & Berks
(1831 – 1843)

Beech & Hancock
(1840 – 1860)

Belford (1892 – 1918)

Bell, J&MP
(1881 – 1928)

Bell, J&MP (1850 – 1860)

Belleek (1863 – 1891)

Bell, J&MP (1850 – 1870)

Belleek
(1863 – 1891)

Bell, J&MP
(1881 – 1928)

Belleek
(1863 – present)

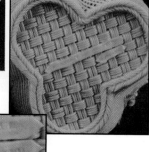

Belleek (1891 – 1926)

Belleek (2000)

Belleek (1927 – 1941)

Bennett, Edwin (1876 – 1936)

Belleek (1946 – 1955)

Bennett, Edwin (1886)

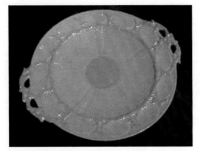

Belleek (1956 – 1965)

Bennett, Edwin (1890+)

Bennett, Edwin
(1895 – 1897)

Bennett, Edwin
(1897 – 1904)

Bennington Potters
(1949 – present)

Berlin Porcelain Manufactory
(1904 – 1911)

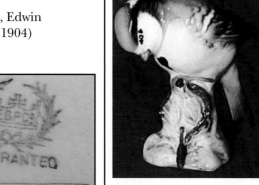

Beswick, John (1936)

Beswick, John (1940+)

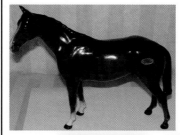

Beswick, John (1946+)

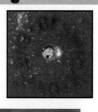

Beswick, John (1949+)

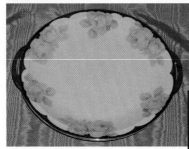

Beyer & Bock
(1905 – 1931)

Beyer & Bock
(1905 – 1931)

Beyer & Bock (1914)

Beyer & Bock
(1931 – present)

Beyer & Bock
(1931 – present)

Biltons (1950 – present)

Biltons (1950 – present)

Biltons (1970 – present)

Bing & Grondahl
(1899+)

Bing & Grondahl
(1915+)

Bing & Grondahl
(1948+)

Bing & Grondahl
(1948+)

Bing & Grondahl
(1952 – 1958)

Bing & Grondahl
(1962+)

Bing & Grondahl
(1970+)

Bing & Grondahl
(1970+)

Birks, Rawlins
(1917 – 1933)

Black, Harding (1957)

Bishop & Stonier
(1891 – 1910)

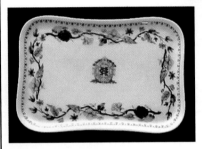

Black Knight
(1925 – 1941)

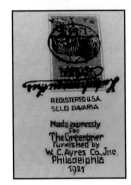

Bishop & Stonier
(1891 – 1936)

Blairs (1914 – 1930)

Bishop & Stonier
(1910)

Blake, Trenle
(1940 – 1966)

Blau (1880 – 1950)

Block China
(1960 – present)

Blin, J. (1920 – 1995)

Bloch, B. (1915 – 1920)

Block China (1997)

Bloch, R. (1954+)

Bloor Derby
(1820 – 1840)

Blyth Porcelain
(1913 – 1935)

Boch Freres (1900 – 1930+)

Boch, B. (1923 – 1940)

Boch Freres (1900 – 1930+)

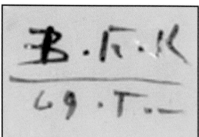

Bock, Josef
(1893 – 1933)

Boch Freres (1900)

Boch Freres (1841+)

Boch Freres (1914+)

Boch Freres (1914+)

Boch Freres (1920 – 1930)

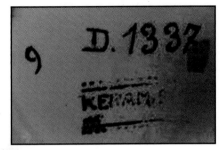

Boch Freres (1920 – 1930)

Boch Freres (1920)

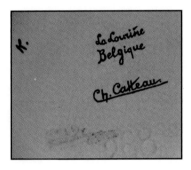

Boch Freres (1920 – 1930)

Boch Freres (1924)

Boch Freres (1920 – 1930)

Boch Freres (1930s – 1940s)

Boch Freres
(1980 – present)

Bodley, E. J. D.
(1875 – 1892)

Bodley, E. F. D. (1887)

Bodley, E. J. D.
(1875 – 1892)

Bodley, E. F. D. (1890)

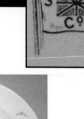

Boehm (1954 – present)

Bodley, E. F. D.
(1875 – 1892)

Boehm (1971+)

Boehm (1971+)

Boehm (1973)

Boehm (1971+)

Boehm (1976)

Boehm (1971+)

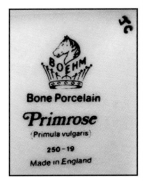

Boehm (1980+)

Boehm (1971+)

Boehm (1989+)

Bohemia Ceramic
(1941 – 1945)

Bohemia Ceramic
(1941 – 1945)

Bohne, Ernst Sons (1878 – 1920)

Bohne, Ernst Sons (1878 – 1920)

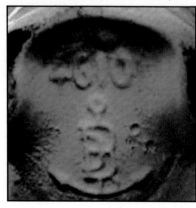

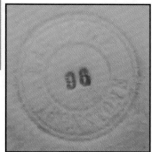

Boote, T. & R.
(1842 – 1863)

Boote, T. & R. (1853)

Boote, T. & R. (1870)

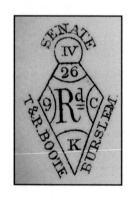

Boote, T. & R.
(1890 – 1906)

Boote, T. & R.
(1890 – 1906)

Boote, T. & R.
(1890 – 1906)

Boote, T. & R.
(1890 – 1906)

Boote, T. & R. (1900)

Boote, T. & R.
(1890 – 1906)

Booth, Thomas
(1876 – 1883)

Boote, T. & R.
(1890 – 1906)

Booths (1891 – 1912)

Booths (1906 – 1912)

Booths & Colcloughs
(1950 – present)

Booths (1912+)

Bopla (1980 – present)

Booths & Colcloughs
(1948 – 1954)

Borgfeldt, George
(1926+)

Booths & Colcloughs
(1950 – presrent)

Borgfeldt, George
(1936 – 1976)

Borgfeldt, George
(1936 – 1976)

Borgfeldt, George (1978)

Bourdois & Bloch (1890 – 1948)

Bourne (1930+)

Bourne (1948 – 1964)

Bourne (1950s)

Bourne (1950s – 1960s)

Bourne & Leigh
(1892 – 1939)

43

Bourne & Leigh
(1912+)

Bourne & Leigh
(1912+)

Bourne & Leigh
(1930s)

Bourne & Leigh (1930s)

Bovey Pottery
(1937 – 1949)

Bovey Pottery
(1949 – 1956)

Bovey Pottery
(1949 – 1956)

Bowker, Arthur
(1950 – 1958)

Boyer, Georges
(1936 – 1953)

Boyle, Zachariah
(1823 – 1828)

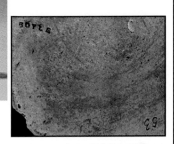

Boyle, Zachariah
(1823 – 1850)

Brannam, C. H. (1914+)

Brannam, C. H. (1980+)

Brentleigh (1950s)

Brentleigh (1950s)

Brian, E. & Co. (1905 – 1930s)

Brian, E. & Co.
(1945 – 1963)

Bridgwood
(1890 – 1920)

Brian, E. & Co. (1953)

Bridgwood & Clarke
(1857 – 1864)

Brian, E. & Co. (1953)

Bristol (1950s)

Brianchon (1864+)

Bristol, Pountney,
Goldney (1836 – 1849)

Bristol Pountney
(1938)

British Anchor Pottery
(1945+)

British Anchor Pottery
(1884 – 1913)

British Anchor Pottery
(1950s)

British Anchor Pottery
(1884 – 1913)

British Anchor Pottery
(1960s)

British Anchor Pottery
(1913 – 1940)

British Anchor Pottery
(1960s)

Broadhurst (1950s)

Brownfield, William
(1850 – 1871)

Broadhurst (current)

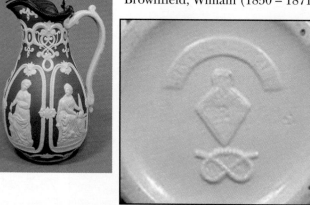

Brownfield, William (1850 – 1871)

Brock (1950 – 1955)

Brownfield, William
(1850 – 1871)

Brough & Blackhurst
(1872 – 1895)

Brownfield, William
(1871 – 1891)

48

Brownfield, William
(1871 – 1891)

Brown-Westhead, Moore
(1869 – 1904)

Brownfield, William
(1871 – 1891)

Brown-Westhead, Moore (1875)

Brownfield, William
(1871 – 1891)

Brown-Westhead,
Moore (1891 – 1920)

Brownhills Pottery (1870 – 1890)

Brown-Westhead,
Moore (1891 – 1920)

Brunt, William Pottery
(1892 – 1911)

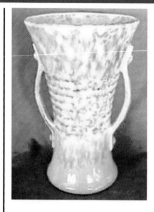

Brush McCoy (1938 – 1965)

Brusche Ceramics
(1950s)

Brush McCoy (1950s)

Brusche Ceramics (1950s)

Buchan, A. W. (1949+)

Brush McCoy (1930s)

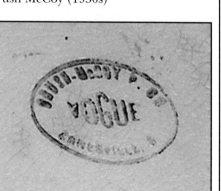

Buchan, A. W. (1949+)

Buchan, A. W. (1949+)

Buffalo China
(1985 – present)

Buckau Porcelain
(1850 – 1920)

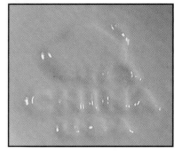

Buffalo China
(1985 – present)

Buckfast Abbey Pottery
(1952 – 1964)

Buffalo Pottery (1905+)

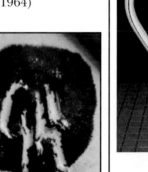

Buffalo Pottery
(1907 – 1940s)

Buffalo China
(1920s – 1930s)

Buffalo Pottery
(1909 – 1925)

Buffalo Pottery (1980)
(questionable origin)

Buffalo Pottery (1911)

Burford Bros. (1895)

Buffalo Pottery
(1915 – 1920+)

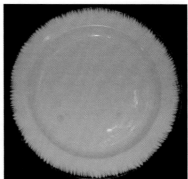

Burford Bros. (1900)

Buffalo Pottery
(1915 – 1920+)

Burgess & Goddard
(1840 – 1860)

Burgess & Goddard
(1878)

Burgess & Leigh (1930+)

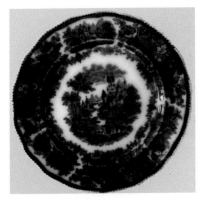

Burgess & Leigh
(1891)

Burgess & Leigh
(1930+)

Burgess & Leigh (1906 – 1912)

Burgess & Leigh (1930+)

Burgess & Leigh (1930+)

Burgess & Leigh
(current)

Burgess Bros. (1920s)

Burgess Campbell
(1904)

Burgess Bros. (1920s+)

Burleigh (1980+)

Burgess Bros.
(1922 – 1939)

Burmantofts (1882 – 1904)

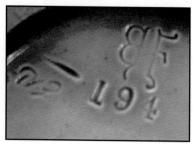

Burgess Campbell
(1860 – 1936)

Burmantofts (1890)

Burmantofts (1890)

Bybee (1900+)

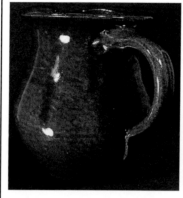

Burroughs & Mountford
(1879 – 1882)

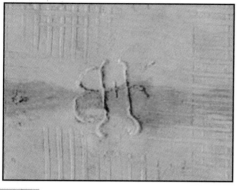

Bybee (1900+)

Bursley Ware (1920s)

Bybee, Selden
(1927 – 1928)

Bursley Ware (1930s)

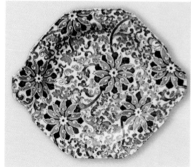

California Faience (1920+)

Camark Pottery (1927+)

Cambridge Art Pottery (1904)

Camark Pottery (1927+)

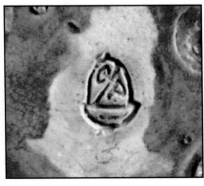

Campbellfield (1850 – 1905)

Cambridge Art Pottery (1895 – 1903)

Canonsburg China (1920s – 1940s)

Cambridge Art Pottery (1895 – 1909)

Canonsburg Pottery (1900 – 1909)

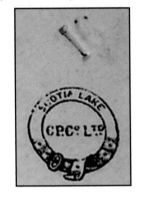

Canonsburg Pottery
(1940s – 1960s)

Canonsburg Pottery
(1950s – 1970s)

Canonsburg Pottery
(1952 – 1954)

Canonsburg Pottery
(1960 – 1978)

Canonsburg Pottery
(1970+)

Cantagalli (1878 – 1901)

Cardew, Michael
Ambrose (1926+)

Cardew, Michael Ambrose
(1939 – 1942)

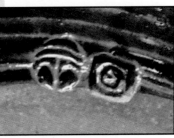

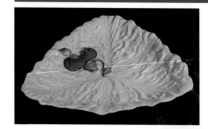

Carlton Ware
(1925 – present)

Carstens, C.&E.
(1933 – 1975)

Carrollton China
(1910 – 1920)

Carstens, C.&E. (1940+)

Carstens, C.&E.
(1918 – 1945)

Carter, Stabler, Adams (1921+)

Carstens, C.&E.
(1918 – 1945)

Cartwright & Edwards
(1870 – 1890)

Cartwright & Edwards
(1880)

Cartwright Bros.
(1888)

Cartwright & Edwards (1900s)

Cartwright China
(1896 – 1927)

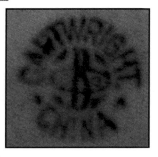

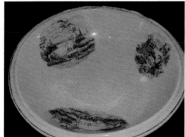

Cartwright Bros.
(1880 – 1927)

Castleton China
(1940 – present)

Cartwright Bros.
(1887 – 1900)

Castleton China
(1940 – present)

Castleton China
(1940+)

Caughley (1775 – 1778)

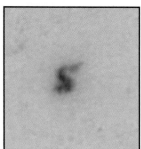

Castleton China
(1968 – 1979)

Caughley (1785)

Catalina Pottery (1935+)

Cauldon (1860 – 1880)

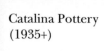

Catalina Pottery
(1935+)

Cauldon (1862 – 1890)

Cauldon (1905 – 1920)

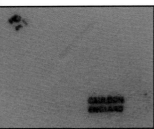

Ceralene (current)

Cauldon (1905 – 1920)

Ceralene (current)

Century House (1950)

Ceramic Arts Studio (1940 – 1955)

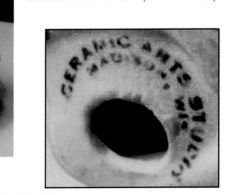

Century Services Corporation (1950+)

Challinor, E.
(1842 – 1867)

Challinor, E. (1842 – 1867)

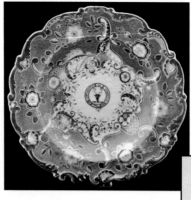

Chamberlains
Worcester (1847 – 1850)

Challinor, E.
(1853 – 1862)

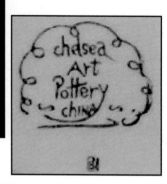

Chelsea Art Pottery
(1952+)

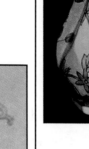

Chamberlains Worcester
(1811 – 1840)

Chelsea-Derby
(1756 – 1775)

Chamberlains
Worcester (1820 – 1840)

Chelsea Keramic Art Works
(1872 – 1889)

Chelsea Keramic Art
Works (1891 – 1895)

Chikusa (1905+)

Chelsea Pottery
(1952+)

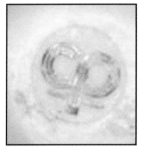

Chessell Pottery (1978 – present)

Chugai China
(1945 – 1952)

Chinese Export
(19th century)

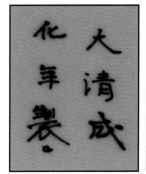

Clark, Edward (1865 – 1877)

Clementson, J. (1839+)

Clementson, J.
(1839 – 1864)

Clementson, J. (1839+)

Clementson, J.
(1839 – 1864)

Clementson, J.
(1839 – 1864)

Clementson Bros.
(1870+)

Clementson, J.
(1839 – 1864)

Clementson Bros.
(1891 – 1910)

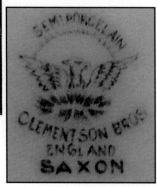

Clementson Bros.
(1901 – 1913)

Clews, George (1947 – 1961)

Clementson Bros.
(1913 – 1916)

Clews, James &
Ralph (1810 – 1820)

Clewell (1906+)

Clews, James & Ralph
(1818 – 1834)

Clewell (1909+)

Clews, James & Ralph
(1818 – 1834)

Clews (1920s – 1930s)

Cliff, Clarice (1920+)

Cliff, Clarice
(1938 – 1966)

Cliff, Clarice (1938 – 1966)

Cliff, Clarice (1938 – 1966)

Cliff, Clarice (1938+)

Clifton (1905 – 1911)

Clifton (1905 – 1911)

Coalport
(1960 – present)

Clinchfield Pottery
(1920 – 1930)

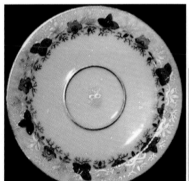

Cockson & Seddon
(1875 – 1877)

Coalport (1820)

Colclough (1919 – 1931)

Coalport (1891 – 1920)

Colclough (1928 – 1937)

Colclough (1937 – 1954)

Colclough
(1955 – present)

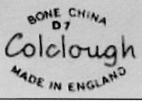

Colclough
(1937 – present)

Colclough (1962+)

Colclough (1939 – 1954)

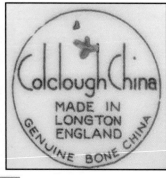

Colclough (1964 – present)

Colclough (1945 – 1948)

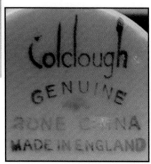

Cone, Thomas
(1960 – present)

Continental Kilns
(1944 – 1954)

Cook Pottery (1894)

Cook & Hancock
(1894 – 1929)

Cook Pottery (1894)

Cook & Hancock (1894 – 1929)

Cook Pottery (1900)

Cook Pottery (1893 – 1926)

Cooper, Susie (1930+)

Cooper, Susie (1932)

Cooper, Susie (1932+)

Cooper, Susie (1932)

Cooper, Susie (1932+)

Cooper, Susie (1932+)

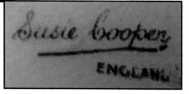

Cooper, Susie (1938)

Cooper, Susie (1932+)

Cooper, Susie (1950+)

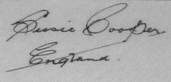

Cooper, Susie (1950+)

Co-Operative
Wholesale Society
(1950 – 1960)

Co-Operative Wholesale
Society (1946 – 1964)

Co-Operative
Wholesale Society
(1950s – 1960s)

Co-Operative
Wholesale Society
(1946 – 1964)

Co-Operative Whole-
sale Society (1952)

Co-Operative Wholesale
Society (1950 – 1960)

Coors (1900 – 1930)

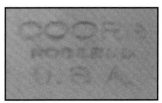

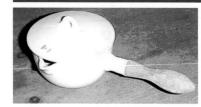

Coors (1920 – present)

Cordey (1942 – 1955)

Coors (1980+)

Corn, W & E
(1900 – 1904)

Cordey (1942 – 1955)

Corning Glass Works
(1962+)

Cordey (1942 – 1955)

Coronado (1939 – 1944)

Coronation Ware
(1940s)

Cowan Pottery
(1912 – 1931)

Count Thun
(1918 – 1939)

Cowan Pottery
(1913 – 1917)

Count Thun (1947+)

Cowan Pottery
(1913 – 1917)

Cowan Pottery (1912 – 1931)

Cox, Paul (1900+)

Coxon Pottery
(1863 – 1884)

Creil & Montereau
(1880 – 1890)

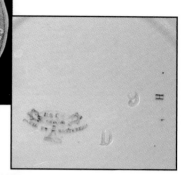

Coxon Pottery
(1926 – 1930)

Creil et Montereau
(1870)

Cranston Pottery (1910)

Crescent Pottery
(1881+)

Creil & Montereau (1880 – 1890)

Crescent Pottery
(1899 – 1902)

Crescent Pottery
(1899 – 1902)

Crown Clarence (1946+)

Cronin China
(1934 – 1956)

Crown Clarence
(1950 – 1962+)

Crooksville China
(1940)

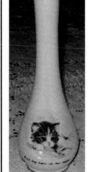

Crown Devon (1972+)

Crosse & Blackwell
(1840 – 1890)

Crown Devon (1972+)

Crown Devon (1972+)

Crown Devon (1972+)

Crown Ducal (1915+)

Crown Ducal
(1916 – 1970+)

Crown Ducal (1925+)

Crown Ducal (1925+)

Crown Ducal (1950+)

Crownford (1930s)

Crownford (1960+)

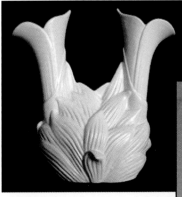

Crownford (1960+)

Crown Lynn Pottery
(1950 – 1960)

Crown Potteries
(1902 – 1962)

Crown Potteries
(1902 – 1962)

Crown Potteries
(1940 – 1962)

Crown Potteries (1891)

Crown Staffordshire
(1930+)

Crown Staffordshire
(1970+)

Dachsel, Paul (1904)

Cumberlidge &
Humphrys (1880 – 1890+)

Dahl Jensen
(1928 – present)

Cybis (1952 – 1966)

Dalpayrat, Adrien
(1876 – 1905)

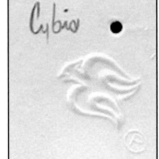

Cybis (1952 – 1966)

Dalpayrat, Adrien (1900)

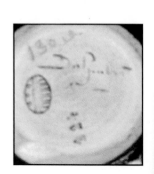

D'Arceau Limoges
(1973 – 1979)

Dartmouth Pottery
(1947 – present)

D'Arceau Limoges
(1973 – 1979)

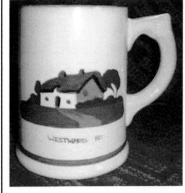

Dartmouth Pottery
(1947 – present)

Dartmouth Pottery
(1920)

Dartmouth Pottery
(current)

Dartmouth Pottery (1947 – present)

Davenport (1793 – 1810)

Davenport
(1800 – 1840)

Davenport (1805 – 1820)

Davenport (1800 – 1860)

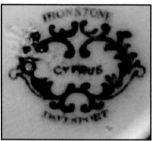

Davenport (1820 – 1860)

Davenport (1800 – 1860)

Davenport (1820 – 1860)

Davenport (1800 – 1860)

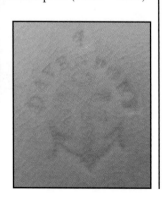

Davenport (1820 – 1860)

Davenport
(1820 – 1860)

Davenport (1840 – 1867)

Davenport (1830 – 1835)

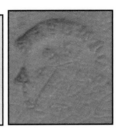

Davenport (1853+)

Davenport (1830 – 1880)

Davenport (1860 – 1870)

Davenport (1840 – 1867)

Davenport (1860 – 1873)

Davenport (1870 – 1886)

Decoeur, Emile (1907+)

Davis, John Heath
(1881 – 1891)

Dedham Pottery (1891+)

Dean, S. W.
(1904 – 1910)

Dedham Pottery
(1895 – 1932)

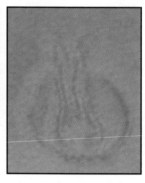

Deck, Theodore
(1859 – 1891)

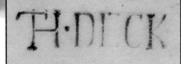

Dedham Pottery
(1895 – 1932)

Dedham Pottery
(1980s – present)

Denbac (1930s+)

Dedham Pottery
(1980s – present)

Denby Tableware
(1980+)

Delaherche, Auguste
(1894 – 1940)

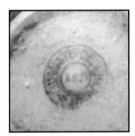

Denver (1893 – 1960)

Delinieres, R.
(1879 – 1900)

Denver (1893 – 1960)

Derby Porcelain Works (1760 – 1825)

Derby Porcelain Works
(1800 – 1820)

Derby Porcelain Works
(1782 – 1825)

Derby Porcelain Works
(1861 – 1935)

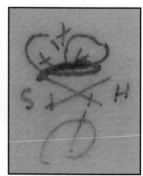

Derby Porcelain Works
(1784 – 1795)

Derby Porcelain
Works (1865)

Derby Porcelain Works (1790)

Derby Porcelain Works
(1878 – 1890)

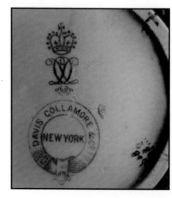

Derby Porcelain
Works (1878 – 1890)

Derby Porcelain Works
(1940 – present)

Derby Porcelain Works
(1890 – 1940)

Derby Porcelain Works
(1959)

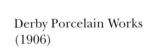

Derby Porcelain Works
(1906)

Derby Porcelain Works
(1964 – 1975)

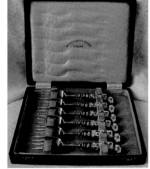

Derby Porcelain Works
(1940 – present)

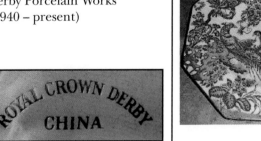

Derby Porcelain
Works (1964)

Derby Porcelain Works (1975+)

Desert Sands Pottery
(1940 – 1978)

Derby Porcelain Works
(1975+)

Desert Sands Pottery
(1940 – 1978)

Desert Sands Pottery
(1940 – 1978)

Desiree Denmark
(1970)

Desert Sands Pottery
(1940 – 1978)

Desvres (1870)

Devonmoor (1922+)

Dillion, Francis
(1834 – 1843)

Dimmock, J.
(1878 – 1904)

Dimmock, Thomas
(1828 – 1859)

Dimmock, Thomas
(1828 – 1859)

Distel (1897 – 1901)

Distel (1897 – 1923+)

Distel (1897 – 1923+)

Donath, P. (1896 – 1922)

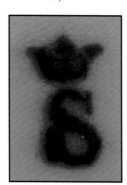

Donath, P.
(1896 – 1922)

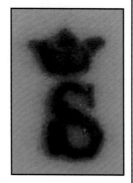

Donath, P.
(1910 – 1916)

Donath & Company
(1893 – 1916)

Dorchester
(1940 – 1970+)

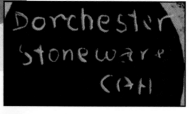

Dorchester
(1950s – 1960s)

Doulton (1853+)

Doulton (1855+)

Doulton (1869 – 1872)

Doulton (1876)

Doulton (1869 – 1872)

Doulton (1877 – 1880)

Doulton (1873 – 1914)

Doulton (1880)

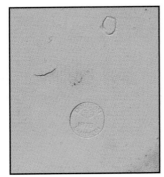

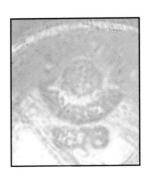

Doulton (1873 – 1914)

Doulton (1880 – 1902)

Doulton (1880 – 1902)

Doulton (1885 – 1902)

Doulton (1881 – 1912)

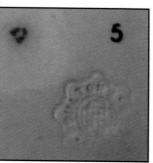

Doulton (1885 – 1902)

Doulton (1885 – 1902)

Doulton (1885 – 1891)

Doulton (1885 – 1910)

Doulton (1885 – 1902)

Doulton (1887 – 1906)

Doulton (1891 – 1910)

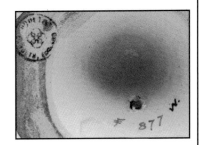

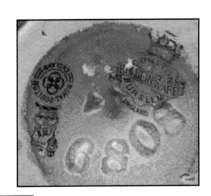

Doulton (1902 – 1922)

Doulton (1900 – 1935)

Doulton (1902+)

Doulton (1900)

Doulton (1902 – 1922)

Doulton (1900+)

Doulton (1902 – 1922)

Doulton (1902 – 1922)

Doulton (1902 – present)

Doulton (1902 – 1922)

Doulton (1905)

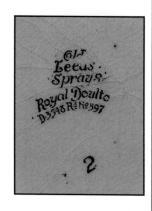

Doulton (1902 – present)

Doulton (1912 – 1956)

Doulton (1902 – present)

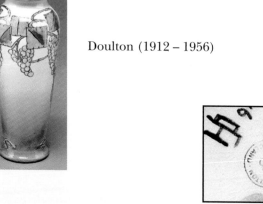

Doulton (1920 – 1936)

Doulton (1922 – 1927)

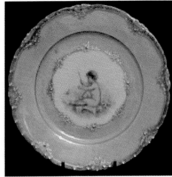

Dresden (1883 – 1893)

Doulton (1922 – 1956)

Dresden (1900)

Dresden Porcelain
(1869 – 1903)

Doulton (1959)

Dick Turpin
D 6528
COPR 1959
DOULTON & CO LIMITED
Rd No 893841
Rd No 39649
Rd No 8313
Rd No 420/59

Doulton (1974+)

Dresden Pottery Co.
(1900 – 1927)

Dresden Pottery Co. (1900)

Dressler, Julius
(1900 – 1945)

Dressel, Kister (1907 – 1922)

Dressler, Julius
(1900)

Dressel, Kister (1907 – 1922)

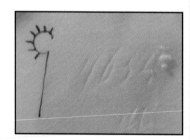

Ducal Brunswick
(1850 – 1894)

Dresser, Ch.
(1879 – 1889)

Dudson, Wilcox & Till
(1902 – 1926)

Dudson, Wilcox & Till
(1902 – 1926)

Dunn, Bennett
(1875 – 1907)

Dunn, Bennett
(1875 – 1907)

Dunn, Bennett
(1937 – 1964+)

Dunn, Bennett
(1875 – 1907)

Durant Kilns
(1911 – 1929)

Dunn, Bennett
(1875 – 1907)

Dux Porcelain
(1900 – 1918)

Dux Porcelain
(1912 – 1918)

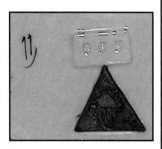

East Liverpool Potteries
(1896+)

Dux Porcelain
(1918 – 1945)

East Liverpool Potteries
(1896 – 1901)

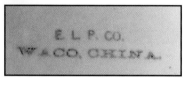

East End Pottery
(1894 – 1901, 1903 – 1907)

East Liverpool Potteries
(1901 – 1907)

East End Pottery
(1894 – 1908)

East Liverpool Potteries
(1907 – 1925)

East Liverpool Potteries
(1907 – 1925)

Ebeling & Reuss
(1955 – present)

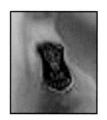

East Trenton Pottery
(1888 – 1905)

Eckert, Richard
(1894 – 1918)

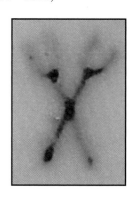

Ebeling & Reuss
(1955 – present)

Edelstein (1931+)

Ebeling & Reuss
(current)

Edelstein (1931+)

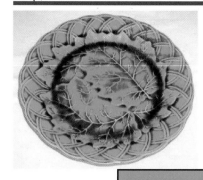

Edge, Malkin (1873+)

Edge, Malkin
(1873 – 1903)

Edge, Malkin (1873+)

Edge, Malkin
(1873 – 1903)

Edge, Malkin
(1873 – 1903)

Edge, Malkin (1890+)

Edwards, James
(1841 – 1851)

Edwards, James (1847)

Edwards, James
(1851 – 1882)

Edwards Bros. (1880+)

Edwards, John (1853)

Efchenbach (1931+)

Edwards, John
(1880 – 1900)

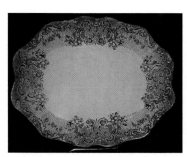

Egersund Pottery
(1880+)

Edwards, John
(1880 – 1900)

Egersund Pottery (1954+)

Egersund Pottery (1954+)

Elfinware (1940s+)

Eichwald (1931+)

Elfinware (1940s+)

Eichwald (1931+)

Elizabethan
(1980 – present)

Elbogen (1900+)

Elkin, Knight, Bridg-
wood (1827 – 1840)

Elsmore & Forster
(1860s)

Empire Pottery
(1884 – 1892)

Elsmore, T. & Sons
(1878)

Empire Pottery (1892)

Elton, Sir Edmund
(1879 – 1930)

Empire Pottery (1930s)

Empire Crockery (1920+)

Empire Pottery (1930s)

Empire Pottery
(1940s – 1960s)

Epiag (1910 – 1945)

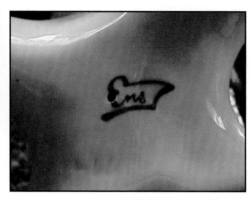

Ens Porcelain (1915 – 1981+)

Epiag (1910 – 1945)

Ens Porcelain, Karl (1919 – 1972)

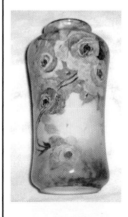

Epiag (1920 – 1939)

Ephraim (1990s+)

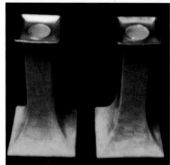

Epiag (1920 – 1939)

 Epiag (1920 – 1939)

 Epiag (1941 – 1945)

 Epiag (1920 – 1939)

Epiag (1941 – 1945)

Epiag (1920 – 1945+)

 Epiag (1941 – 1945)

Epiag (1920 – 1945+)

Eschenbach
(1945 – present)

Eschenbach
(1945 – present)

Faience Manufacturing Co.
(1884 – 1890)

Ewenny Pottery (1956)

Fasold & Stauch
(1914 – 1972)

Exeter Art Pottery (1891 – 1895)

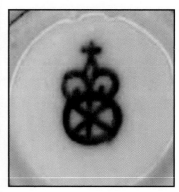

Fasold & Stauch (1972)

Faience Manufacturing Co.
(1880 – 1892)

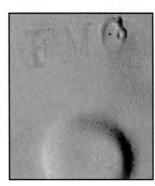

Fielding, S. (1891 – 1913)

Fielding, S. (1891 – 1913)

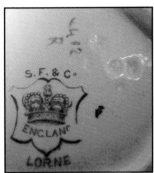

Fielding, S.
(1913 – 1930s)

Fielding, S. (1891 – 1913)

Fielding, S.
(1917 – 1930)

Fielding, S. (1913)

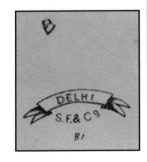

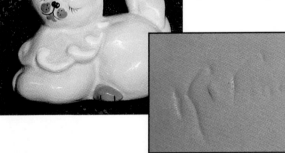

Finch, Kay
(1939 – 1963)

Fielding, S.
(1913 – 1930s)

Finney, A. T.
(1961 – present)

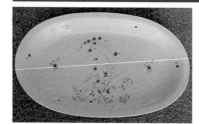

Fischer, Bruce
(1933 – 1940,
1949 – present)

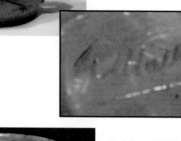

Fishley, George (1955+)

Fischer, Christian (1846 – 1857)

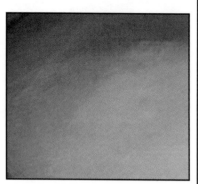

Fishley, William (1900+)

Fischer, Emil (1866 – 1908+)

Fitz and Floyd (1985+)

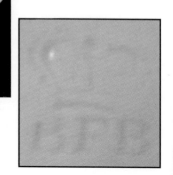

Fischer & Mieg (1810 – 1846)

Flight, Barr, Barr
Worcester (1807 – 1813)

Flight, Barr, Barr
Worcester (1807 – 1813)

Flight, Barr, Barr Worcester
(1813 – 1840)

Flight, Barr, Barr
Worcester (1813 – 1840)

Flintridge China
(1945 – present)

Flintridge China
(1945 – present)

Florence Ceramics (1940s – 1950s)

Florence Ceramics
(1940s – 1950s)

Ford & Riley
(1882 – 1964+)

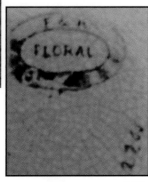

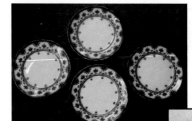

Ford & Sons
(1839 – 1938)

Forrester, Rembrandt & Son
(1890 – 1910)

Forester, Thomas
(1883+)

T.F.&S.Ld
ENGLAND

Frankoma (1931)

Forester, Thomas (1891 – 1912)

Frankoma (1972+)

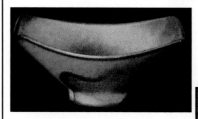

FRANKOMA
FJ4

ORIGINAL
CREATION
by
FRANKOMA

Forester, Thomas
(1930+)

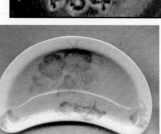

Fraureuther
(1898 – 1928)

Fraureuther (1898 – 1935)

French China
(1916 – 1929)

French China
(1900 – 1916)

French China
(1916 – 1929)

French China (1900 – 1916)

French China
(1916 – 1929)

French China
(1900 – 1916)

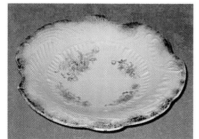

French Saxon China
(1935 – 1964)

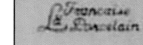

French Saxon China
(1935 – 1964)

Fryer, J.
(1954 – present)

French Saxon China
(1940 – 1958)

Fukagawa
(1950 – present)

Frie Onnaing (1890+)

Fukagawa
(1950 – present)

Fritsch & Weidermann
(1921 – 1939)

Fukagawa
(1950 – present)

Fulham Pottery (1864 – 1869)

Furnivals (1818 – 1890)

Fulper Pottery
(1910 – 1929)

Furnivals
(1868 – 1883)

Fulper Pottery (1910 – 1929)

Furnivals (1880+)

Furnivals
(1818 – 1890)

Furnivals
(1890 – 1910)

Furnivals (1890)

Furstenberg
(1922 – present)

Furnivals
(1900 – 1915+)

Galle (1874 – 1904)

Furnivals
(1905 – 1913)

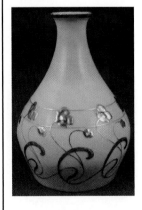

Galle (1874 – 1904)

Furnivals (1913)

Galluba & Hoffman (1895 – 1927)

Galluba & Hoffman
(1895 – 1927)

Gebr. Kuhnlenz (1884)

Gater Hall
(1895 – 1907)

Gefle (1931 – 1950+)

Gater Hall (1900)

George, W. S. (1932+)

Gater Hall (1914+)

George, W. S. (1934+)

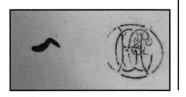

George, W. S. (1950s)

George Grainger
Worcester (1850 – 1860)

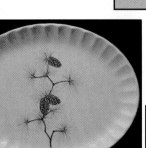

George, W. S. (1954)

George Grainger Worcester
(1870 – 1879)

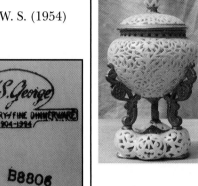

George Grainger
Worcester (1810 – 1820)

George Grainger
Worcester (1870 – 1879)

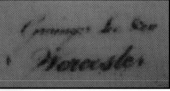

George Grainger
Worcester (1840 – 1860)

George Grainger Worcester
(1889 – 1902)

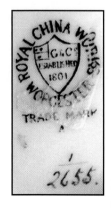

George Grainger Worcester
(1889 – 1902)

Gibson & Sons
(1896 – 1920)

Georgia Art Pottery
(20th century)

Gibson & Sons (1912+)

Gerz, Simon Peter (1910+)

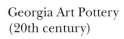

Gibson & Sons (1912+)

Gesetzlitch Geschutzt (1897 – 1900)

Gibson & Sons (1928+)

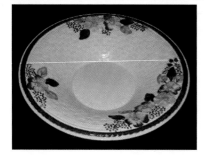

Gibson & Sons (1940+)

Gien (1864+)

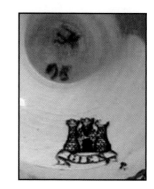

Gibsons (1930+)

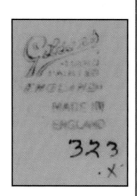

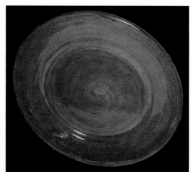

Gien (1970+)

Gien (1864+)

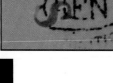

Gladding, McBean
(1923+)

Gien (1864+)

Gladding, McBean
(1934 – 1962)

Gladding, McBean
(1937 – 1942)

Gladding, McBean
(1937 – 1942)

Gladding, McBean
(1939+)

Gladding, McBean
(1939 – 1947)

Gladding, McBean
(1939 – 1947)

Gladding, McBean
(1939 – 1947)

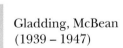

Gladding, McBean
(1939 – 1947)

Gladding, McBean
(1939 – 1947)

Gladding, McBean (1947 – 1953)

Glasgow Pottery
(1863+)

Gladding, McBean
(1963 – 1964)

GREY
RENAISSANCE

GLADDING, McBEAN & CO

Franciscan
MASTERPIECE
CHINA

MADE IN U.S.A.

Glasgow Pottery
(1863+)

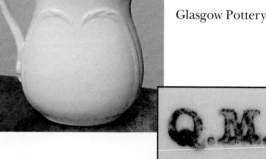

IRONSTONE CHINA
J.M. & Co.

Gladding, McBean
(1963 – 1964)

Cloud Nine

GLADDING McBEAN & CO

Franciscan
WHITESTONE
WARE

Glasgow Pottery (1899)

Q. M. D

Glasgow Pottery (1863)

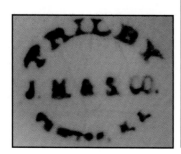

TRILBY

J. M. & CO.

Glasgow Pottery
(1904+)

GLASGOW POTTERY
& CO
TRENTON.
N.J.

118

Glidden Pottery
(1947 – 1957)

Globe Pottery (1914)

Glidden Pottery
(1947 – 1957)

Globe Pottery
(1930 – 1934)

Glidden Pottery
(1947 – 1957)

Gloria (1947 – 1981+)

Globe Pottery (1900 – 1912)

Gmundner Keramik
(1909 – 1922)

Goebel (1914 – 1920)

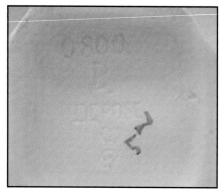

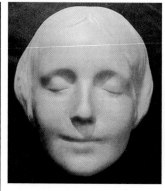

Goebel (1923 – 1949)

Goebel (1919)

Goebel (1940 – 1955)

Goebel (1923 – 1949)

Goebel (1950 – 1955)

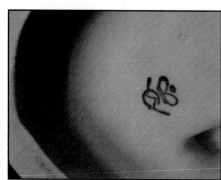

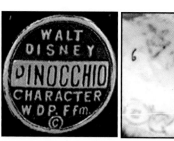

Goebel (1923 – 1949)

Goebel (1950 – 1955)

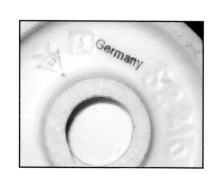

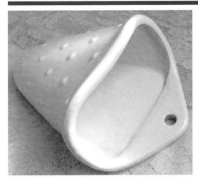

Goebel (1950 – 1955)

Goebel (1968 – 1979)

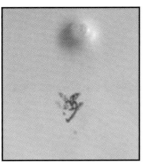

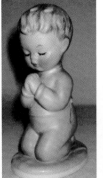

Goebel (1956)

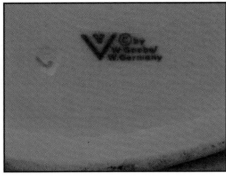

Goebel (1972 – 1979)

Goebel (1956)

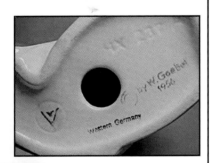

Goebel
(1980 – present)

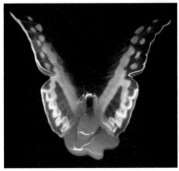

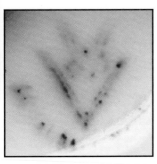

Goebel (1957)

Goedewaagen (1902)

Goldscheider (1885 – 1897)

Goldscheider (1885 – 1897)

Goldscheider (1937 – 1941)

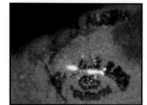

Goldscheider (1937 – 1941)

Goldscheider (1946 – 1959+)

Goldscheider (1946 – 1959+)

Goldscheider (1946 – 1959+)

Goldscheider (1946 – 1959+)

Gonder Originals (1941 – 1957)

Goodwin Pottery
(1893 – 1906)

Gonder Originals (1941 – 1957)

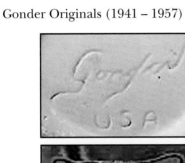

Goodwin Pottery
(1893 – 1906)

Gonder Originals
(1941 – 1957)

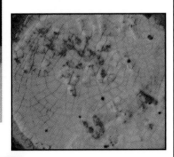

Goodwin Pottery
(1893 – 1906)

Goodwin Pottery
(1852)

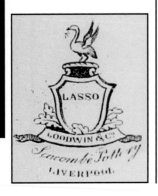

Goss, William Henry
(1862 – 1930)

Gouda, Holland (1891+)

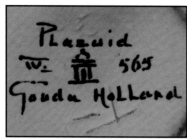

Gouda, Holland
(1913)

Gouda, Holland (1891+)

Gouda, Holland (1916)

Gouda, Holland (1895 – 1910)

Gouda, Holland
(1923 – 1930)

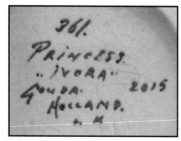

Gouda, Holland
(1898 – 1910)

Goumot-Labesse
(1955 – 1977)

Goumot-Labesse
(1955 – 1977)

Greber, Charles (1899 – 1933)

Gray, A. E. Pottery
(1934 – 1961)

Greber, Charles
(1899 – 1933)

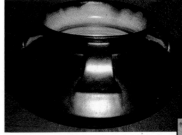

Gray, A. E. Pottery
(1934 – 1961)

Green, T. G. (1892+)

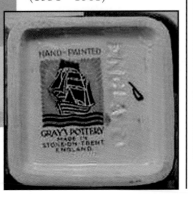

Gray, A. E. Pottery
(1934 – 1961)

Green, T. G. (1930 – present)

125

Green, T. G. (1930 – present)

Green, T. G. (1930 – present)

Green, T. G. (1980+)

Greenwood Pottery
(1868 – 1933)

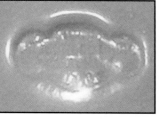

Greenwood Pottery
(1904)

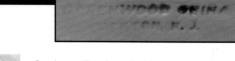

Greiner, Frederick Christian
(1894 – 1936)

Griffen, Smith & Hall
(1878 – 1889)

Griffen, Smith & Hall
(1878 – 1889)

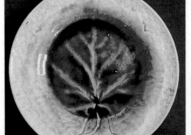

Grimwades (1900+)

Grimwades (1906+)

Grimwades (1906+)

Grimwades (1930+)

Grimwades (1906+)

Grimwades (1931)

Grimwades (1906 – 1910)

Grimwades (1934 – 1950)

Grimwades (1951+)

Grindley (1891 – 1914)

Grindley (1891 – 1914)

Grindley (1908+)

Grindley (1891 – 1914)

Grindley (1908+)

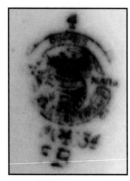

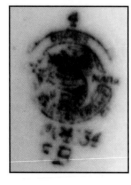

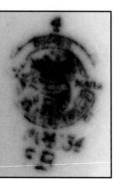

Grindley (1891 – 1914)

Grindley (1925)

Grindley (1925+)

Grindley
(1954 – 1960+)

Grindley (1925+)

Grindley Hotelware
(1980 – present)

Grindley
(1950s – 1960s)

Groschel & Stethmann
(1892 – 1915)

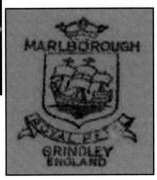

Grindley (1954 – 1960+)

Grosvenor, F.
(1879 – 1926)

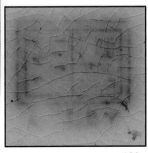

Grosvenor China
(1930s – 1964+)

Grueby Pottery
(1897 – 1911)

Grosvenor China
(1930s – 1964+)

Grueby Pottery
(1897 – 1911)

Grosvenor China
(1930s – 1964+)

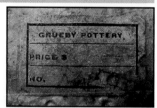

Grueby Pottery (1904)

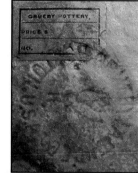

Grosvenor China (1934)

Grueby Pottery (1910+)

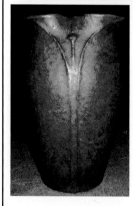

Grueby Pottery (1910+)

Gustafsberg
(1860 – 1890)

Guernsey Pottery
(1964+)

Gustafsberg
(1880 – 1925)

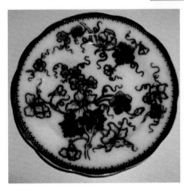

Guernsey Pottery (1964+)

Gustafsberg
(1880 – 1925)

Gustafsberg
(1839 – 1860)

Gustafsberg
(1895 – 1900)

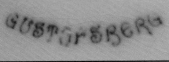

Gustafsberg
(1895 – 1930)

Gustafsberg (1903)

Gustafsberg (1900 – 1929)

Gustafsberg
(1910 – 1940)

Gustafsberg (1900 – 1929+)

Gustafsberg (1931+)

Gustafsberg (1902)

Gustafsberg (1932+)

Gustafsberg (1932+)

Gustafsberg (1950s – 1960s)

Gustafsberg (1932+)

Gustafsberg (1970+)

Gustafsberg
(1937 – 1978)

Gutherz, Oscar &
Edgar (1899 – 1918)

Gustafsberg
(1937 – 1978)

Haas & Czjzek (1918+)

Haas & Czjzek
(1939 – 1945)

Hackefors Porcelain
(1957 – present)

Hache, Alfred (1903)

Hadley, James
(1896 – 1897)

Hache & Pepin
(1845 – 1872)

Hadley, James (1902 – 1905)

Hackefors Porcelain
(1929 – 1957)

Hadley, M. A.
(1939 – present)

Haeger (1915 – present)

Haeger (1940 – present)

Haeger (1930 – present)

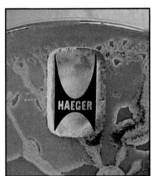

Haeger
(1940 – present)

Haeger
(1940 – present)

Haeger
(1940 – present)

Haeger
(1940 – present)

Haeger
(1940 – present)

Haeger
4060
U.S.A.

Haeger
(1940 – present)

Hall China
(1930 – 1972)

Hall, Ralph & Son (1825)

Hall China
(1930 – 1972)

Hall, Ralph & Son
(1843 – 1849)

Hall China
(1930 – 1972)

Hall China (1916 – 1930)

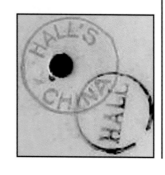

Hall China (1932 – 1963)

Hall China (1933 – 1976)

Hall China
(1937 – present)

Hall China (1933 – 1976)

Hall China
(1938 – 1953)

Hall China
(1933 – 1976)

Hall China (1950+)

Hall China
(1937 – present)

Hall China (1950 – 1955)

Hall China
(1969 – 1980+)

Hammersley (1939 – present)

Hall China (1969 – 1980+)

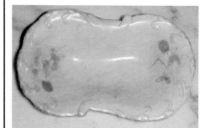

Hammersley
(1939 – present)

Hammersley
(1912 – 1939)

Hampshire Pottery
(1871 – 1923)

Hammersley
(1939 – present)

Hampshire Pottery (1871+)

Hampshire Pottery
(1883+)

Hampshire Pottery (1900 – 1920)

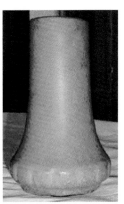

Hampshire Pottery
(1900 – 1920)

Hancock, Sampson
(1906 – 1912)

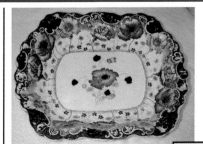

Hancock, Sampson
(1906 – 1912)

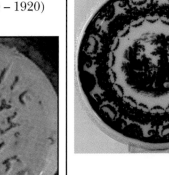

Hancock, Sampson (1910)

Hanke, Robert (1882 – 1914)

Harker Pottery (1890)

Harker Pottery
(1890 – 1900)

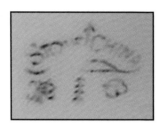

Harker Pottery
(1935 – 1950)

Harker Pottery (1929)

Harker Pottery
(1935 – 1950)

Harker Pottery
(1930 – 1935)

Harker Pottery
(1936 – 1948)

Harker Pottery
(1935 – 1950)

Harker Pottery
(1939 – 1947)

Harker Pottery
(1940 – 1948)

Harker Pottery (1950)

Harker Pottery
(1948 – 1955)

Harker Pottery (1950s)

Harker Pottery
(1948 – 1963)

Harker Pottery
(1954 – 1965)

Harker Pottery
(1950)

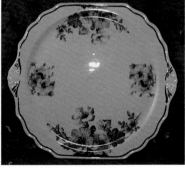

Harker Pottery (1954 – 1965)

141

Harker Pottery
(1955 – 1960)

Harrison & Shaw
(1800+)

Harker Pottery (1960 – 1972)

Hautin & Boulanger (1880+)

Harker Pottery
(1960 – 1972)

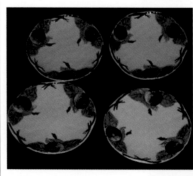

Hautin & Boulanger
(1880+)

Harker Pottery (1965)

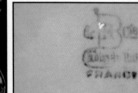

Hautin & Boulanger
(1930s)

Haviland, Johann
(1946)

Haynes, D. F.
(1882 – 1885)

Haviland, Johann
(1972)

Haynes, D. F. (1900+)

Haynes, Bennett
(1881 – 1895)

Heath, J. (1802 – 1850)

Haynes, D. F.
(1882 – 1884)

Heath Ceramics
(1941+)

143

Heinrich
(1896 – present)

Heinrich
(1976 – present)

Heinrich (1900)

Heinrich
(1976 – present)

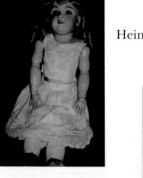

Heinrich (1976 – present)

Heinrich, Franz (1911+)

Heinrich
(1976 – present)

Henneberg Porcelain
(1973 – present)

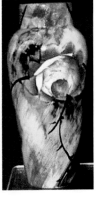

Heron, Robert (1883 – 1929)

Herculaneum
(1796 – 1833)

Heron, Robert
(1883 – 1929)

Herculaneum
(1790 – 1830)

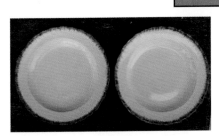

Hertel, Jacob (1969+)

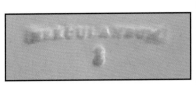

Herend (1980s)

Heubach & Koppelsdorf
(1882+)

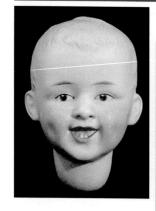

Heubach Bros. (1882+)

Heubach Bros. (1904+)

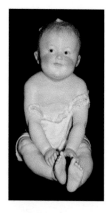

Heubach Bros. (1882+)

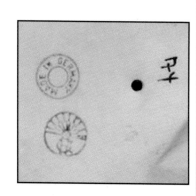

Heubach Bros. (1915)

Heubach Bros. (1882+)

Hewitt & Leadbeater (1907 – 1926)

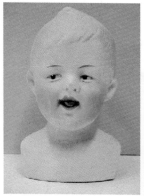

Heubach Bros. (1904+)

Hibel Studio (1979+)

Hibel Studio (1979+)

Hoganas Ceramics (1976+)

Hicks, Meigh & Johnson (1822 – 1835)

Holland, John (1852 – 1854)

Hochst (1965 – present)

Hollinshead & Kirkham (1900 – 1924)

Hoganas Ceramics (1976+)

Honition Pottery (1947 – 1956+)

Honition Pottery
(1947 – 1956+)

Honiton Pottery
(current)

Honition Pottery
(1947 – 1956+)

Honiton Pottery
(current)

Honition Pottery
(1947 – 1956+)

Hopper, Robin (1980+)

Honition Pottery
(1956+)

Horn Bros.
(1830 – 1860)

Horn Bros. (1830 – 1860)

Howard Pottery (1925 – 1964+)

Horn Bros. (1860s)

Howard Pottery (1950+)

Horn Bros. (1870)

Hubbe Brothers (1882 – 1898)

Hornsea (1951+)

Hudson, William (1889+)

149

Hudson, William
(1892 – 1912)

Hughes, Thomas
(1910 – 1930)

Hudson, William
(1936 – 1941+)

Hughes, Thomas
(1930 – 1935)

Hughes, E. (1908 – 1912)

Hughes & Sons (1850s)

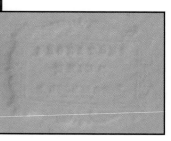

Hughes, Thomas (1895+)

Hull Pottery (1910 – 1935)

Hull Pottery (1930+)

Hull Pottery (1958+)

Hull Pottery (1930+)

Hull Pottery (1960+)

Hull Pottery (1950+)

Hull, A. E. (1960+)

Hull Pottery (1950+)

Hulme, William
(1891 – 1936)

Hutschenreuther (1882+)

Hutschenreuther
(1910)

Hutschenreuther
(1884 – 1909)

Hutschenreuther (1914+)

Hutschenreuther
(1886 – 1945)

Hutschenreuther
(1920 – 1945)

Hutschenreuther (1887)

Hutschenreuther
(1928 – 1963)

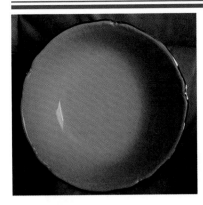

Hutschenreuther
(1928 – 1963)

Hutschenreuther (1938)

Hutschenreuther (1930)

Hutschenreuther (1939)

Hutschenreuther
(1930)

Hutschenreuther
(1940)

Hutschenreuther (1934)

Hutschenreuther
(1948+)

Hutschenreuther
(1950 – 1963)

Hutschenreuther
(1955 – 1969)

Hutschenreuther (1955)

Hutschenreuther
(1963 – present)

Hutschenreuther (1955)

Hutschenreuther (1970)

Hutschenreuther
(1955 – 1969)

Hutschenreuther (1975)

Weihnachtsteller 1975   Christmas Plate 1975
Serie: „Die Heilige Familie"   Series: "The Holy-Family"
Motiv: Mariä Verkündigung   Motive: The Annunciation
Design: Ole Winther, Dänemark Design: Ole Winther, Denmark
Modell: Uwe Netzsch   Model: Uwe Netzsch
Begrenzte Auflage   Limited Edition

Hutschenreuther (1975)

Hutschenreuther (1985)

Hyalyn
(1940s – present)

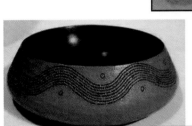

Hyalyn
(1940s – present)

Hyalyn
(1940s – present)

Hyalyn (1950s)

Iden Pottery (1961 – present)

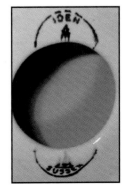

Iden Pottery (1961 – present)

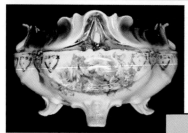

Ilmenau Porcelain
(1905 – 1938)

International Pottery
(1903+)

Imperial China
(1885 – 1896)

Interpace Corporation
(1974 – 1979)

International Pottery
(1860 – 1940+)

Iron Mountain (1968+)

International Pottery
(1903+)

Iron Mountain (1968+)

156

Iroquois China (1946+)

Isle of Wight (1950s)

Iroquois China
(1946+)

Isle of Wight (1950s+)

Iroquois China
(1950+)

Jackson China
(1923 – 1946)

Iroquois China
(1950+)

Jackson China
(1923 – 1946)

Jackson Vitrified China
(1930)

Jaeger (1900 – 1978)

Jackson Vitrified China
(1930s)

Jaeger (1902+)

Jaeger (1902+)

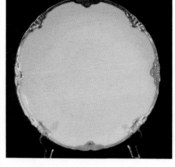

Jackson Vitrified China
(1939 – 1960)

Jaeger (1900 – 1978)

Jaeger (1902+)

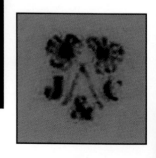

Jersey Pottery (1946+)

Johnson Bros. (1900+)

Johnson, Samuel
(1916 – 1931)

Johnson Bros. (1904+)

Johnson Bros. (1890)

Johnson Bros. (1913+)

Johnson Bros. (1900+)

Johnson Bros. (1950s)

159

Johnson Bros.
(current)

Jones, A. B. (1949+)

Jones, A. B. (1900 – 1913)

Jones, A. B. (1949+)

Jones, A. B. (1905 – 1935)

Jones, A. B. (1949+)

Jones, A. B. (1935+)

Jones, A. B.
(1957 – present)

Jones, A. G. Harley (1907+)

Jones, George
(1861 – 1873)

Jones, A. G. Harley
(1923 – 1934)

Jones, George (1873)

Jones, George
(1861 – 1873)

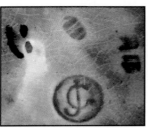

Jones, George
(1891 – 1924)

Jones, George (1861 – 1873)

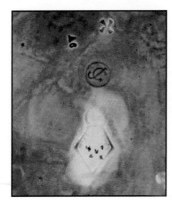

Jones, George
(1924 – 1951)

Jones, George
(1924 – 1951)

Jonroth Studios (1900+)

Jones, George
(1924 – 1951)

Josef Originals
(1945 – 1960)

Jones, George
(1924 – 1951)

Josef Originals (1960 – 1985)

Jonroth Studios (1900)

Josef Originals
(1960 – 1985)

Jugtown (1920s – 1930s)

Kahla Porcelain
(1957 – 1964)

Jugtown (1950s – 1970s)

Kahla Porcelain
(1957 – 1964)

Jugtown (1978)

Kahla Porcelain
(1957 – 1964)

Kaestner, Friedrich (1884 – 1929)

Kaiser Porcelain
(1970 – present)

Kalk Porcelain (1904+)

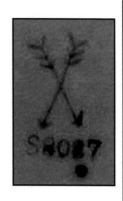

Karlskrona (1933 – 1968)

Kammer, Rudolf
(1961 – 1972)

Karlskrona
(1961 – 1970s)

Karlskrona (1924 – 1933)

Keeling & Co.
(1886 – 1899)

Karlskrona (1924 – 1933)

Keeling & Co.
(1886 – 1899)

Keeling & Co.
(1912 – 1936)

Keller & Guerin
(1890+)

Keller & Guerin (1889+)

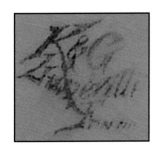

Keller & Guerin
(1890+)

Keller & Guerin (1889+)

Keller & Guerin
(1891+)

Keller & Guerin (1889+)

Keller & Guerin
(1891+)

Keller & Guerin (1900+)

Keller & Guerin (1900+)

Keller & Guerin (1940s – 1950s)

Kensington (1900+)

Kent, James (1897 – 1901)

Kent, James (1901+)

Kent, James (1901+)

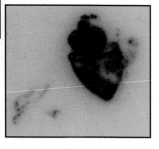

Kent, James (1901 – 1910)

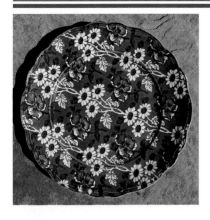

Kent, James (1913+)

Kent, James (1950 – current)

Kent, James (1930+)

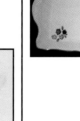

Kent, James
(1950 – current)

Kent, James (1930+)

Kent, James
(1950 – current)

Kent, James (1930+)

Kent, James (current)

Kerafina (1950+)

Keramos (1945+)

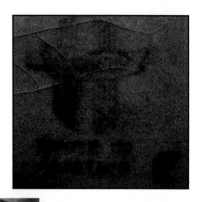

Kerafina (1950 – 1958)

Keramos (1945+)

Kerafina (1950+)

Keramos (1945+)

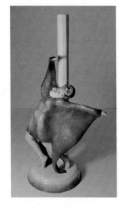

Keramos (1920+)

Kern Collectibles
(current)

168

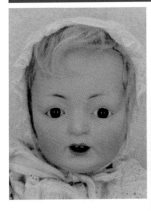

Kestner, J. D. (1900+)

Klemm, Richard
(1886 – 1916)

Kirkham (1946 – 1961)

Knowles, Edwin
(1900 – 1948)

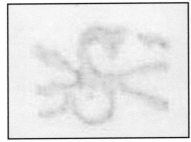

Kister, A. W. (1900 – 1972)

Knowles, Edwin
(1910 – 1948)

Kister, Fr. (1887)

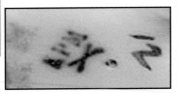

Knowles, Edwin (1953+)

Knowles, Edwin (1953+)

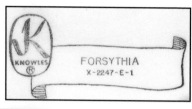

Knowles, Edwin (1956)

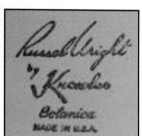

Knowles, Edwin
(1974 – present)

Knowles, Taylor &
Knowles (1890)

Knowles, Taylor &
Knowles (1890 – 1905)

Knowles, Taylor & Knowles
(1890 – 1907)

Knowles, Taylor &
Knowles (1891 – 1898)

Knowles, Taylor &
Knowles (1925)

Kokura (1921 – 1940)

Krautheim & Adelberg
(1945 – present)

Kranichfeld Porcelain
Factory (1903+)

Krautheim & Adelberg
(1945 – present)

Krautheim (1945+)

Krautheim & Adelberg
(1945 – present)

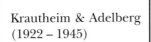

Krautheim & Adelberg
(1922 – 1945)

Krister (1939 – 1945)

Krister Porcelain Manu-
factory (1904 – 1927)

Kuba (1947 – present)

Krister Porcelain Manu-
factory (1904 – 1927)

Krister Porcelain
Manufactory (1930+)

Kunst (current)

Kunst (current)

Kronester
(1969 – present)

Kuznetsov (1875 – 1900)

Laeuger, Max (1920)

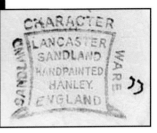

Lancaster
(1930 – 1964+)

Lancaster (1906+)

Lancaster (1954)

Lancaster (1906+)

Lang, Anton (1880 – 1938)

Lancaster
(1930 – 1964+)

Lang, Anton
(1880 – 1938)

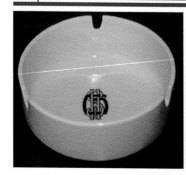

Langenthal (1930+)

Laughlin, Homer (1900)

Late Mayers (1876)

Laughlin, Homer (1900)

Laughlin, Homer (1873 – 1877)

Laughlin, Homer (1901 – 1915)

Laughlin, Homer (1900)

Laughlin, Homer (1907)

Laughlin, Homer
(1912)

Laughlin, Homer
(1939)

Laughlin, Homer
(1934)

Laughlin, Homer
(1940 – 1965)

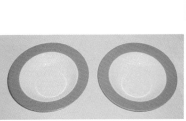

Laughlin, Homer (1935)

Laughlin, Homer
(1940 – 1965)

Laughlin, Homer
(1935 – 1941)

Laughlin, Homer
(1940 – 1965)

175

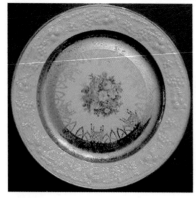

Laughlin, Homer
(1940 – 1965)

Laughlin, Homer (1953)

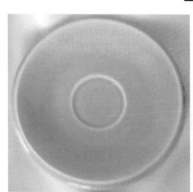

Laughlin, Homer
(1941 – 1945)

Laughlin, Homer
(1954)

Laughlin, Homer
(1946 – 1960)

Laughlin, Homer
(1955)

Laughlin, Homer
(1950 – 1960)

Laughlin, Homer
(1960)

Laughlin, Homer (1960)

Laughlin, Homer (1960)

Laughlin, Homer
(1970 – 1980+)

Laughlin, Homer
(1970 – present)

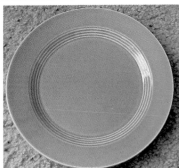

Laughlin, Homer
(1970 – present)

Laughlin, Homer
(1970 – present)

Lawrence, Thomas
(1936+)

Leach, Bernard
(1921 – 1964+)

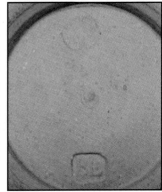

177

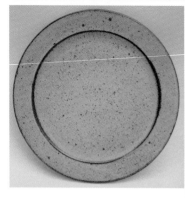

Leach, Bernard
(1921 – 1964+)

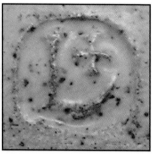

Leach, David (1956+)

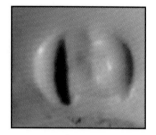

Leach, Bernard
(1921 – 1964+)

Leach, David (1956+)

Leach, Bernard
(1921 – 1964+)

Lebeau Porcelain (1879 – 1910)

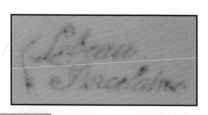

Leach, David (1956+)

Lefton
(1940 – present)

Lefton (1940 – present)

Lenox (1906 – present)

Lefton (1940 – present)

Lenox (1970+)

Leigh Potters
(1926 – 1931)

Lenox (current)

Lenox (1906 – 1924)

Leonard, P. H.
(1890 – 1908)

Levy, Ch. (1876)

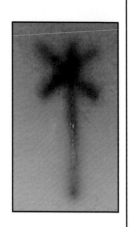

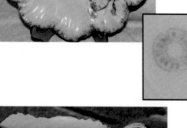

Limoges, A. Lanternier
(1890s)

Lietzke Porcelains
(1950s)

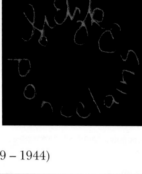

Limoges, A. Lanternier
(1891 – 1914)

Limbach (1919 – 1944)

Limoges, A. Lanternier
(1891 – 1914)

Limoges, A. Lanternier
(1890s)

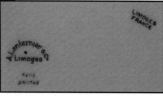

Limoges, A. Lanternier
(1900)

Limoges, A. Lanternier
(1915+)

Limoges, Bawo & Dotter
(1900+)

Limoges, Bawo & Dotter
(1891 – 1900)

Limoges, Bawo & Dotter
(1900 – 1914)

Limoges, Bawo & Dotter
(1891 – 1900)

Limoges, Bawo &
Dotter (1900 – 1914)

Limoges, Bawo &
Dotter (1900+)

Limoges, Beaux-Arts
(1900)

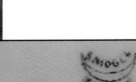

Limoges, Bernardaud & Co. (1900)

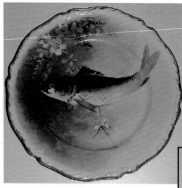

Limoges, Blakeman & Henderson (1900 – 1910)

Limoges, Bernardaud & Co. (1914 – 1930s+)

Limoges, Blakeman & Henderson (1900 – 1910)

Limoges, Bernardaud (1900 – 1929)

Limoges, Blakeman & Henderson (1900 – 1910)

Limoges, Bernardaud (1900 – 1929)

Limoges, Camille Tharaud (1920s)

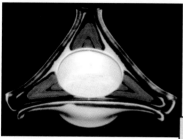

Limoges, Camille Tharaud (1922+)

Limoges, Charles Ahrenfeldt (1886 – 1910)

Limoges, Camille Tharaud (1980 – present)

Limoges, Charles Ahrenfeldt (1893+)

Limoges, Castel (1979+)

Limoges, Charles Ahrenfeldt (1894 – 1930s)

Limoges, Castel (1980s – 1990s)

Limoges, Charles Ahrenfeldt (1894 – 1930s)

Limoges, Charles Ahrenfeldt (1894 – 1930s)

Limoges, Charles Ahrenfeldt (1946 – 1969)

Limoges, Charles Ahrenfeldt (1894 – 1930s)

Limoges, Charles Field Haviland (1882 – 1890)

Limoges, Charles Ahrenfeldt (1894 – 1930s)

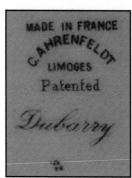

Limoges, Charles Field Haviland (1900 – 1941)

Limoges, Charles Ahrenfeldt (1918)

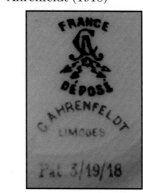

Limoges, Charles Field Haviland (1900)

Limoges, Charles Field
Haviland (1900)

Limoges, Delinieres &
Bernardaud (1900)

Limoges, Charles Field
Haviland (1941+)

Limoges, Delinieres & Co. (1870s)

Limoges, Coiffe
(1891 – 1914)

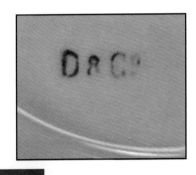

Limoges, Delinieres &
Co. (1894 – 1900)

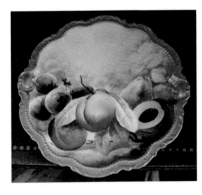

Limoges, Comte
D'Artois (1930s+)

Limoges, Delinieres &
Co. (1894 – 1900)

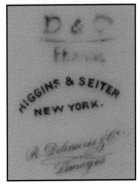

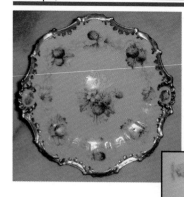

Limoges, Flambeau China
(1890s – 1900s)

Limoges, Fontanille &
Marraud (1935+)

Limoges, Flambeau
China (1900 – 1914)

Limoges, Frank Havi-
land (1910 – 1914)

Limoges, F. Legrand
(1924 – 1944)

Limoges, G. Demartine
(1891 – 1910)

Limoges, F. Legrand
(1924 – 1962+)

Limoges, George
Bassett (1890 – 1914)

Limoges, George Borgfeldt (1906 – 1920)

Limoges; Gerard, Dufraisseix & Abbot (1980 – current)

Limoges; Gerard, Dufraisseix & Abbot (1937+)

Limoges; Gerard, Dufraisseix & Morel (1882 – 1890)

Limoges; Gerard, Dufraisseix & Abbot (1937 – 1976)

Limoges, Haviland & Co. (1879 – 1889)

Limoges; Gerard, Dufraisseix & Abbot (1937 – 1976)

Limoges, Haviland & Co. (1888 – 1896)

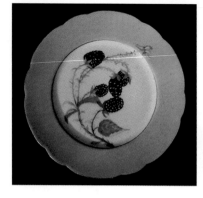

Limoges, Haviland & Co. (1888 – 1896)

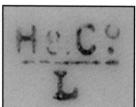

Limoges, Haviland & Co. (1893 – 1930)

Limoges, Haviland & Co. (1941 – current)

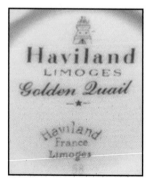

Limoges, Jean Pouyat (1900 – 1906)

Limoges, Jean Pouyat (1906 – 1932)

Limoges, Jean Pouyat (1908)

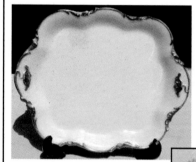

Limoges, Klingenberg & Charles Dwenger (1880s – 1890s)

Limoges, Klingenberg & Charles Dwenger (1900 – 1910)

Limoges, Latrille Freres
(1908 – 1913)

Limoges; Lazeyras,
Rosenfeld & Lehman
(1920s)

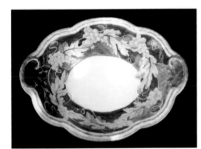

Limoges, Latrille
Freres (1908 – 1913)

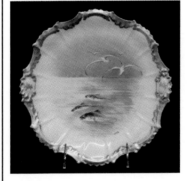

Limoges, Leon Sazerat
(1891 – 1900)

Limoges, Laviolette
(1896 – 1905)

Limoges, L.W. Levy
(1915 – 1920+)

Limoges; Lazeyras,
Rosenfeld & Lehman
(1920s)

Limoges, Martial Redon
(1891 – 1896)

Limoges, Martial Redon
(1905 – 1939)

Limoges, Paroutaud
Freres (1903 – 1917)

Limoges, Mavaleix &
Granger (1922 – 1938)

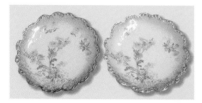

Limoges, Porcelaine Limousine (1930)

Limoges, P. M. Mavaleix
(1908 – 1914)

Limoges, Raynaud &
Co. (1980 – present)

Limoges, Pallas
(1980 – present)

Limoges, Ribes (1891+)

Limoges, Robert
Haviland (1924+)

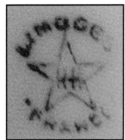

Limoges, Theodore
Haviland (1893+)

Limoges, Robert
Haviland (1949+)

Limoges, Theodore Havi-
land (1893+)

Limoges, Tharaud
(1977+)

Limoges, Theodore
Haviland (1893+)

Limoges, Theodore
Haviland (1893+)

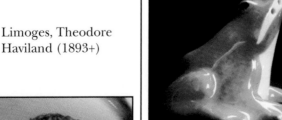

Limoges, Theodore Havi-
land (1904 – 1925)

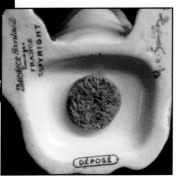

Limoges, Theodore Haviland
(1920 – 1936)

Limoges, Tressemanes
& Vogt (1891 – 1907)

Limoges, Theodore
Haviland (1925+)

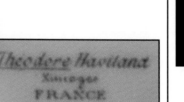

Limoges, Tressemanes &
Vogt (1892 – 1907)

Limoges, Theodore
Haviland (1925 – 1945)

Limoges, Tressemann
& Vogt (1892 – 1907)

Limoges, Theodore Havi-
land (1937 – present)

Limoges, Tressemann &
Vogt (1905 – 1910)

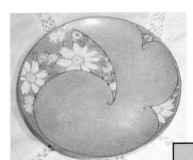

Limoges, Union Ceramique (1909 – 1938)

Limoges, Union Ceramique (1909 – 1938)

Limoges, Vignaud Freres (1911 – 1938)

Limoges, Vignaud Freres (1911 – 1938+)

Limoges, Vignaud Freres (1938+)

Limoges, Wannamakers (1906 – 1932)

Limoges, William Guerin (1900 – 1932)

Limoges, William Guerin (1900 – 1932)

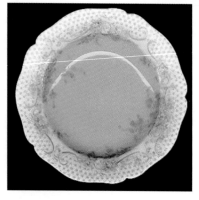

Limoges, William
Guerin (1900 – 1932)

Lindner (1948 – 1981+)

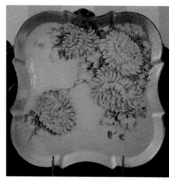

Limoges, William Guerin
(1900 – 1932)

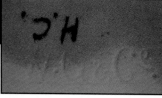

Lindner
(1948 – 1981+)

Limoges, William
Guerin (1908)

Lindner (1948 – 1981+)

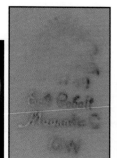

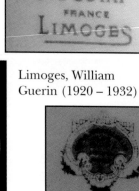

Limoges, William
Guerin (1920 – 1932)

Lindner (1948 – 1981+)

Linthorpe Pottery
(1879 – 1889)

Lladro (1965 – present)

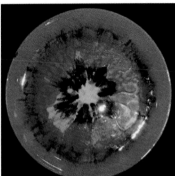

Linthorpe Pottery
(1879 – 1889)

Lladro (1965 – present)

Linthorpe Pottery
(1879 – 1889)

Lladro (1965+)

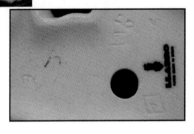

Linthorpe Pottery
(1879 – 1889)

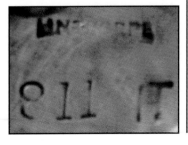

Lladro (1987 – 1991)

L. Lourioux (1971+)

L. Lourioux (1971+)

Locke & Co.
(1895 – 1900)

Lomonosov Porcelain
Factory (1917 – present)

Lomonosov Porcelain Factory
(1917 – present)

Longwy Faience (1875+)

Longwy Faience
(1875+)

Longwy Faience (1875+)

Longwy Faience
(1878+)

Longwy Faience (1890s)

Longwy Faience (1878+)

Longwy Faience (1891+)

Longwy Faience (1878+)

Longwy Faience (1910)

Longwy Faience (1881 – 1889)

Longwy Faience
(1920 – 1940)

197

Longwy Faience
(1920 – 1940)

Longwy Faience
(1940+)

Longwy Faience
(1920 – 1940)

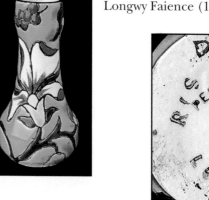

Longwy Faience (1940+)

Longwy Faience
(1920 – 1940)

Longwy Faience (1940+)

Longwy Faience
(1920 – 1940)

Lord Nelson Pottery
(1940 – 1960+)

198

Lord Nelson Pottery
(1940 – 1960+)

Los Angeles Potteries
(1948 – 1954)

Los Angeles Potteries
(1948 – 1954)

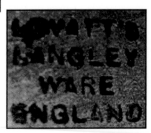

Lovatts Potteries
(1895+)

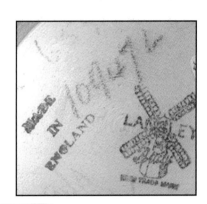

Lovatts Potteries (1931 – 1962)

Lovatts Potteries
(1960 – present)

Low Art Tile
(1877 – 1893)

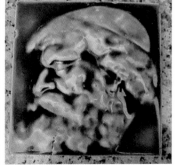

Low Art Tile
(1881 – 1885)

Low Art Tile
(1881 – 1885)

MacIntosh, Harrison
(1950 – 1955)

Ludwigsburg (1918+)

MacIntyre, James
(1868 – 1883)

Ludwigsburg
(1948 – present)

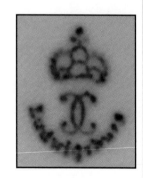

MacIntyre, James
(1894 – 1928)

Lyman, Fenton & Co. (1849)

MacIntyre, James
(1894 – 1928)

MacIntyre, James (1898 – 1904)

Maddock, John (1900+)

Maddock, John
(1842 – present)

Maddock, John (1907+)

Maddock, John
(1891 – 1912)

Maddock, John (1907+)

Maddock, John (1896+)

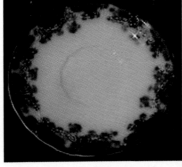

Maddock, John (1907+)

Maddock, John
(1907+)

Maddock, John
(1907+)

Maddock, John
(1940s – 1950s)

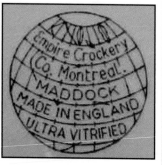

Maddock, John (1960+)

Maddock, John
(1980+)

Maddock Pottery
(1900 – 1929)

Maddock Pottery (1904+)

Maddux
(1935 – 1964+)

202

Mafra & Son (1853+)

Maling, C. T. (1890+)

Maling, C. T. (1817 – 1853)

Maling, C. T. (1900)

Maling, C. T. (1817 – 1853)

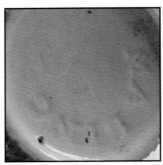

Maling, C. T. (1930 – 1955)

Maling, C. T. (1875 – 1908)

Maling, C. T. (1930 – 1955)

Maling, C. T. (1930 – 1955)

Marblehead Pottery
(1908 – 1936)

Maling, C. T.
(1949 – 1963)

Marblehead Pottery (1908 – 1936)

Manka, Franz
(1936 – 1945)

Maria Pottery
(1956 – 1958)

Manzoni, Carlo (1895 – 1898)

Mark & Gutherz
(1890 – 1900)

Marseille, Armand (1900 – 1930)

Martin Bros. (1882 – 1914)

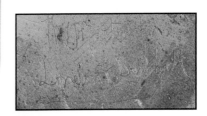

Marseille, Armand
(1900 – 1930)

Martin Bros.
(1882 – 1914)

Martin Bros.
(1847 – 1918)

Martin Bros. (1882 – 1914)

Martin Bros. (1882 – 1914)

Martin Bros. (1882 – 1914)

Martin Bros. (1882 – 1914)

Masons (1813 – 1825)

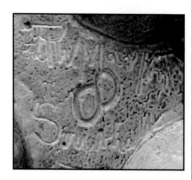

Martin Bros. (1900+)

Masons (1820)

Martin Bros. (1900+)

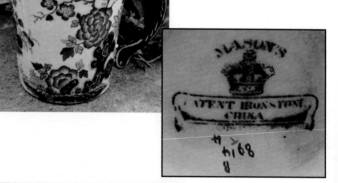

Masons (1845+)

Masons (1813 – 1825)

Massier, Clement
(1883 – 1917)

Massier, Clement (1883 – 1917)

Massier, Clement (1883 – 1917)

Massier, Clement (1917+)

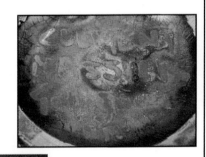

Matsumura (1960s+)

Matthews & Clark
(1890 – 1920)

Mayer, T. J. & J. (1830+)

Mayer, T. J. & J. (1834 – 1848)

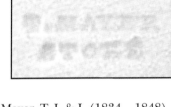

Mayer, T. J. & J.
(1840 – 1860)

Mayer, T. J. & J. (1847)

Mayer, T. J. & J. (1851)

Mayer China
(1881 – 1891)

Mayer China
(1881 – 1930+)

McCoy (1906+)

McCoy (1920s – 1930s)

McCoy (1935)

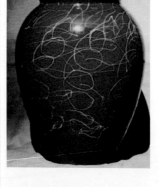

McCoy (1925 – 1929)

McCoy (1925 – 1929)

McCoy (1940 – 1966)

McCoy (1930+)

McCoy (1940s)

McCoy (1935)

McCoy (1940s – 1960s)

McCoy (1940 – 1966)

McCoy (1960s – 1970s)

McCoy (1960s – 1970s)

McCoy (1970s – 1980s)

McCoy (1967 – 1974)

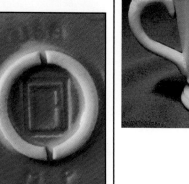

McNicol, D. E.
(1892 – 1910)

McCoy (1970s – 1980s)

McNicol, D. E.
(1892 – 1910)

McCoy (1970s – 1980s)

McNicol, D. E.
(1892 – 1910)

McNicol, D. E.
(1892 – 1920)

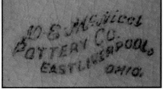

McNicol, D. E.
(1897 – 1915)

McNicol, D. E.
(1915 – 1929)

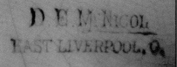

McNicol, D. E.
(1915 – 1929)

McNicol, D. E.
(1930 – 1954)

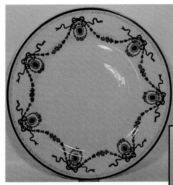

McNicol, D. E.
(1933 – 1950)

McNicol, D. E. (1935+)

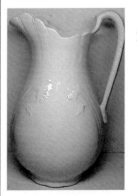

McNicol, D. E. (1935 – 1950)

McNicol, D. E. (1950s)

McNicol, T. A. (1924)

McNicol-Smith (1901)

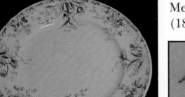

Meakin, Alfred
(1875 – 1897)

Meakin, Alfred
(1875 – 1897)

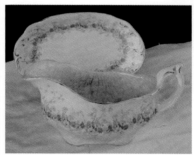

Meakin, Alfred
(1875 – 1897)

Meakin, Alfred
(1875 – 1897)

Meakin, Alfred (1891)

Meakin, Alfred (1891+)

Meakin, Alfred (1900)

Meakin, Alfred
(1891 – 1930)

Meakin, Alfred
(1907+)

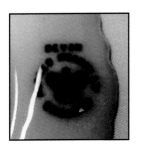

Meakin, Alfred
(1891 – 1930)

Meakin, Alfred (1907+)

Meakin, Alfred
(1897+)

Meakin, Alfred
(1907+)

Meakin, Alfred (1930s)

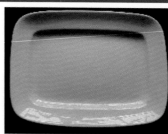

Meakin, Charles
(1883 – 1889)

Meakin, Alfred (1930s)

Meakin, Charles
(1883 – 1889)

Meakin, Alfred (1930s)

Meakin, J.&G. (1870 – 1890)

Meakin, Alfred (1930s)

Meakin, J.&G. (1890)

Meakin, J.&G. (1890+)

Meakin, J.&G. (1907+)

Meakin, J.&G. (1907+)

Meakin, J.&G. (1912+)

Meakin, J.&G. (1912+)

Meakin, J.&G. (1962)

Meakin, J.&G. (1980 – present)

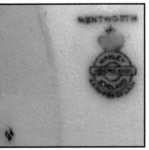

Meakin, J.&G. (1980 – present)

Mehlem, Franz Anton
(1887 – 1920)

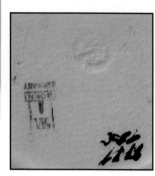

Mehlem, Franz Anton
(1887 – 1920)

Mehlem, Franz Anton
(1887 – 1920)

Mehlem, Franz Anton
(1888 – 1920)

Mehlem, Franz Anton
(1887 – 1920)

Mehlem, Franz Anton
(1890 – 1920)

Mehlem, Franz Anton
(1887 – 1920)

Mehlem, Franz Anton (1890 – 1920)

Meigh, Charles (1835 – 1849)

Meir, John
(1848 – 1863)

Meigh, Charles
(1851 – 1861)

Meir, John
(1848 – 1863)

Meigh, Charles
(1851 – 1861)

Meir, John
(1848 – 1863)

Meigh, Charles
(1851 – 1861)

Meir, John
(1848 – 1863)

Mercer Pottery (1868 – 1937)

Mercer Pottery
(1868 – 1937)

Mercer Pottery
(1868 – 1937)

Mercer Pottery
(1900+)

Mercer Pottery
(1900 – 1937)

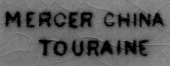

Mercer Pottery (1902)

Meredith, Roper
(1913 – 1924)

Merkelbach, Reinhold (1895+)

Merkelbach, Reinhold (1910)

Merkelbach, Reinhold (1925 – 1945)

Merkelbach, Reinhold (1910)

Merkelbach, Reinhold (1964 – 1968)

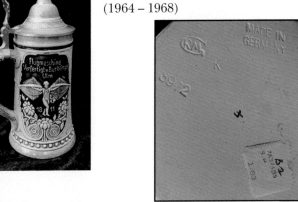

Merkelbach, Reinhold (1925 – 1945)

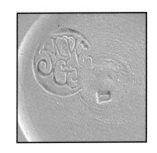

Merkelbach & Wick (1872 – 1921)

Merkelbach, Reinhold (1925 – 1945)

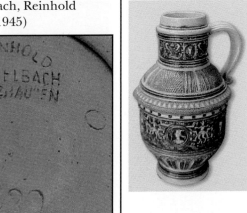

Merkelbach & Wick (1872 – 1921)

Merkelbach & Wick (1872 – 1921)

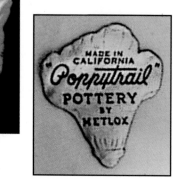

Metlox Pottery (1980)

Merrimac Pottery (1902 – 1908)

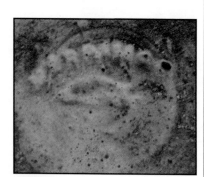

Metlox Pottery
(1980 – present)

Metenier, Gilbert
(1896 – 1939)

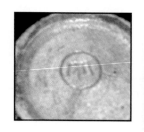

Metthey, Andre (1901)

Metzler & Ortloff (1970+)

Metlox Pottery
(1958 – 1978+)

Middleton, J. H.
(1930 – 1941+)

Midwinter (current)

Midwinter
(1910 – present)

Midwinter (current)

Midwinter
(1940s – 1960s)

Mikasa (1980 – present)

Midwinter
(1940s – 1960s)

Mikasa
(1980 – present)

221

Minton (1800 – 1830)

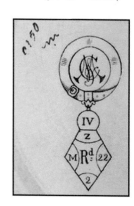

Minton (1841 – 1873)

Minton (1830 – 1860)

Minton (1843)

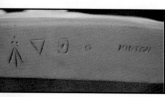

Minton (1836 – 1841)

Minton (1845 – 1860)

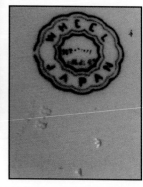

Minton (1840 – 1860)

Minton (1845)

Minton (1850+)

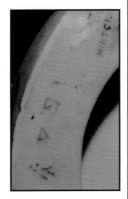

Minton (1862)

Minton (1853)

Minton (1863 – 1872)

Minton (1862 – 1871)

Minton (1863 – 1872)

Minton (1862)

Minton (1863 – 1872)

Minton (1864)

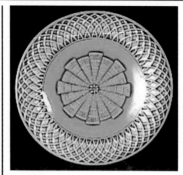

Minton (1870)

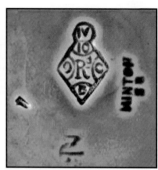

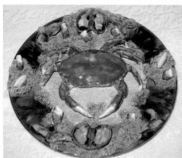

Minton (1865)

Minton (1870)

Minton (1869)

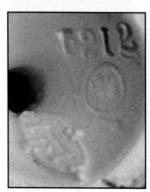

Minton (1871 – 1875)

Minton (1870)

Minton (1873)

Minton (1873+)

Minton (1881)

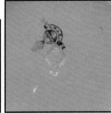

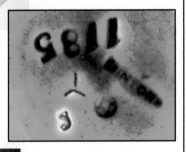

Minton (1873+)

Minton (1881)

Minton (1877)

Minton (1890+)

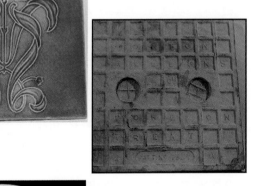

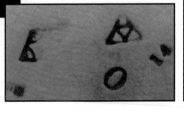

Minton (1879)

Minton (1900 – 1908)

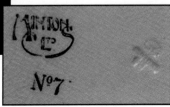

Minton (1908)

Minton, Hollins & Co. (1870+)

Minton (1912 – 1950)

Miramar (1935 – 1964)

18th., Cent., Staffordshire Salt-glaze

Minton (1912 – 1950)

Mitterteich (1918+)

Minton (1951 – present)

GRASMERE

MINTON
1793

FINE BONE CHINA
MADE IN ENGLAND
© MINTON LIMITED 1973

Mitterteich (1918+)

Mitterteich (1938+)

Moorcroft (1913 – present)

Mitterteich (1946+)

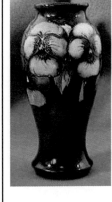

Moorcroft (1913 – present)

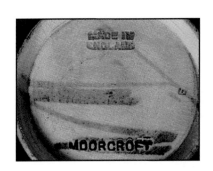

Moira Pottery (1922+)

Moorcroft (1919 – 1945)

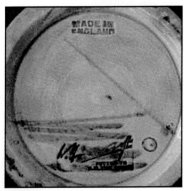

Moira Pottery (1922+)

Moorcroft (1919+)

Moorcroft (1919+)

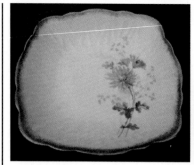

Moore (1891+)

Moorcroft (1919 – 1945)

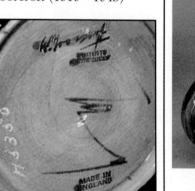

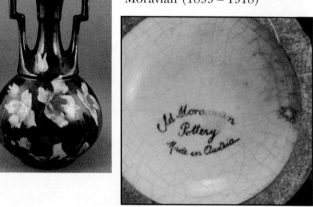

Moravian (1899 – 1918)

Moorcroft (1930 – 1949)

Morgan, William De
(1882 – 1888)

Moorcroft (1945+)

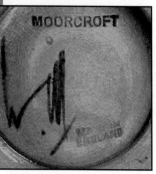

Morgan, William De
(1888 – 1897)

Morgan, William De
(1888+)

Morley, Francis
(1845 – 1858)

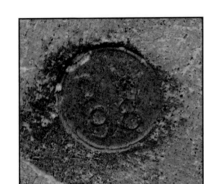

Morgan, William De (1898+)

Morley, Francis
(1845 – 1858)

Morimura Bros. (1891+)

Morley & Co.
(1879 – 1884)

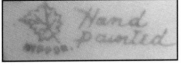

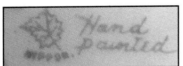

Morley & Co. (1879 – 1884)

Morley, Francis
(1845 – 1858)

Morris, Thomas (1912+)

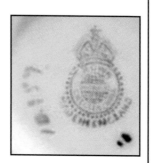

Mosa Maastricht (1930s+)

Mortlock, John (1877)

Mosaic Tile Co. (1894 – 1964)

Mortlock, John (1877)

Mosa Maastricht
(1883 – present)

Mosaic Tile Co. (1894+)

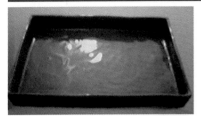

Mosaic Tile Co.
(1930 – 1964)

Muller, Paul
(1920 – 1928)

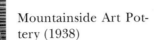

Mountainside Art Pottery (1938)

Muller & Co. (1907 – present)

Muller, Carl (1920)

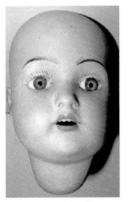

Muller & Co.
(1907 – present)

Muller, E.&A. (1890+)

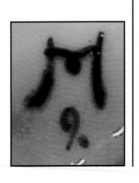

Muncie Pottery (1922+)

231

Musterschutz (1930s+)

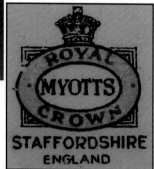

Myott (1936+)

Myott (1930+)

Myott (1936+)

Myott (1930+)

Myott (1936+)

Myott (1930+)

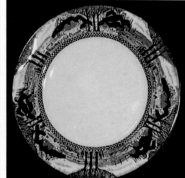

Myott (1940s – 1960s)

Myott (1940s – 1960s)

National Potteries (1938+)

Myott (1980 – present)

National Potteries (1970+)

National Potteries
(1938 – present)

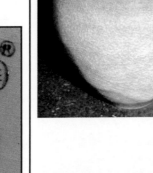

Natzler (1930s+)

National Potteries
(1938 – present)

Naudot, Camille
(1904 – 1919)

Nautilus Porcelain
(1896 – 1913)

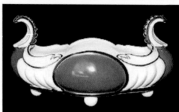

Neu-Tettau
(1904 – 1935)

Nautilus Porcelain
(1903 – 1913)

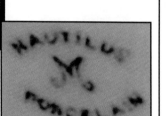

New Chelsea (1919+)

Neuerer, Hans (1943+)

New Chelsea (1943+)

Neukirchner, Franz
(1916 – 1977)

New Chelsea (1943+)

Newcomb Pottery
(1896 – 1945)

New England Pottery
(1889 – 1895)

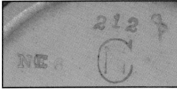

Newcomb Pottery
(1896 – 1945)

New Hall Pottery
(1930 – 1951)

New Devon (1957+)

New Hall Pottery
(1930 – 1951)

New England Pottery
(1887+)

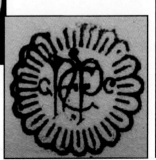

New Porcelain Factory
(1935 – 1948)

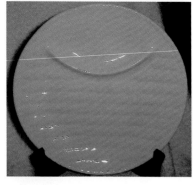

New Porcelain Factory
(1948 – 1981+)

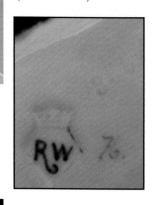

New York & Rudolstadt
(1887 – 1918)

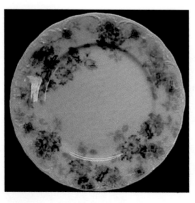

Newport Pottery
(1920+)

New York & Rudolstadt
(1904 – 1924+)

New Wharf Pottery
(1890 – 1894)

New York & Rudol-
stadt (1904 – 1924+)

New York & Rudolstadt
(1887 – 1918)

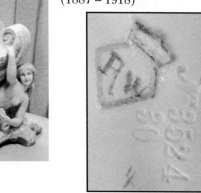

Nicodemis, Chester (1965+)

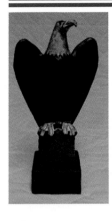

Nicodemis, Chester (1965+)

Nippon, Toki
(1876 – present)

Niloak Pottery (1909 – 1944)

Nippon, Rising
Sun (1890 – 1921)

Niloak Pottery (1909 – 1944)

Nippon, Royal Kaga
(1890 – 1921)

Niloak Pottery
(1930 – 1942)

Nippon, Royal Kinran
Crown (1890 – 1921)

Nippon, Japan
(1891 – 1921)

Nippon, Shofu Industrial
Co. (1921 – 1965)

Nippon, Nihon Yoko Boeki
Co. (1891 – present)

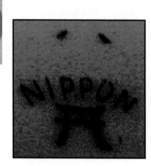

Nippon, Torii
(1894 – 1921)

Nippon, RC (1911+)

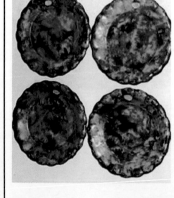

Nittsjo Earthenware
(1934+)

Nippon, Royal Nishiki (1890 – 1921)

Nittsjo Earthenware
(1947+)

Northwestern Terra Cotta (1920)

Nymolle (1942+)

Norton Pottery
(1845 – 1847)

Nymolle (1942+)

Nymphenburg (1895+)

Nove (1727 – 1835)

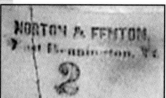

Nymolle (1942+)

Nymphenburg (1895+)

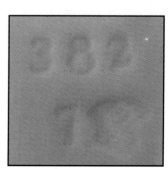

Occupied Japan
(1945 – 1952)

Occupied Japan
(1945 – 1952)

Occupied Japan
(1945 – 1952)

Occupied Japan
(1945 – 1952)

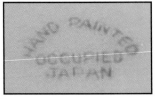

Occupied Japan (1945 – 1952)

Occupied Japan
(1945 – 1952)

SANGO CHINA
MADE IN OCCUPIED
JAPAN

FLORADEL

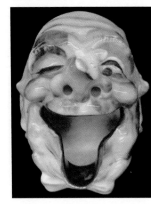

Occupied Japan (1945 – 1952)

Ohme, Hermann
(1882+)

OLD IVORY
117

Ohme, Hermann (1882+)

Ohr, George (1883+)

Ohme, Hermann (1882+)

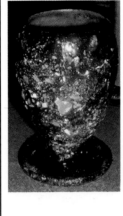

Ohr, George (1883+)

Ohme, Hermann (1882+)

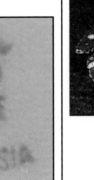

Ohr, George (1899 – 1906)

Ohme, Hermann (1882+)

Onondaga Pottery (1874 – 1893)

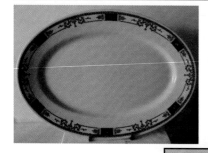

Onondaga Pottery
(1900 – 1966)

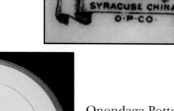

Onondaga Pottery
(1900 – 1966)

Bracelet

Onondaga Pottery
(1900 – 1966)

Ott & Brewer
(1863 – 1894)

Ott & Brewer
(1863 – 1894)

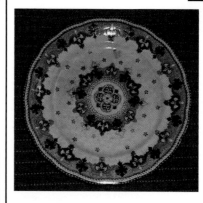

Ott & Brewer
(1863 – 1894)

Ott & Brewer (1863+)

Ott & Brewer (1866)

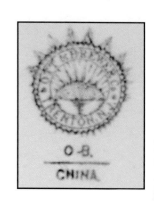

Ott & Brewer (1876)

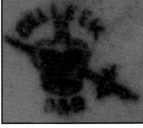

Owens Pottery
(1891 – 1907)

Ott & Brewer (1882)

Owens Pottery
(1891 – 1907)

Ott & Brewer (1886)

O.B.
CHINA

Owens Pottery (1901+)

Owens
1 4 4

Owens Pottery (1885+)

1157

Owens Pottery (1906+)

OWENSART

Paden City Pottery
(1930 – 1956)

Paden City Pottery
(1940)

Paden City Pottery
(1930 – 1956)

Paden City Pottery
(1940)

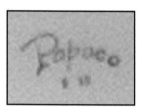

Paden City Pottery
(1930 – 1956)

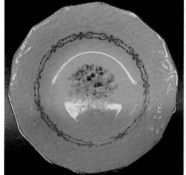

Paden City Pottery
(1940+)

Paden City Pottery
(1930 – 1956)

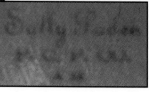

Palissy Pottery
(1908 – 1936)

Palissy Pottery
(1908 – 1936)

Palissy Pottery
(1940s – 1960s)

Palissy Pottery
(1937 – 1946+)

Palissy Pottery
(1970 – present)

Palissy Pottery
(1940s – 1960s)

Palissy Pottery
(1970 – present)

Palissy Pottery
(1940s – 1960s)

Palissy Pottery
(1970 – present)

247

Pankhurst, J. W. (1870s)

Paragon China
(1915 – 1919)

Paragon China
(1893 – 1920+)

Paragon China (1915)

Paragon China
(1893 – 1920+)

Paragon China
(1932+)

Paragon China
(1904 – 1919)

Paragon China
(1939 – 1949)

Paragon China
(1940 – present)

Pech, R.&E. (1945+)

Paragon China
(1940 – present)

Pennsbury Pottery
(1951 – 1971)

Pauline Pottery (1883+)

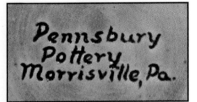

Pennsbury Pottery
(1951 – 1971)

Pearl China (1930 – present)

Pennsbury Pottery
(1951 – 1971)

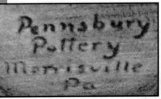

Pennsbury Pottery
(1951 – 1971)

Pewabic Pottery
(1903 – present)

Peoria Pottery (1873 – 1902)

Pewabic Pottery (1920)

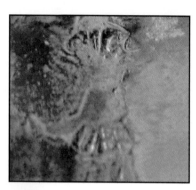

Peoria Pottery
(1873 – 1902)

Pfaltzgraff (1940+)

Petit, Jacob (1830 – 1862)

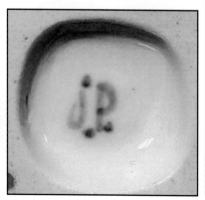

Pfaltzgraff
(1950 – present)

Pfaltzgraff (current)

Pfeffer Bros. (1900+)

Pfeiffer & Lowenstein
(1914 – 1918)

Pfeiffer & Lowenstein
(1914 – 1918)

Philadelphia City
Pottery (1868)

Phillips, G.
(1834 – 1848)

Phillips, G.
(1834 – 1848)

Phillips, G. (1845)

Picasso (1946+)

Pickard China
(1925 – 1938)

Pick, Albert (1935)

Pickard China
(1938 – present)

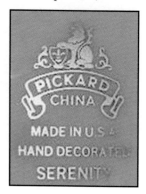

Pickard China (1895 – 1898)

Pierce, Howard
(1941+)

Pickard China
(1919 – 1922)

Pierce, Howard (1941+)

Pierce, Howard (1993)

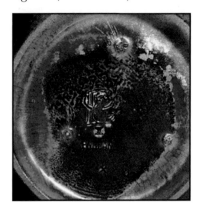

Pilkingtons (1904 – 1914)

Pigeon Forge (1946+)

Pilkingtons (1914 – 1938)

Pigeon Forge (1946+)

Pillin Pottery (1950s – 1980s)

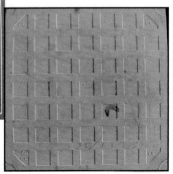

Pilkingtons (1900)

Pillivuyt, Charles (1854+)

Pinder Bourne
(1862 – 1882)

Pioneer Pottery
(1894 – 1900)

Pinder Bourne
(1862 – 1882)

Pioneer Pottery
(1935 – 1958)

Pinder Bourne
(1862 – 1882)

Pioneer Pottery
(1935 – 1958)

Pinder Bourne
(1862 – 1882)

Pisgah Forest
(1920 – 1961)

Pisgah Forest (1920 – 1961)

Plankenhammer
(1920 – 1978)

Pisgah Forest
(1920 – 1961)

Plant, R. H. & S. L.
(1947 – present)

Pisgah Forest
(1920 – 1961)

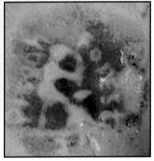

Plant, R. H. & S. L.
(1947 – present)

Pisgah Forest
(1920 – 1961)

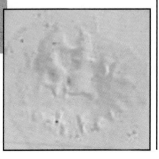

Plant, R. H. & S. L.
(1947 – present)

Plaue Porcelain
(1974 – present)

Podmore, Walker
(1849 – 1859)

Podmore, Walker
(1834 – 1859)

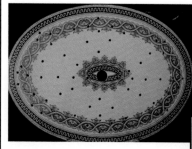

Podmore, Walker
(1849 – 1859)

Podmore, Walker
(1834 – 1859)

Podmore, Walker
(1849 – 1859)

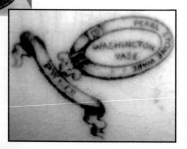

Podmore, Walker
(1834 – 1859)

Podmore, Walker
(1849 – 1859)

Poole, Thomas (1912+)

Poole Pottery (1960s – 1970s)

Poole Pottery
(1921 – 1925)

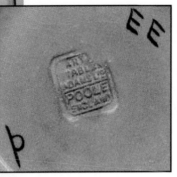

Poole Pottery (1960s – 1970s)

Poole Pottery
(1952 – present)

Poole Pottery (1972+)

Poole Pottery
(1956 – 1966)

Poole Pottery (1972+)

257

Poole Pottery (1973+)

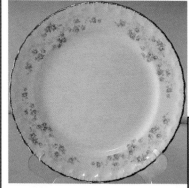

Pope-Gosser
(1902 – 1958)

Pope-Gosser (1900)

Pope-Gosser (1930s)

Pope-Gosser (1902)

Pope-Gosser (1950)

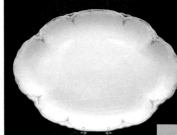

Pope-Gosser
(1902 – 1958)

Pope-Gosser (1950)

Porcelain Factory
Konigszelt (1912 – 1928)

Porcelain Union
(1921 – 1927)

Porcelain Factory
Konigszelt (1912 – 1928)

Porcelain Union
(1921 – 1927)

Porcelain Fles (1800+)

Porcelier (1928 – 1949)

Porcelain Fles (1900+)

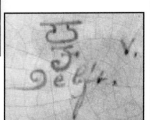

Porcelier
(1928 – 1949)

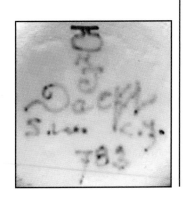

Porquier, Adolphe
(1897 – 1904)

Portheim & Son
(1860 – 1870)

Porquier, Adolphe
(1897 – 1904)

Portmeirion Pottery
(1962+)

Porquier Beau
(1875 – 1900)

Portmeirion Pottery
(1962 – present)

Porsgrund (current)

Portmeirion Pottery
(1962 – present)

Portmeirion Pottery
(1972 – 1977)

Potters Co-Operative
(1920+)

Portmeirion Pottery
(1972 – present)

Potters Co-Operative (1959)

Potters Co-Operative
(1896)

Pottery Guild
(1937 – 1946)

Potters Co-Operative
(1915)

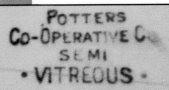

Pottery Guild
(1937 – 1946)

Pountney
(1840s – 1860s)

Powell, Bishop &
Stonier (1856)

Pountney (1889+)

Powell, Bishop &
Stonier (1876 – 1936)

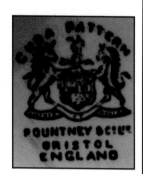

Pountney
(1900 – 1930s+)

Powell, Bishop &
Stonier (1878 – 1891)

Pouplard-Beatrix
(1890 – 1898)

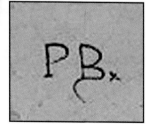

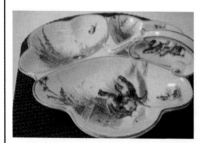

Powell, Bishop &
Stonier (1880+)

Powell, Bishop &
Stonier (1899 – 1936)

Precious Moments (cross, 1977+)

Pratt (1800+)

Precious Moments (diamond, 1986+)

Precious Moments
(bow and arrow, 1988+)

Precious Moments
(dove, 1984+)

Precious Moments (butterfly, 1993+)

Precious Moments (fish, 1981+)

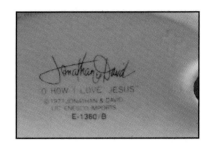

Precious Moments (flame, 1978+)

MY HAPPINESS
© 1989 Samuel J. Butcher
All rights reserved worldwide
Licensee Enesco Corporation
C0010

Precious Moments (three balls, 1987+)

YOU ARE MY MAIN EVENT
© 1987 Samuel J. Butcher
All rights reserved worldwide
Licensee Enesco Imports Corp.
115231

Precious Moments (hourglass, 1982+)

1981 Charter Member

© 1982 JONATHAN & DAVID
LICENSEE ENESCO IMPORTS CORP
E-0102

Precious Moments
(treble clef, 1992+)

BRING THE LITTLE ONES TO JESUS
Exclusively designed in Honor of
the Child Evangelism Fellowship
by Artist Samuel J. Butcher
© 1991 Samuel J. Butcher
All rights reserved worldwide
Licensee Enesco Corporation
527556

Precious Moments
(olive branch, 1982+)

Jonathan David
"SOMEBUNNY CARES"
© 1982 JONATHAN & DAVID
LIC. ENESCO IMPORTS
E-9266

Precious Moments (tree, 1986+)

PRECIOUS™ MOMENTS
THE SPIRIT IS WILLING
BUT THE FLESH IS WEAK
© 1986 Samuel J. Butcher
All rights reserved worldwide
Licensee Enesco Imports Corp.
100196

Precious Moments (sailboat, 1994+)

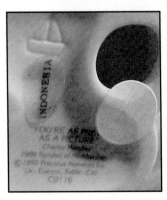

INDONESIA
YOU'RE AS PRETTY
AS A PICTURE
Charter Member
1996 Symbol of Membership
© 1993 Precious Moments
Lic. Enesco. Suble, CA
C0116

Precious Moments (triangle, 1979+)

Jonathan David
"...BUT LOVE
GOES ON FOREVER"
© 1979 JONATHAN & DAVID
LIC. ENESCO IMPORTS

Precious Moments
(trumpet, 1994+)

Purinton Pottery
(1941+)

Price & Kensington
(1963 – present)

Quarry Tile (1892 – 1908)

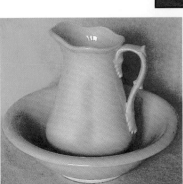

Price & Kensington
(1963 – present)

Quimper
(1922 – 1968)

Prospect Hill Pottery
(1880+)

Quimper
(1922 – 1968)

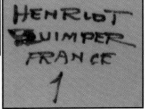

Quimper (1922 – 1968)

Quimper (1984+)

Quimper (1968 – 1983)

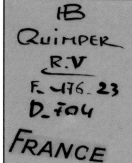

Radford, E. (1930s+)

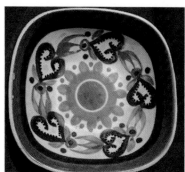

Quimper (1968 – 1983)

Radford, E. (1930s+)

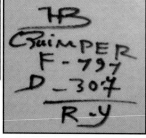

Quimper (1968 – 1983)

Radford, Samuel (1880+)

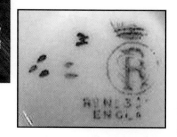

Radford, Samuel
(1891+)

R. J. Ernst Enterprises
(1976 – present)

Radford, Samuel (1928+)

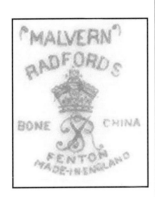

Rappsilber, A.
(1900 – 1912)

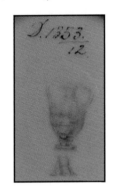

Radford Pottery (1896+)

Rathbone, T. (1912)

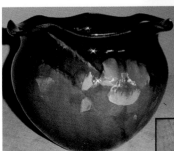

Radford Pottery
(1903 – 1912)

Rauschert, Paul
(1971 – 1981+)

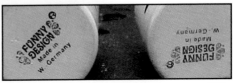

Rauschert, Paul
(1971 – 1981+)

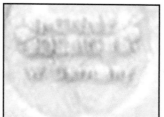

Red Wing (1906 – 1936)

Redware (1830 – 1860)

Red Wing (1930+)

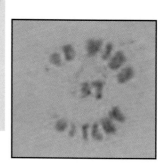

Red Wing (1878 – 1892)

Red Wing (1933 – 1938)

Red Wing (1906 – 1936)

Red Wing (1933 – 1938)

Red Wing (1933 – 1938)

Red Wing (1936 – 1967, molded)

Red Wing (1933 – 1938)

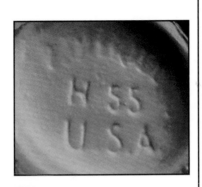

Red Wing (1946+)

Red Wing (1935+)

Red Wing (1967)

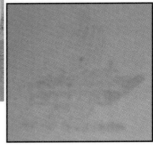

Red Wing (1936 – 1967, impressed)

Regal China (1938 – 1990)

Regal China
(1938 – 1990)

Regout, Petrus (1870)

Regency China
(1953+)

Regout, Petrus
(1891+)

Registry mark
(1842 – 1883)

Regout, Petrus
(1929 – 1931+)

Registry mark
(1842 – 1883)

Regout, Petrus
(1970+)

Regout, Petrus
(1970+)

Revere, Paul Pottery
(1906 – 1942)

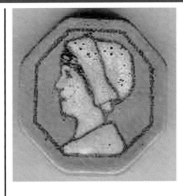

Reichenbach
(1949 – 1968)

Revere, Paul Pottery
(1908+)

Reutter
(1948 – present)

Revere, Paul Pottery
(1906+)

Revere, Paul Pottery
(1906 – 1942)

Revere, Paul Pottery
(1906 – 1942)

Revere, Paul Pottery
(1906+)

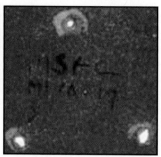

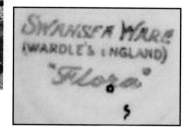

Rhead, Frederick
(1920s – 1930s)

Rhead, Charlotte (1920s – 1930s)

Rhead Pottery (1913)

Rhead, Charlotte
(1920s – 1930s)

Rhodes, Daniel (1930 – 1989)

Rhead, Charlotte
(1920s – 1930s)

Richardson, A. G.
(1916 – 1970+)

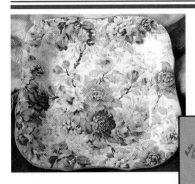

Richardson, A. G.
(1916 – 1970+)

Ridgway Pottery
(1950s)

Richter, Fenkl & Hahn
(1900+)

Ridgway Pottery (1950s)

Ridgewood China
(1948 – 1976)

A nostalgic world of children
created by Romantic Artist
LORRAINE TRESTER

"SING A SONG OF SPRING"
Spring 1976

Limited Edition /5000
2503

© MASTERPIECES

Ridgway Pottery
(1950s)

Ridgway Pottery
(1940 – 1960)

Ridgway Pottery
(1950s – 1960s)

Ridgway Pottery (1960)

Ridgway Pottery
(John, 1841+)

Ridgway Pottery (1962)

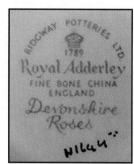

Ridgway Pottery
(John, 1841+)

Ridgway Pottery
(1964 – present)

Ridgway Pottery
(John, 1841+)

Ridgway Pottery
(John, 1835 – 1845)

Ridgway Pottery
(John & William,
1814 – 1830)

Ridgway Pottery
(John & William,
1814 – 1830)

Ridgway Pottery
(Morley, 1842 – 1844)

Ridgway Pottery
(Morley, 1836 – 1842)

Ridgway Pottery (William,
1830 – 1854)

Ridgway Pottery
(Morley, 1836 – 1842)

Ridgway Pottery (William,
1830 – 1854)

Ridgway Pottery
(Morley, 1842 – 1844)

Ridgway Pottery
(William, 1838 – 1848)

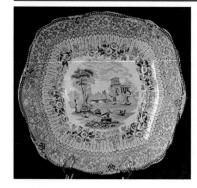

Ridgway Pottery
(William, 1891+)

Robertson Pottery
(1934 – 1952)

Ridgway Pottery
(William, 1912+)

Robertson Pottery (1940)

River Shore
(1975 – present)

Robinson, W. H.
(1901 – 1904)

Robertson Pottery
(1934 – 1952)

Robinson Ransbottom
(1900+)

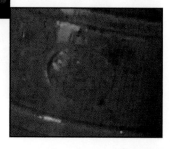

Robinson Ransbottom
(1920 – present)

Robinson Ransbottom
(1920 – present)

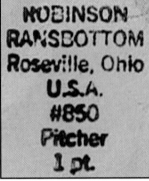

Robinson Ransbottom
(1920 – present)

Robinson Ransbottom
(1920 – present)

ROBINSON
RANSBOTTOM
Roseville, Ohio
U.S.A.
#850
Pitcher
1 pt.

Robinson Ransbottom
(1920 – present)

Robj (1920)

Robj
Paris
Made in France

Robinson Ransbottom
(1920 – present)

Rockingham Works
(1826 – 1830)

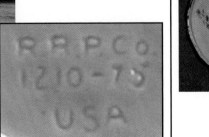

Roman Ceramic Corporation
(1940 – 1982)

Rookwood
(1901 – 1967)

Rookwood (1881 – 1882)

Rorstrand (1884)

Rookwood (1882)

Rorstrand (1885+)

Rookwood (1886 – 1900)

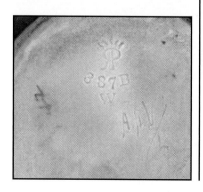

Rorstrand (1885+)

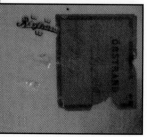

Rorstrand (1890)

Rorstrand (1940+)

Rorstrand (1910+)

Rorstrand
(1950 – present)

Rorstrand (1930s – 1940s)

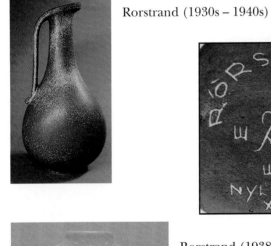

Rorstrand (1980 – present)

Rorstrand (1938+)

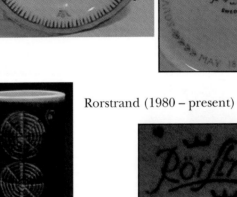

Roselane
(1938 – 1977)

Roselane (1938 – 1977)

Rosemeade (1940 – 1961)

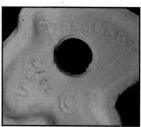

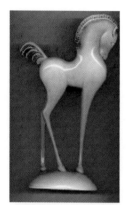

Roselane (1938 – 1977)

Rose Medallion (1850)

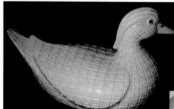

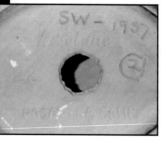

Roselane (1938 – 1977)

Rosenthal (1897 – 1939)

Rosemeade (1940 – 1961)

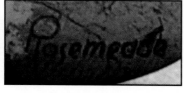

Rosenthal (1900+)

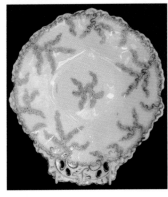

Rosenthal (1900+)

Rosenthal
(1907 – 1956)

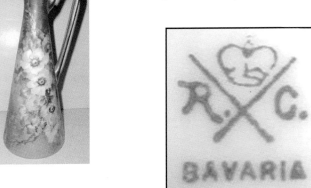

Rosenthal (1901 – 1956)

Rosenthal (1907 – 1956)

Rosenthal
(1901 – 1956)

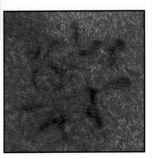

Rosenthal (1907 – 1956)

Rosenthal (1901 – 1956)

Rosenthal
(1962 – present)

Rosenthal
(1969 – 1981+)

Rosenthal
(1980 – present)

Rosenthal
(1969 – present)

Roseville Pottery (1892 – 1904)

Rosenthal
(1980 – present)

Roseville Pottery (1892 – 1904)

Rosenthal
(1980 – present)

Roseville Pottery (1904)

Roseville Pottery (1904)

Roseville Pottery (1915+)

Roseville Pottery (1904)

Roseville Pottery (1930)

Roseville Pottery (1905)

Roseville Pottery (1930+)

Roseville Pottery
(1914 – 1930)

Roseville Pottery
(1935 – 1954)

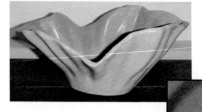

Roseville Pottery
(1935 – 1954)

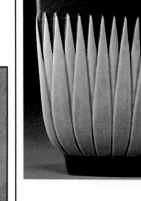

Roseville Pottery
(1950s)

Roseville Pottery (1939 – 1953)

Rosina (1946+)

Roseville Pottery
(1950s)

Rowland & Marsellus
(1860 – 1912+)

Roseville Pottery
(1950s)

Rowland & Marsellus
(1860 – 1912+)

Royal Bayreuth
(1887 – 1902)

Royal Bayreuth (1902+)

Royal Bayreuth (1919)

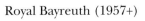

Royal Bayreuth (1957+)

Royal Bayreuth
(1968 – present)

Royal Bayreuth
(1968 – present)

Royal Bayreuth (1972+)

Royal Bayreuth (Germany,
US Zone, 1919)

Royal Bayreuth (Germany, US Zone, 1972+)

Royal China
(1934 – 1960)

Royal China
(1933 – present)

Royal China
(1940 – 1950)

Royal China
(1934 – 1955)

Royal China
(1949 – 1960)

Royal China
(1934 – 1960)

Royal China
(1950 – 1960)

Royal China
(1951 – 1960)

Royal China (1970)

Royal China (1965)

Royal Copenhagen
(1863 – 1920)

Royal China (1968)

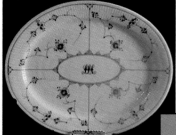

Royal Copenhagen (1889+)

Royal China (1968)

Royal Copenhagen
(1894 – 1900)

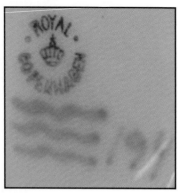

Royal Copenhagen (1897 – 1922)

Royal Copenhagen
(1921)

Royal Copenhagen
(1903 – present, brown)

Royal Copenhagen (1922 – present)

Royal Copenhagen
(1903 – present, green)

Royal Copenhagen (1950s)

Royal Copenhagen
(1919)

Royal Copenhagen (1955+)

Royal Copley (1942 – 1957)

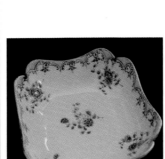

Royal Porcelain Manufactory (1750 – 1775)

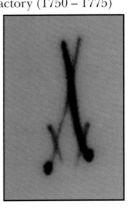

Royal Kendal
(1980 – present)

Royal Porcelain Manufactory (1766 – 1780)

Royal Porcelain Manufactory (1725 – 1763)

Royal Porcelain Manufactory (1770)

Royal Porcelain Manufactory (1740 – 1745)

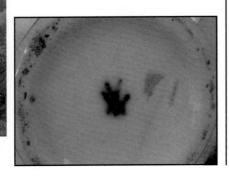

Royal Porcelain Manufactory (1774 – 1817)

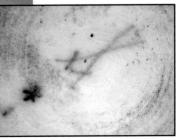

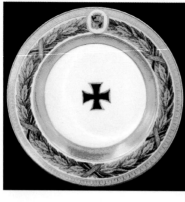

Royal Porcelain Manufactory (1800 – 1850)

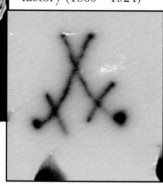

Royal Porcelain Manufactory (1860 – 1924)

Royal Porcelain Manufactory (1814 – 1860)

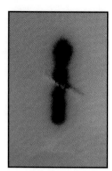

Royal Porcelain Manufactory (1870 – present)

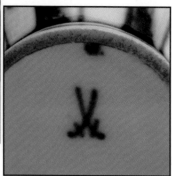

Royal Porcelain Manufactory (1814 – 1860)

Royal Porcelain Manufactory (1870 – present)

Royal Porcelain Manufactory (1832 – present)

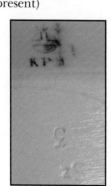

Royal Porcelain Manufactory (front mark, 1880+)

Royal Windsor
(1980 – present)

Ruskin Pottery (1904 – 1930+)

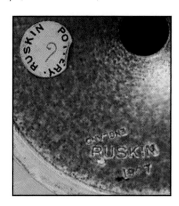

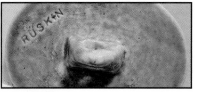

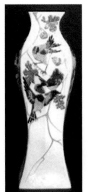

Rozenberg (1890 – 1914)

Ruskin Pottery (1904 – 1930+)

Ruskin Pottery (1904 – 1930+)

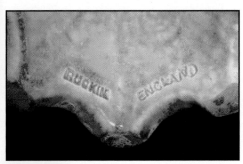

Russian (1900)

Ruskin Pottery
(1904 – 1930+)

Russian (1903)

Russian (1920s)

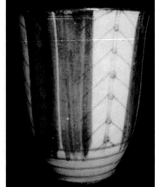

Rye Pottery (1947 – 1956)

Russian (1940s – 1960s)

Rye Pottery (1947 – 1956)

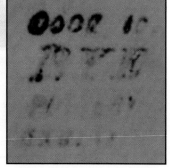

Russian Imperial
Porcelain Factory
(1894 – 1917)

Rye Pottery
(1947 – 1956)

Rye Pottery (1947 – 1953)

Rye Pottery (1955 – 1956)

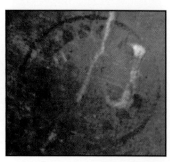

Rye Pottery
(1980 – present)

Sadler, James
(1947 – present)

Sabin Industries (1970+)

Sadler, James (1947 – present)

Sabin Industries (1970+)

Sadler, James (1947 – present)

Sadler, James
(1947 – present)

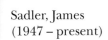

Sadler, James
(1980 – present)

Sadler, James (2002)

Salem China (1918+)

Salem China (1918+)

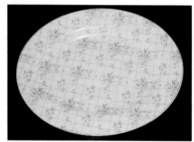

Salem China (1940 – 1967)

Salem China
(1940 – 1967)

Salem China
(1940 – 1967)

Salem China
(1940 – 1967)

Salem China
(1940 – 1967)

Salem China
(1940 – 1967)

Salem China
(1940 – 1967)

Salt & Nixon
(1921 – 1934)

Salem China
(1940 – 1967)

Sampson Bridgwood
(1853 – 1897+)

Salem China
(1940 – 1967)

Sampson Bridgwood
(1870+)

Salem China
(1940 – 1967)

Sampson Bridgwood
(1885)

Sampson Bridgwood
(1885+)

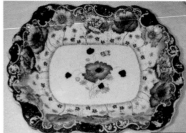

Sampson Hancock
(1906 – 1912)

Sampson Bridgwood
(1885+)

Sampson Hancock (1910)

Sampson Bridgwood (1950+)

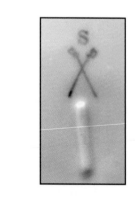

Samson (1873 – 1905)

Sampson Hancock
(1906 – 1912)

Samson (1875)

Samson (1885+)

Samson (1885+)

Sandizell (1951 – present)

Santa Anita Pottery
(1948+)

Schachtel, Joseph
(1896 – 1919)

Schafer & Vater
(1896 – 1962)

Schaller, Oscar
(1892 – 1918)

Schaller, Oscar (1918+)

Schaller, Oscar (1918+)

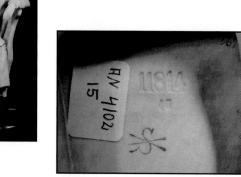

Scheibe-Alsbach (1972+)

Schaller, Oscar
(1921+)

Scheibe-Alsbach
(1972+)

Schaller, Oscar
(1950 – 1981+)

Scheier (1940 – 1960+)

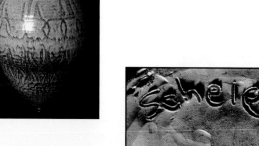

Schau Bach Kunst
(1950 – present)

Scheier (1980s+)

Schierholz, Von (1907+)

Schierholz, Von (1907+)

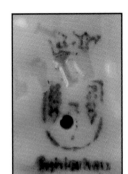

Schierholz, Von (1907+)

Schierholz, Von (1907+)

Schierholz, Von (1907+)

Schierholz, Von (1967 – 1972)

Schierholz, Von (1907+)

Schiller, W. & Sons (1895+)

Schiller, W. & Sons (1895+)

Schiller & Gerbing
(1829 – 1885)

Schirnding (1974 – present)

Schlegelmilch,
Erdmann (1891+)

Schlegelmilch,
Erdmann (1891+)

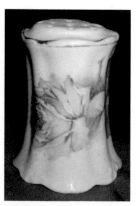

Schlegelmilch, Erdmann
(1900 – 1938)

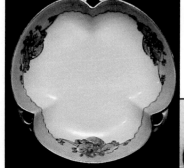

Schlegelmilch, Erdmann
(1902 – 1938)

Schlegelmilch,
Erdmann (1938)

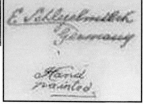

Schlegelmilch, Oscar
(1892+)

Schlegelmilch, Oscar
(1950 – 1972)

Schlegelmilch, Oscar
(1904+)

Schlegelmilch, Reinhold
(1870s – 1880s)

Schlegelmilch, Oscar (1904+)

Schlegelmilch, Reinhold
(1904 – 1938)

Schlegelmilch, Oscar
(1904+)

Schlegelmilch, Reinhold
(1904 – 1938)

Schlegelmilch, Reinhold (1904 – 1938)

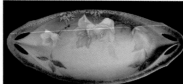

Schlegelmilch, Reinhold (1904 – 1938)

Schlegelmilch, Reinhold (1904 – 1938)

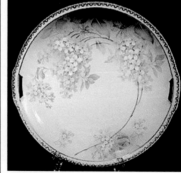

Schlegelmilch, Reinhold (1919 – 1921)

Schlegelmilch, Reinhold (1904 – 1938)

Schlegelmilch, Reinhold (1932 – 1938)

Schlegelmilch, Reinhold (1904 – 1938)

Schmid (1979 – present)

Schmid
(1979 – present)

Schmider, Georg (1930+)

Schmid (1979 – present)

Schmider, Georg
(1930+)

Schmider, Georg
(1907 – 1928)

Schmidt (1918 – 1939)

Schmider, Georg (1907+)

Schmidt, Hugo
(1919 – 1945)

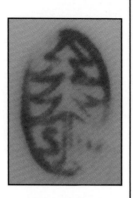 Schnabel & Sons (1900 – 1931)

 Schoenau & Hoffmeister
(1909 – 1952)

 Schneider, Carl (1879 – 1954)

 Schonwald Porcelain
(1911 – 1945)

 Schneider, Carl (1879 – 1954)

 Schonwald Porcelain (1920 – 1927)

 Schneider, Carl (1879 – 1954)

 Schonwald Porcelain
(1968 – present)

Schonwald Porcelain
(1968 – present)

Schramberger Majolica
Factory (1918+)

Schonwald Porcelain
(1968 – present)

Schumann, Carl (1918+)

Schonwald Porcelain
(1968 – present)

Schumann, Carl
(1918+)

Schoonhoven (1900)

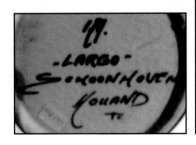

Schumann, Carl
(1918+)

305

Schumann, Carl (1918+)

Schwarzburg (1908 – 1938)

Schumann, Carl
(1980 – present)

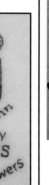

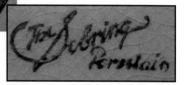

Sebring Pottery
(1890 – 1905)

Schumann, Carl
(1980 – present)

Sebring Pottery (1895)

Schutzmeister & Quendt
(1899 – 1927)

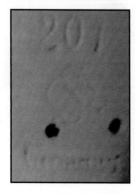

Sebring Pottery
(1925 – 1942)

Sebring Pottery
(1925 – 1942)

Seltmann, Christian
(1946 – 1975)

Sebring Pottery (1925 – 1942)

Seltmann, Johann
(1901+)

Sebring Pottery
(1925 – 1942)

Seltmann, Johann
(1980 – present)

Sebring Pottery
(1925 – 1942)

Seltmann, Johann
(1980 – present)

Seltmann, Johann
(1980 – present)

Sevres (1765)

Seltmann, Johann (2002)

Sevres (1814)

Sevres (1753)

Sevres (1820)

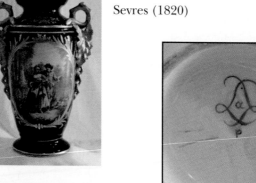

Sevres (1756)

Sevres (1830 – 1848)

Sevres (1843 – 1845)

Sevres (1910)

Sevres (1897+)

Sevres (1917)

Sevres (1897+)

Sevres (1928 – 1940)

Sevres (1900)

Sevres China
(1900 – 1908)

Sewell (1804 – 1878)

Shaw, Anthony (1851+)

Shaw, Anthony
(1851 – 1856)

Shaw, Anthony (1851+)

Shaw, Anthony
(1851 – 1860)

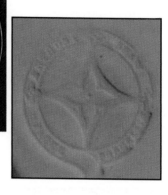

Shawnee (1936 – 1961)

Shaw, Anthony
(1851 – 1856)

Shearwater (1920s+)

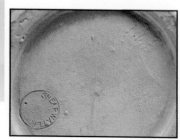

Shearwater (1920s+)

Shenango Pottery
(1905 – 1912)

Shelley (1925 – 1940)

Shenango Pottery
(1930 – present)

Shenango Pottery (1901+)

Shenango Pottery
(1930 – present)

Shenango Pottery (1901+)

Shenango Pottery
(1930 – present)

Shenango Pottery
(1935+)

Shorter & Son (1930s)

Shenango Pottery
(1940 – 1960)

Silver Springs (1924+)

Silver Springs (1938)

Shenango Pottery
(1980 – present)

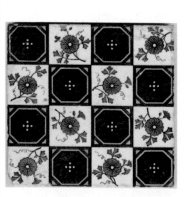

Simpson, T. A.
(1870 – 1880)

Simpson, T. A. (1900)

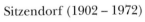

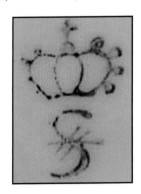

Sitzendorf
(1902 – 1972)

Sitzendorf (1887 – 1900)

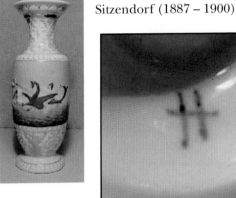

Sitzendorf (1902 – 1972)

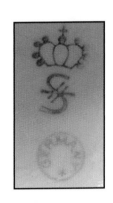

Sitzendorf (1887 – 1900)

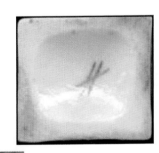

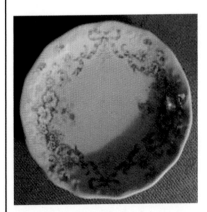

Smith, W. T. H.
(1898 – 1905)

Sitzendorf (1902 – 1972)

Smith Phillips
(1901 – 1929)

Smith Phillips
(1901 – 1929)

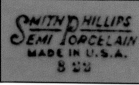

Smith Phillips
(1901 – 1929)

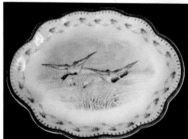

Smith Phillips
(1901 – 1929)

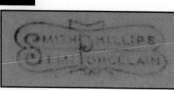

Smith Phillips
(1901 – 1929)

Societa Ceramica
(1842 – 1860)

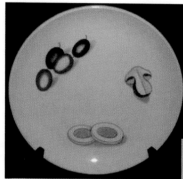

Societa Ceramica
(1856 – present)

Societa Ceramica (1883+)

Societa Ceramica
(1920 – 1931)

Societa Ceramica
(1980 – present)

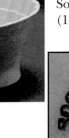

Sohn, Ernest (1963+)

Societe Ceramique
(1887+)

Solly, John (1953 – 1986)

Societe Ceramique
(1887+)

Solon and Schemmel
(1920)

Sohn, Ernest
(1950 – 1955)

Southern Potteries
(1920+)

Southern Potteries
(1930)

Spode (1814 – 1833)

Southern Potteries
(1950s)

Spode (1928+)

Spode (1790 – 1827)

Spode (1940 – 1956)

Spode (1805 – 1815)

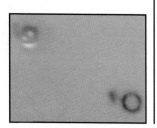

Spode (1950 – 1960+)

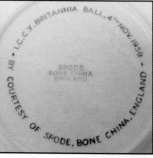

Spode
(1970 – present)

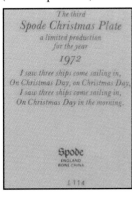

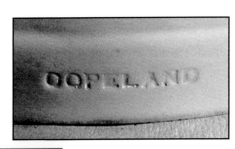

Spode (Copeland, 1848)

Spode
(1970 – present)

Spode (Copeland, 1850)

Spode (1970 – present)

Spode (Copeland,
1851 – 1885)

Spode (Copeland,
1833 – 1847)

Spode
(Copeland, 1867+)

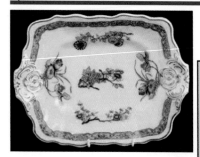

Spode
(Copeland, 1867+)

Spode (Copeland,
1890 – 1920)

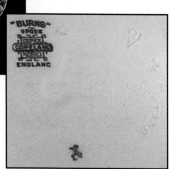

Spode (Copeland,
1875 – 1890)

Spode (Copeland,
1890 – 1920)

Spode (Copeland,
1882 – 1890+)

Spode (Copeland, 1900)

Spode (Copeland,
1882 – 1890+)

Spode
(Copeland, 1928+)

Spode
(Copeland, 1930s)

Spode (Copeland &
Garrett, 1833 – 1847)

Spode (Copeland &
Garrett, 1833 – 1847)

Spode (Copeland &
Garrett, 1833 – 1847)

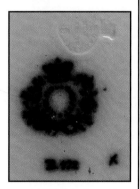

Spode (Copeland &
Garrett, 1833 – 1847)

Spode (Copeland &
Garrett, 1833 – 1847)

Spode (Copeland &
Garrett, 1833+)

Spode (Copeland &
Garrett, 1850 – 1867)

Spode (Copeland
& Garrett, 2000)

Stanfordware
(1945 – 1961)

Springer & Co.
(1891 – 1918)

Stangl (1930)

Stafford Pottery
(1840 – 1860)

Stangl (1972+)

Standard China
(1930 – 1949)

Stangl (1972+)

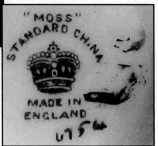

State's Porcelain Manu-
factory (1934 – present)

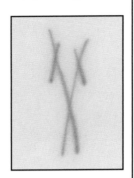

St. Clements (1930s+)

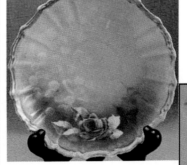

State's Porcelain Manu-
factory (1943 – 1957)

St. Clements (1930s+)

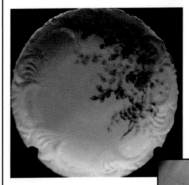

State's Porcelain Manu-
factory (1924 – 1934)

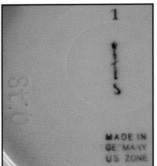

Steinmann, K.
(1868 – 1938)

St. Clements (1930s+)

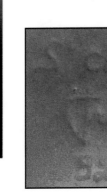

Steinmann, K.
(1900 – 1938)

Steinmann, K. (1914 – 1932)

Stellmacher
(1895 – 1905, gold)

Stellmacher (1859 – 1897)

Stellmacher
(1895 – 1905)

Stellmacher (1885 – 1897)

Stellmacher
(1904 – 1912)

Stellmacher (1895 – 1905)

Sterling China (1917+)

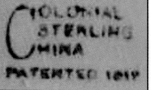

Sterling China (1917+)

Sterling China
(1946 – present)

Sterling China (1920+)

Sterling China
(1946 – present)

Sterling China (1940)

Sterling China (1947 – 1948)

Sterling China
(1946 – present)

Sterling China (1949)

Sterling China (1949)

Stetson China (1919 – 1965)

Sterling China
(1980 – 1990+)

Stetson China
(1940s – 1950s)

Sterling China
(1980 – present)

Stetson China (1946+)

Sterling China
(1980 – present)

Stetson China (1950+)

Stetson China (1958)

Steubenville Pottery
(1939+)

Steubenville Pottery
(1920 – 1930s)

Steubenville Pottery (1939+)

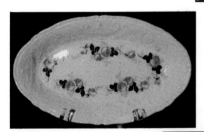

Steubenville Pottery
(1930 – 1959)

Steubenville Pottery
(1939+)

Steubenville Pottery
(1930 – 1960)

Steubenville Pottery
(1940 – 1960)

Steubenville Pottery
(1960 – 1978)

Steventon, John (1880)

Steubenville Pottery
(1966)

Steventon, John
(1923 – 1936)

Stevenson, Ralph
(1832 – 1835)

Stnact, Josef
(1881 – 1932)

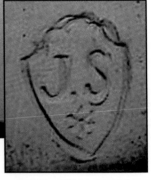

Stevenson & Williams
(1825)

Stnact, Josef (1881 – 1932)

Stockhardt & Schmidt-Eckert
(1912 – present)

Stubbs, Joseph (1830)

Stockton Art Pottery
(1895 – 1902)

Swasey, E. (1886 – 1891)

Straub, Paul
(1948 – 1970)

Swasey, E. (1886 – 1891)

Straus, Lewis & Sons
(1895 – 1917)

Swasey, E. (1890+)

Swastika Keramos (1904+)

Swinnertons (1946+)

Swastika Keramos (1904+)

Swinnertons (1946+)

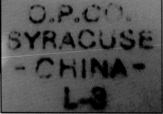

Swift, John (1843)

Syracuse China
(1886 – 1898)

Swillington Bridge
(1820 – 1850)

Syracuse China
(1886 – 1898)

Syracuse China
(1893 – 1898)

Syracuse China
(1966+)

Syracuse China (1930+)

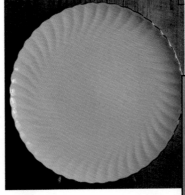

Syracuse China (1972)

Syracuse China
(1935+)

Syracuse China
(1980 – present)

Syracuse China
(1940s – 1960s)

Syracuse China
(1980 – present)

Szeiler Studio
(1980 – present)

Taylor, Tunnicliffe
(1875 – 1898)

Szeiler Studio (1980 – present)

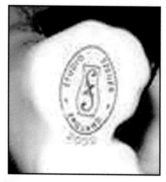

Taylor, Tunnicliffe (1875 – 1898)

Takito (1880 – 1948)

Taylor, Tunnicliffe (1875 – 1898)

Tamac (1950s – 1960s)

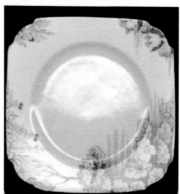

Taylor & Kent (1912+)

Taylor Bros.
(1860 – 1880)

Taylor Smith & Taylor
(1925)

Taylor Smith & Taylor
(1901 – 1930)

Taylor Smith & Taylor
(1928 – 1945)

Taylor Smith & Taylor
(1908 – 1915)

Taylor Smith & Taylor
(1935 – 1955)

Taylor Smith & Taylor
(1908 – 1915)

Taylor Smith & Taylor
(1935 – 1981)

Taylor Smith & Taylor
(1935 – 1981)

Taylor Smith & Taylor
(1940s – 1960s)

Taylor Smith & Taylor (1938 – 1945)

Taylor Smith & Taylor
(1940s – 1960s)

Taylor Smith & Taylor
(1940s – 1960s)

Taylor Smith & Taylor
(1960)

Taylor Smith & Taylor
(1940s – 1960s)

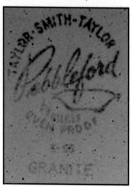

Taylor Smith & Taylor
(1963 – 1968)

Taylor Smith & Taylor
(1963 – 1968)

Taylor Smith & Taylor
(1972)

Taylor Smith & Taylor
(1970)

Teichert, C.
(1882 – 1930)

Taylor Smith & Taylor
(1970)

Teichert, C.
(1890 – 1914)

Taylor Smith & Taylor
(1970)

Teichert, C.
(1892 – 1914)

Teichert, Ernst (1884+)

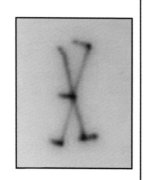

Terra Nigra (1930s)

Tharaud, Justin
(1948 – 1953)

Thewalt, Albert Jacob
(1920 – 1930)

Thieme, Carl
(1888 – 1901)

Thieme, Carl (1902+)

Thieme, Carl (1902+)

Thieme, Carl (1902+)

Thomas, F. Porcelain
(1908+)

Thomas, F. Porcelain (1908+)

Thomas, Mark (1950s)

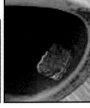

Thomas & Co.
(1937 – 1957)

Thomas China
(1902 – 1905)

Thompson, C. C.
(1890 – 1910)

Thompson, C. C.
(1916 – 1938)

Thompson, C. C. (1927 – 1938)

Thorley, Palen (1940s)

Tielsch, C.
(1875 – 1934)

Tielsch, C.
(1875 – 1918)

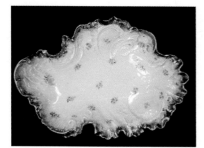

Tielsch, C. (1875 – 1934)

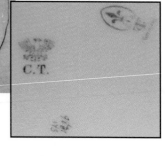

Tielsch, C.
(1875 – 1934)

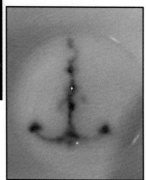

Tielsch, C.
(1895 – 1918)

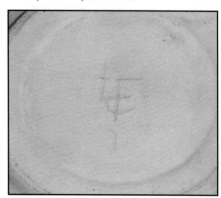

Tielsch, C.
(1875 – 1934)

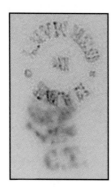

Tiffany Pottery (1904+)

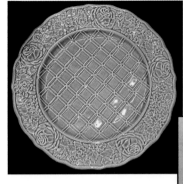

Tiffany Pottery (1980+)

Tirschenreuth (1927+)

Till, Thomas (1861+)

Tirschenreuth (1970s)

Till, Thomas (1919)

Tirschenreuth (1903 – 1981+)

Tomkinson Bros.
(1860 – 1872)

Torquay (Aller Vale,
1887 – 1901)

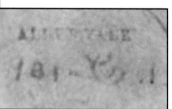

Torquay (Watcombe,
1880 – 1901)

Torquay (Aller Vale,
1887 – 1901)

Torquay (Watcombe,
1918 – 1927)

Torquay (Longpark,
1904 – 1918)

Torquay (Watcombe,
1935 – 1962)

Torquay (Longpark,
1918 – 1925)

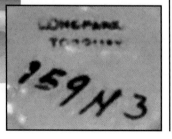

Torquay (Watcombe,
1958 – 1962)

Trenle Blake China
(1940 – 1966)

Trent Tile (1882+)

Trenle Blake China
(1940 – 1966)

Trenton Potteries (1930s)

Trenle China
(1909 – 1917)

Trenton Potteries
(1930s)

Trent Tile (1882+)

Triebner, Ens, Eckert
(1884 – 1894)

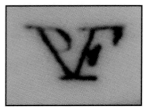

Triebner, Ens, Eckert
(1886 – 1894+)

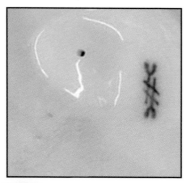

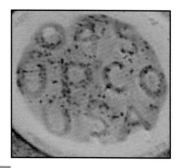

Ungemach Pottery (1937 – 1966+)

Turner, John
(1800 – 1805)

Ungemach Pottery
(1937 – 1966+)

Turner's Patent.
Nº 12

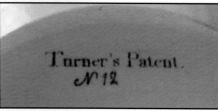
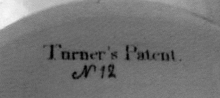

Turner & Tomkinson
(1860 – 1872)

PEARL
IRONSTONE CHINA
TURNER & TOMKINSON

Union Porcelain Works
(1878+)

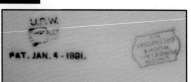

U.P.W.

PAT. JAN. 4 · 1881.

Twisted Rope
(1865 – 1935)

Union Porcelain Works
(1879)

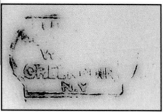

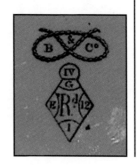

Union Porcelain Works
(1879)

United States Pottery
(1852 – 1858)

Union Porcelain Works
(1891 – 1904)

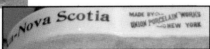

Universal Potteries
(1934 – 1956)

United China
(1953 – present)

Universal Potteries
(1934 – 1956)

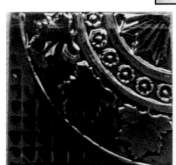

United States Encaustic
Tile (1893)

Universal Potteries
(1934 – 1956)

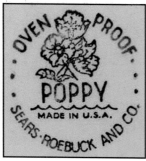

Universal Potteries
(1934 – 1956)

Universal Potteries
(1947 – 1956)

Universal Potteries
(1934 – 1956)

University City Pottery
(1910 – 1915)

Universal Potteries
(1934 – 1956)

Universal Potteries
(1947 – 1956)

University of North
Dakota (1892 – 1963)

Universal Potteries
(1947 – 1956)

University of North Dakota
(1892 – 1963)

Unterweissbach
(1959 – present)

Upsala-Ekeby
(1918 – 1942)

Upchurch Pottery
(1913 – 1961)

Utzchneider & Co.
(1850 – 1870)

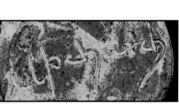

Upchurch Pottery
(1913 – 1961)

Utzchneider & Co.
(1890 – 1915+)

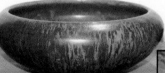

Upper Hanley
(1895 – 1910)

Utzchneider & Co. (1900)

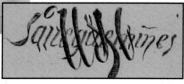

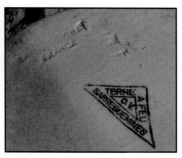

Utzchneider & Co. (1935+)

Van Briggle (1900 – 1920)

Utzchneider & Co. (1940+)

Van Briggle (1901 – 1949)

Utzchneider & Co.
(1965+)

Van Briggle (1902)

Utzchneider & Co. (1965+)

Van Briggle (1955 – 1968)

Vance (1900)

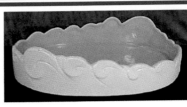
Vernon Kilns (1930s)

Variazioni, Tema
(1950 – 1955)

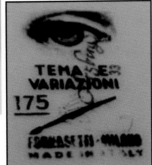

Vernon Kilns (1930s)

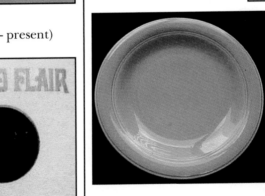

Veneto Flair (1975 – present)

VENETO FLAIR

EASTER

1975

Vernon Kilns (1930s)

Vernon Kilns (1930s)

Vernon Kilns (1931+)

VERNON KILNS
CALIFORNIA
MADE IN U. S. A.

Vernon Kilns
(1938 – 1940)

Vernon Kilns (1947 – 1956)

Vernon Kilns
(1942 – 1947)

Vernon Kilns
(1950 – 1954)

Vernon Kilns
(1942 – 1947)

Vernon Kilns (1950)

ORGANDIE NO. T-511

Vernon Kilns
(1947 – 1956)

Vernon Kilns (1950)

Vernon Kilns
(1953 – 1954)

Vernon Kilns (1956+)

Vernon Kilns (1955)

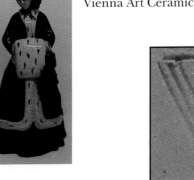

Victoria Porcelain
(1891 – 1918)

Vernon Kilns (1955)

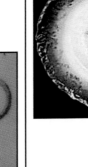

Vienna Art Ceramic (1899 – 1940)

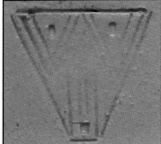

Vernon Kilns
(1956 – 1960+)

Vienna Porcelain
(1923 – 1981+)

Vienna Workshops
(1913 – 1923+)

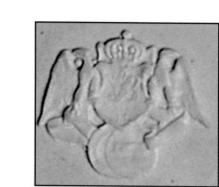

Villeroy & Boch (1850)

Viletta (current)

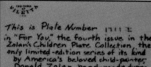

This is Plate Number 1711 I
in "For You" the fourth issue in the
Zolan's Children Plate Collection, the
only limited-edition series of its kind
by America's beloved child-painter,
Donald Zolan, hand-made during
a 22-day firing schedule
permanently closing in 1981.

Villeroy & Boch
(1874 – present)

Fasan
Unterglasur

Viletta (current)

Villeroy & Boch (1880 – 1883)

Villeroy & Boch
(1836 – 1855)

Villeroy & Boch
(1880s – 1890s)

Villeroy & Boch
(1883 – 1930s)

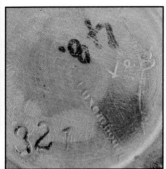

Villeroy & Boch
(1885 – 1895)

Villeroy & Boch (1885 – 1895)

Villeroy & Boch
(1887 – 1945)

Villeroy & Boch (1885)

Villeroy & Boch
(1890 – 1920)

Villeroy & Boch (1885)

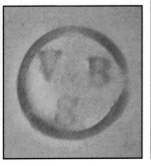

Villeroy & Boch (1890)

Villeroy & Boch (1890)

Villeroy & Boch (1980 – present)

Villeroy & Boch ©
1748
Paon
handausgemalt
W. – Germany

Villeroy & Boch
(1895 – 1912)

Vodrey & Brothers
(1876 – 1896)

Villeroy & Boch
(1895 – 1912)

Vodrey & Brothers
(1876 – 1896)

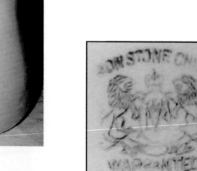

Villeroy & Boch (1897)

Vodrey & Brothers
(1896 – 1920)

Vohann of California (1950+)

Volkstedt (1915 – 1981+)

Vohann of California (1950+)

Volkstedt (1915+)

Volkmar Ceramic (1895)

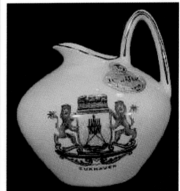

Wachter, R. (1927+)

Volkstedt (1915 – 1981+)

Wachtersbach (1914 – present)

Wachtersbach
(1914 – present)

Wade (1980 – present)

Wachtersbach
(1914 – present)

Wade, George (1936+)

Waco (1900 – 1930)

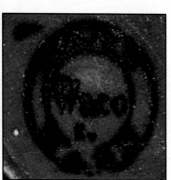

Wade, Heath (1934 – 1945)

Waco (1900 – 1930)

Wade, Heath (1953)

Wade, Heath (1953)

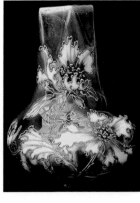

Wahliss, Ernest (1899 – 1918)

Wagner & Apel (1954)

Wahliss, Ernest
(1899 – 1918)

Wahliss, Ernest (1894 – 1921)

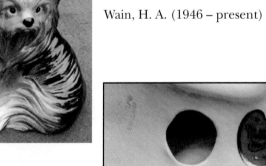

Wain, H. A. (1946 – present)

Wahliss, Ernest (1897 – 1906)

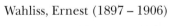

Wain, H. A. (1946 – present)

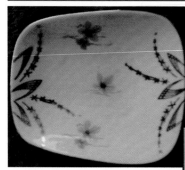

Waldsassen Porcelain
(1960 – 1970)

Waldsassen Porcelain
(1960 – 1970)

Waldsassen Porcelain
(1970+)

Walker China
(1923 – present)

Walker China
(1923 – present)

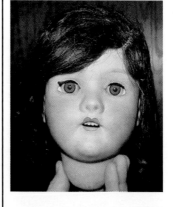

Walkure (1920+)

Walkure (1920+)

Wallace & Chetwynd
(1882 – 1901)

Wallace & Chetwynd
(1882 – 1901)

Walley, Edward
(1845 – 1865)

Wallace & Chetwynd (1882 – 1901)

Walley Pottery
(1898 – 1919)

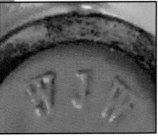

Wallace China
(1931 – 1964)

Walrath, Frederick
(1900 – 1920)

Wallendorf (1964+)

Walrich Pottery (1922)

Walton (1800)

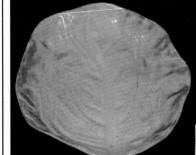

Wannopee Pottery (1901+)

Wannopee Pottery (1886 – 1903)

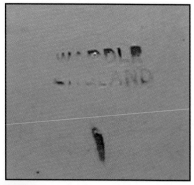

Wardle (1882 – 1909)

Wannopee Pottery (1886 – 1903)

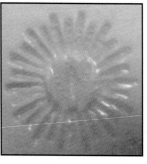

Wardle (1900)

Wannopee Pottery (1900)

Wardle (1930)

Warwick China
(1893 – 1898)

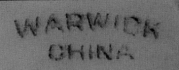

Warwick China
(1893 – 1898)

Warwick China
(1893 – 1898)

Warwick China
(1920s – 1940s)

Warwick China (1940s)

Warwick China (1944)

Watt Pottery
(1936 – 1965)

Watt Pottery
(1936 – 1965)

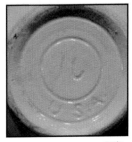

Watt Pottery
(1936 – 1965)

Watt Pottery
(1936 – 1965)

Watt Pottery
(1936 – 1965)

Watt Pottery
(1936 – 1965)

Watt Pottery
(1936 – 1965)

Watt Pottery
(1936 – 1965)

Weatherby, J. H.
(1892 – present)

Watt Pottery
(1936 – 1965)

Weatherby, J. H.
(1980+)

Wedge Wood, John
(1841 – 1860)

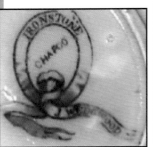

Wedgwood (1769 – present)

Wedgwood
(1769 – present)

Wedgwood
(1780 – 1795)

Wedgwood
(1769 – present)

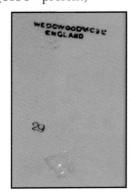

Wedgwood
(1834 – present)

Wedgwood
(1769 – present)

Wedgwood (1840)

Wedgwood (1861)

Wedgwood (1900+)

Wedgwood
(1862 – 1890)

Wedgwood (1906+)

Wedgwood
(1870 – 1880)

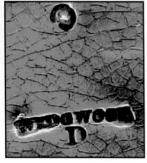

Wedgwood
(1908 – 1920s)

Wedgwood (1890+)

Wedgwood (1908+)

Wedgwood (1930s+)

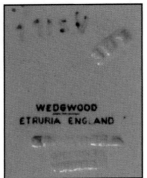

Wedgwood
(1930 – present)

Wedgwood
(1940 – present)

Wedgwood (2000)

Wedgwood
(1940s – 1960s)

Wedgwood, Enoch
(1925+)

Wedgwood
(1930 – present)

Wedgwood, Enoch
(1965 – present)

Wedgwood & Bentley
(1768 – 1780)

Weller Pottery
(LonHuda, 1894 – 1895)

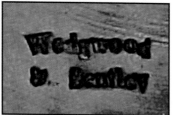

Wehinger, H.
(1905 – 1945)

Weller Pottery
(1894 – 1895, 1900 – 1905)

Weil (1950+)

Weller Pottery (1895 – 1915)

Weller Pottery (1882+)

Weller Pottery (1895 – 1918)

Weller Pottery
(1895 – 1918)

Weller Pottery (1902 – 1907)

Weller Pottery (1897 – 1910)

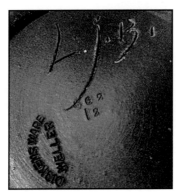

Weller Pottery (1902 – 1907)

Weller Pottery
(1900 – 1925)

Weller Pottery (1903)

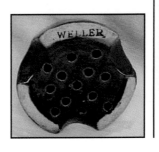

Weller Pottery
(1900 – 1925)

Weller Pottery (1904)

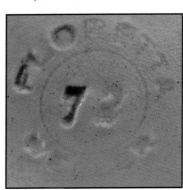

Weller Pottery (1910)

Weller Pottery (1925+)

Weller Pottery (1920+)

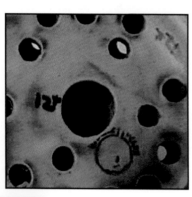

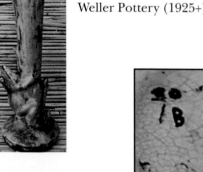

Weller Pottery (1925+)

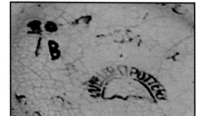

Weller Pottery (1920+)

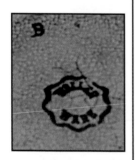

Weller Pottery (1928)

Weller Pottery (1925)

Weller Pottery (1930+)

Weller Pottery (1935+)

Wellsville China
(1940 – 1950)

Wellington China (1930s)

Wellsville China (1955)

Wellsville China
(1933 – 1960)

Wessel, Friedrich Wilhelm
(1949 – 1964)

Wellsville China
(1933 – 1960)

Wessel, Ludwig
(1887 – 1907)

Wessel, Ludwig (1887 – 1907)

West End Pottery
(1893 – 1910)

Wessel, Ludwig
(1893+)

West End Pottery
(1893 – 1910)

Wessel, Ludwig
(1893+)

West End Pottery
(1893 – 1938)

Wessel, Ludwig (1905+)

West End Pottery
(1928 – 1938)

Western Pottery (1905 – 1936)

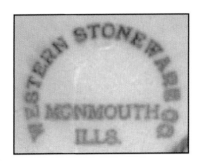

Western Stoneware (1930 – 1935)

Western Stoneware
(1892 – 1906)

Western Stoneware (1930+)

Western Stoneware
(1906 – 1936)

Western Stoneware
(1930+)

Western Stoneware
(1921 – 1928)

Western Stoneware (1930+)

Western Stoneware (1930+)

West Germany
(1949 – 1990)

Western Stoneware (1930+)

West Germany
(1949 – 1990)

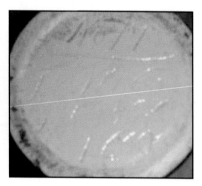

GRÜNSTADT
KERAMIK

WESTERN GERMANY

Western Stoneware (1950s)

Wheatley Pottery (1879 – 1882)

Western Stoneware (1950s)

Wheatley Pottery (1903 – 1936)

Wheeling Pottery
(1879)

Wheeling Pottery
(1893+)

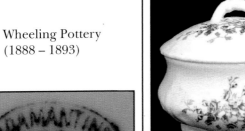

Wheeling Pottery
(1888 – 1893)

Wheeling Pottery (1894+)

Wheeling Pottery
(1893)

Wheeling Pottery
(1900+)

Wheeling Pottery (1893+)

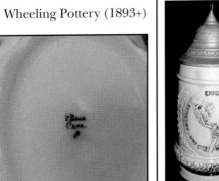

Whites Pottery (1901)

Whittaker & Co. (1886)

Wild, Thomas C. and Sons (1935 – 1945)

Wild, Thomas C. and Sons (1927 – 1934)

Wild, Thomas C. and Sons (1935 – 1945)

Wild, Thomas C. and Sons (1927 – 1934)

Wild, Thomas C. and Sons (1980 – present)

Wild, Thomas C. and Sons (1934)

Wileman (1869 – 1892)

Wileman
(1892 – 1925)

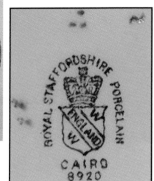

Wilkinson, Arthur
(1891+)

Wileman (1892+)

Wilkinson, Arthur (1896+)

Wileman (1892+)

Wilkinson, Arthur
(1907)

Wilkes, V. M.
(1895 – 1922)

Wilkinson, Arthur
(1907)

Wilkinson, Arthur
(1930+)

Willets (1879 – 1884)

Wilkinson, Arthur
(1930+)

Willets (1879 – 1912+)

Wilkinson, Arthur
(1930+)

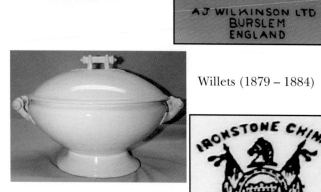

Willets (1879 – 1912+)

Willets (1879 – 1884)

Willets (1879 – 1930+)

Willets (1884)

Williamson, H. M. & Sons (1903+)

Williamsons, H. W. & Sons (1928)

Wilton & Robinson (1894)

Wilton & Robinson (1894)

Wiltshaw & Robinson (1890 – 1957)

Wiltshaw & Robinson (1890+)

Winfield Pottery (1937 – 1960)

Winfield Pottery
(1937 – 1960)

Winkle, F. (1890+)

Winfield Pottery
(1937 – 1960)

Winkle, F. (1890 – 1920)

Winfield Pottery
(1937 – 1960)

Winkle, F. (1890 – 1920)

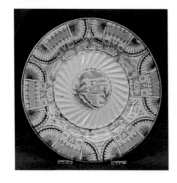

Winkle, F. (1885)

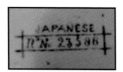

Winkle, F. (1890 – 1920)

Winkle, F.
(1890 – 1920)

Winterling (1970 – present)

Winkle, F. (1890+)

Winterling
(1970 – present)

Winkle, F. (1908 – 1925)

Wolfsohn, Helena
(1850 – 1881)

Winkle, F. (1908 – 1925)

Wolfsohn, Helena
(1850 – 1881)

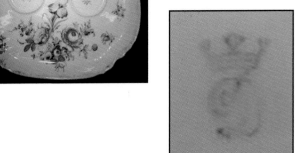

Wood, Arthur
(1904 – 1928)

Wood, Enoch
(1818 – 1846)

Wood, Arthur (1930s)

Wood, Enoch
(1818 – 1846)

Wood, Arthur
(1980 – present)

Wood, Enoch
(1818 – 1846)

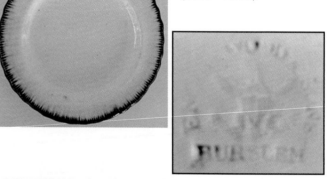

Wood, Enoch (1781)

Wood, Enoch (1830)

Wood, H. J. (1960)

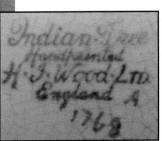

Wood & Sons (1917+)

Wood & Sons (1886)

Wood & Sons (1917+)

Wood & Sons
(1891 – 1907)

Wood & Sons (1917+)

Wood & Sons (1917+)

Wood & Sons
(1920s – 1930s)

377

Wood & Sons (1930+)

Wood & Sons (1931+)

Wood & Sons
(1980 – present)

Worcester
(1755 – 1792)

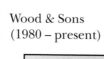

Worcester
(1762 – 1785)

Worcester (1770)

Worcester (1852 – 1875)

Worcester (1862 – 1875)

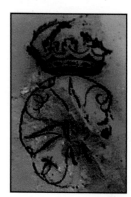

Worcester (1862 – 1875)

Worcester (1887)

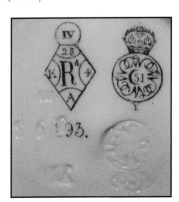

Worcester (1870 – 1887)

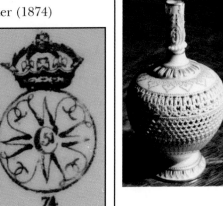

Worcester (1889)

Worcester (1874)

Worcester (1891 – 1915)

Worcester (1891+)

Worcester (1878)

Worcester (1897)

1941

Worcester (1897)

991

Worcester
(1960 – present)

Worcester
(1960 – present)

Worcester
(1960 – present)

Worcester
(1960 – present)

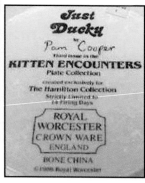

Worcester
(1960 – present)

Worcester Royal Porcelain
(1865 – 1886)

Wranitzky, P. A.
(1900 – 1910)

Zdekauer, Moritz
(1884 – 1909)

Zaneware (1920 – 1941)

Zeh, Scherzer (1880+)

Zaneware (1920 – 1941)

Zeh, Scherzer (1880+)

Zark (1900+)

Zeh, Scherzer
(1899 – 1909)

381

Zeh, Scherzer (1930s)

Zsolnay (1862+)

Zsolnay (1862 – 1900)

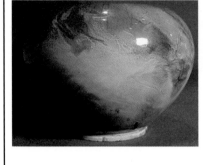

Zsolnay (1865)

Zsolnay (1862+)

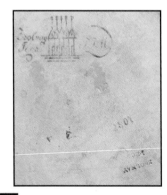

Zsolnay (1904)

Zsolnay (1862+)

Dating English Registry Marks

The following was obtained at the Drexel Grapevine Antiques website and is used with permission.

Starting in 1842, England has offered registration of its decorative designs for pottery, china, wood, paper, porcelain, glass, and more. By using the information below, you can find the date a design was registered. Not every piece registered was marked. Remember, this date is just when the design was registered. An item with a registry mark or number could have been produced before (less likely, as the design would not be protected) or after the date of the registry mark. The following two diamond-shaped marks were used from 1842 – 1883:

Mark I: Used from 1842 – 1867

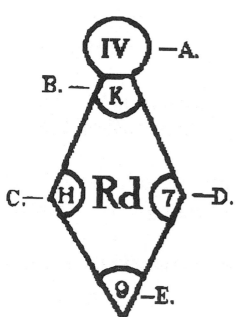

Each letter on the diagram represents one of the tables below:

A — Materials		B — Year				C — Month	
I	Metal	A	1845	N	1864	A	December
II	Wood	B	1858	O	1862	B	October
III	Glass	C	1844	P	1851	C	January
IV	Ceramics	D	1852	Q	1866	D	September
V	Paper Hangings	E	1855	R	1861	E	May
VI	Carpets	F	1847	S	1849	G	February
VII	Printed Shawls	G	1863	T	1867	H	April
VIII	Other Shawls	H	1843	U	1848	I	July
IX	Yarn	I	1846	VEE	1850	K	November
X	Printed Fabrics	J	1854	W	1865	M	June
XI	Furniture	K	1857	X	1842	R	August
XII i	Other Fabrics	L	1856	Y	1853	W	March
XII ii	Damasks	M	1859	Z	1860		
XIII	Lace	D — Day of the Month				E — Bundle Number	

Exceptions:

In 1857, the letter R was used during 1 – 19 of September; during 1860 the letter K was used for December.

To give an example, using the mark next to the chart you get the following information: Material — Ceramics, Design registered — April 7, 1857.

The Bundle number is unimportant to most collectors.

Each letter on the diagram represents on of the tables below:

Mark II: Used from 1868 – 1883

A — Materials		B — Year				C — Month	
I	Metal	A	1871	K	1883	A	December
II	Wood	C	1870	L	1882	B	October
III	Glass	D	1878	P	1877	C	January
IV	Ceramics	E	1881	S	1875	D	September
V	Paper Hangings	F	1873	U	1874	E	May
VI	Carpets	H	1869	VEE	1876	G	February
VII	Printed Shawls	I	1872	X	1868	H	April
VIII	Other Shawls	J	1880	Y	1879	I	July
IX	Yarn					K	November
X	Printed Fabrics					M	June
XI	Furniture					R	August
XII i	Other Fabrics					W	March
XII ii	Damasks	D — Day of the Month					
XIII	Lace	E — Bundle Number					

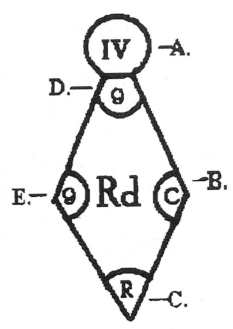

Exceptions:

In 1878, During 1 – 6 of March, the letter W was used for the year instead of the letter D, and the letter G was used for the month in place of the letter W.

To give an example, using the mark next to the chart you get the following information: Material — Ceramics, Design registered — August 9, 1870.

The Bundle number is unimportant to most collectors.

English Registry Numbers

After 1883, a numerical mark was used in the following form:
Rd 742833 or Rd No. 742833

1884 — 1	1913 — 612431	1942 — 839230	1971 — 950046
1885 — 19754	1914 — 630190	1943 — 839980	1972 — 955342
1886 — 40480	1915 — 644935	1944 — 841040	1973 — 960708
1887 — 64520	1916 — 653521	1945 — 842670	1974 — 965185
1888 — 90483	1917 — 658988	1946 — 845550	1975 — 969249
1889 — 116648	1918 — 622872	1947 — 849730	1976 — 973838
1890 — 141273	1919 — 666128	1948 — 853260	1977 — 978426
1891 — 163767	1920 — 673750	1949 — 856999	1978 — 982815
1892 — 185713	1921 — 680147	1950 — 860854	1979 — 987910
1893 — 205240	1922 — 687144	1951 — 863970	1980 — 993012
1894 — 224720	1923 — 694999	1952 — 866280	1981 — 998302
1895 — 246975	1924 — 702671	1953 — 869300	1982 — 1004456
1896 — 268392	1925 — 710165	1954 — 872531	1983 — 1010583
1897 — 291241	1926 — 718057	1955 — 876067	1984 — 1017131
1898 — 311658	1927 — 726330	1956 — 879282	1985 — 1024174
1899 — 331707	1928 — 734370	1957 — 882949	1986 — 1031358
1900 — 351202	1929 — 742725	1958 — 887079	1987 — 1039055
1901 — 368154	1930 — 751160	1959 — 891665	1988 — 1047478
1902 — 385180	1931 — 760583	1960 — 895000	1989 — 1056076
1903 — 403200	1932 — 769670	1961 — 899914	1989 — 1061406
1904 — 424400	1933 — 779292	1962 — 904638	July 1989 — 2000000 (last no.)
1905 — 447800	1934 — 789019	1963 — 909364	Aug. 1990 — 2003720
1906 — 471860	1935 — 799097	1964 — 914536	1991 — 2012047
1907 — 493900	1936 — 808794	1965 — 919607	1992 — 2019933
1908 — 518640	1937 — 817293	1966 — 924510	1993 — 2028110
1909 — 535170	1938 — 825231	1967 — 929335	1994 — 2036116
1910 — 552000	1939 — 832610	1968 — 934515	1995 — 2044229
1911 — 574817	1940 — 837520	1969 — 939875	
1912 — 594195	1941 — 838500	1970 — 944932	

The number listed for each year in the table is the first number issued that year. If your number is higher, but less than the number for the next year, then your item had its design registered during that year.

In July 1990, the numbering sequence changed, as indicated on the chart. The last number issued in July 1990 was 1061406, and the numbering began again in August, starting with number 2000000.

Using the number above the chart as an example, Rd 742833 means: Design of your item was registered during 1929.

Used with permission, Copyright Drexel Grapevine Antiques, www.drexelantiques.com.

Bibliography

Barber, Edwin Atlee. *The Pottery and Porcelain of the United States: an Historical Review of American Ceramic Art from the Earliest Times to the Present Day.* New York, NY: Feingold & Lewis, 1976.

Burton, William. *Collectors Handbook to Marks on Porcelain and Pottery.* Green Farms, CT: Modern Books and Crafts, 1974.

Cameron, Elisabeth. *Encyclopedia of Pottery & Porcelain, 1800-1960.* From Facts on File News Service, 1986.

Chaffers, William. *Marks & Monograms on European and Oriental Pottery & Porcelain.* Los Angeles, CA: Borden Publishing, 1946.

DeBolt, C. Gerald. *DeBolt's Dictionary of American Pottery Marks, Whiteware & Porcelain.* Paducah, KY: Collector Books, 1994.

Evans, Paul. *Art Pottery of the United States: an Encyclopedia of Producers and Their Marks.* New York, NY: Scribner, 1974.

Gaston, Mary Frank. *The Collector's Encyclopedia of Limoges Porcelain.* Paducah, KY: Collector Books, 1998.

_____. *R.S. Prussia Popular Lines: Identifcation and Value Guide.* Paducah, KY: Collector Books, 1999.

Godden, Geoffrey. *The Handbook of British Pottery and Porcelain Marks.* New York, NY: Praeger, 1968.

_____. *The Concise Guide of British Pottery and Porcelain.* London, England: Barrie & Jenkins, 1990.

Hanson, Bob, Craig Nissen, and Margaret Hanson. *McCoy Pottery: Reference & Value Guide.* Paducah, KY: Collector Books, 1997.

Huxford, Bob and Sharon. *The Collector's Encyclopedia of McCoy Pottery.* Paducah, KY: Collector Books, 1995.

Keno, Leigh and Leslie. *Hidden Treasures: Searching for Masterpieces of American Furniture.* New York, NY: Warner Books, 2000.

Kovel, Ralph and Terry. *Kovel's New Dictionary of Marks.* New York, NY: Crown Publishers, 1986.

_____. *Kovel's Dictionary of Marks: Pottery & Porcelain.* New York, NY: Crown Publishers, 1995.

Kowalsky, Arnold A. and Dorothy E. *Encyclopedia of Marks on American, English, and European Earthenware, Ironstone, and Stoneware 1780-1980.* Atglen, PA: Schiffer Publishing Ltd., 1999.

Lehner, Lois. *Lehner's Encyclopedia of U.S. Marks on Pottery, Porcelain & Clay.* Paducah, KY: Collector Books, 1988.

Maloney, David. *Maloney's Antiques & Collectibles Resource Directory.* Iola, WI: Krause Publications Inc., 2000.

Miller, Judith and Martin. *Miller's Pocket Antiques Fact File.* Australia: Reed International Books, 1995.

Moyer, Patsy. *Doll Values: Antique to Modern.* Paducah, KY: Collector Books, 1998.

Poche, Emanuel. *Porcelain Marks of the World.* Arco Publishing Co., 1974.

Savage, Jeff. *Dating English Registry Marks.* www.drexelantiques.com. Drexel Grapevine Antiques, 2003.

Alphabetical Index

A

Abbeydale 5
Abingdon 5
Adams, William 5–9
Adderleys 9, 10
Alboth & Kaiser 10
Alcock, Henry 10
Alcock, John 10, 11
Alcock, Samuel 11
Allerton, Charles 11
Allertons Ltd. 11
Altenburg 11
Altenkunstadt 12
Altrohlau Porcelain 12
American Bisque 12
American China 12
American Chinaware 12
American Encaustic Tile 12, 13
American Limoges China 13, 14
American Terra Cotta & Ceramic . . .14
Amison, Charles 15
Amphora 15, 16
Anchor Pottery 16
Anna Perenna 17
Arabia Porcelain 17
Arcadian China 17, 18
Arequipa Pottery 18
Arkinstall & Sons 18, 19
Arklow Pottery 19
Arnart Imports 19, 20
Artists of the World 20
Arzberg Porcelain 20
Ashtead Potters 20
Ashworth, G. L. & Bros. . . . . . .20 – 22
Augarten Porcelain 22
Ault 22, 23
Aultcliff .23
Avon Art Pottery 23
Avon Faience 23
Axe Vale Pottery 23
Aynsley .24

B

Baggaley, E. 24
Baker & Chetwynd 24
Baker & Co. 24
Balleroy, Julien 24, 25
Balsham, Leah 25
Banko Pottery 25
Bareuther 25
Barker Bros. 25, 26
Barluet & Cie 26
Barons Pottery 26
Barratts .27
Batchelder, Ernest 27
Bauer Pottery 27, 28
Bauscher Bros. 28
Bawo & Dotter 28
Beadmore & Berks 28

Beech & Hancock 28
Belford 29
Bell, J&MP 29
Belleek 29, 30
Bennett, Edwin 30, 31
Bennington Potters 31
Berlin Porcelain Manufactory 31
Beswick, John 31
Beyer & Bock 32
Biltons 32
Bing & Grondahl 33
Birks, Rawlins 34
Bishop & Stonier 34
Black, Harding 34
Black Knight 34
Blairs 34
Blake, Trenle 34, 35
Blau 35
Blin, J. 35
Bloch, B. 35
Bloch, R. 35
Block China 35
Bloor Derby 35
Blyth Porcelain 36
Boch, B. .36
Bock, Josef 36
Boch Freres . . . . .36 – 38
Bodley, E. F. D. 38
Bodley, E. J. D. 38
Boehm 38, 39
Bohemia Ceramic 40
Bohne Sons, Ernst 40
Boote, T. & R. 40, 41
Booth, Thomas 41
Booths 41, 42
Booths & Colcloughs 42
Bopla 42
Borgfeldt, George 42, 43
Bourdois & Bloch 43
Bourne 43
Bourne & Leigh 43, 44
Bovey Pottery 44
Bowker, Arthur 44
Boyer, Georges 45
Boyle, Zachariah 45
Brannam, C. H. 45
Brentleigh 45
Brian, E. & Co. 45, 46
Brianchon 46
Bridgwood 46
Bridgwood & Clarke 46
Bristol 46
Bristol, Poutney, Goldney 46
Bristol Poutney 47
British Anchor Pottery 47
Broadhurst 48
Brock 48
Brough & Blackhurst 48
Brownfield, William 48, 49
Brownhills Pottery 49

Brown-Westhead, Moore 49
Brunt, William Pottery 50
Brusche Ceramics 50
Brush McCoy 50
Buchan, A. W. 50, 51
Buckau Porcelain 51
Buckfast Abbey Pottery 51
Buffalo China 51
Buffalo Pottery 51, 52
Burford Bros. 52
Burgess & Goddard 52, 53
Burgess & Leigh 53
Burgess Bros. 54
Burgess Campbell 54
Burleigh .54
Burmantofts 54, 55
Burroughs & Mountford 55
Bursley Ware 55
Bybee 55
Bybee, Selden 55

C

California Faience 55
Camark Pottery 56
Cambridge Art Pottery 56
Campbellfield 56
Canonsburg China 56
Canonsburg Pottery . . . . .56 – 57
Cantagalli 57
Cardew, Michael Ambrose 57
Carlton Ware 58
Carrollton China 58
Carstens, C. & E. 58
Carter, Stabler, Adams 58
Cartwright & Edwards 58, 59
Cartwright Bros. 59
Cartwright China 59
Castleton China 59, 60
Catalina Pottery 60
Caughley .60
Cauldon 60, 61
Century House 61
Century Services Corporation 61
Ceralene .61
Ceramic Arts Studio 61
Challinor, E. 61, 62
Chamberlains Worcester 62
Chelsea Art Pottery 62
Chelsea-Derby 62
Chelsea Keramic
  Art Works 62, 63
Chelsea Pottery 63
Chessell Pottery 63
Chikusa .63
Chinese Export 63
Chugai China 63
Clark, Edward 63
Clementson, J. 64
Clementson Bros. 64, 65
Clewell 65

Clews 65
Clews, George 65
Clews, James & Ralph 65, 66
Cliff, Clarice 66
Clifton 66, 67
Clinchfield Pottery 67
Coalport .67
Cockson & Seddon 67
Colclough 67, 68
Cone, Thomas 68
Continental Kilns 69
Cook & Hancock 69
Cook Pottery 69
Cooper, Susie . . . . .69 – 71
Co-Operative Wholesale Society 71
Coors 71, 72
Cordey 72
Corn, W & E 72
Corning Glass Works 72
Coronado 72
Coronation Ware 73
Count Thun 73
Cowan Pottery 73
Cox, Paul 73
Coxon Pottery 74
Cranston Pottery 74
Creil & Montereau 74
Crescent Pottery 74, 75
Cronin China 75
Crooksville China 75
Crosse & Blackwell 75
Crown Clarence 75
Crown Devon 75, 76
Crown Ducal 76
Crownford 76, 77
Crown Lynn Pottery 77
Crown Potteries 77
Crown Staffordshire 77, 78
Cumberlidge & Humphrys 78
Cybis 78

D

Dachsel, Paul 78
Dahl Jensen 78
Dalpayrat, Adrien 78
D'Arceau Limoges 79
Dartmouth Pottery 79
Davenport . . . . .79 – 82
Davis, John Heath 82
Dean, S.W. 82
Deck, Theodore 82
Decoeur, Emile 82
Dedham Pottery 82, 83
Delaherche, Auguste 83
Delinieres, R. 83
Denbac .83
Denby Tableware 83
Denver .83
Derby Porcelain Works . . . . . .84 – 86
Desert Sands Pottery 86
Desiree Denmark 86
Desvres .86

Devonmoor 87
Dillion, Francis 87
Dimmock, J. 87
Dimmock, Thomas 87
Distel 87
Donath, P. 88
Donath & Company 88
Dorchester 88
Doulton . . . . .88 – 93
Dresden .93
Dresden Porcelain 93
Dresden Pottery Co 93, 94
Dressel, Kister 94
Dresser, Ch. 94
Dressler, Julius 94
Ducal Brunswick 94
Dudson, Wilcox & Till 94, 95
Dunn, Bennett 95
Duraline Hotel Ware 129
Durant Kilns 95
Dux Porcelain 95, 96

E

East End Pottery 96
East Liverpool Pottery 96, 97
East Trenton Pottery 97
Ebeling & Reuss 97
Eckert, Richard 97
Edelstein 97
Edge, Malkin 98
Edwards, James 98, 99
Edwards, John 99
Edwards Bros. 99
Efchenbach 99
Egersund Pottery 99, 100
Eichwald 100
Elbogen 100
Elfinware 100
Elizabethan 100
Elkin, Knight, Bridgwood 100
Elsmore & Forster 101
Elsmore & Sons, T. 101
Elton, Sir Edmund 101
Empire Crockery 101
Empire Pottery 101, 102
Ens Porcelain 102
Ens Porcelain, Karl 102
Ephraim 102
Epiag 102, 103
Eschenbach 103, 104
Ewenny Pottery 104
Exeter Art Pottery 104

F

Faience Manufacturing Co. 104
Fasold & Stauch 104
Fielding, S. 104, 105
Finch, Kay 105
Finney, A. T. 105
Fischer, Bruce 106
Fischer, Christian 106
Fischer, Emil 106

Fischer & Mieg 106
Fishley, George 106
Fishley, William 106
Fitz and Floyd 106
Flight, Barr, Barr Worcester 106, 107
Flintridge China 107
Florence Ceramics 107
Ford & Riley 107
Ford & Sons 108
Forester, Thomas 108
Forrester, Rembrandt & Son 108
Frankoma 108
Fraureuther 108, 109
French China 109
French Saxon China 109, 110
Frie Onnaing 110
Fritsch & Weidermann 110
Fryer, J. 110
Fukagawa 110
Fulham Pottery 111
Fulper Pottery 111
Furnivals 111, 112
Furstenberg 112

G

Galle 112
Galluba & Hofmann 112, 113
Gater Hall 113
Gebr. Kuhnlenz 113
George, W. S. 113, 114
George Grainer Worcester . . .114, 115
Georgia Art Pottery 115
Gerz, Simon Peter 115
Gesetzlitch Geschutzt 115
Gibson & Sons 115, 116
Gibsons 116
Gien 116
Gladding McBean . . . . .116 – 118
Glasgow Pottery 118
Glidden Pottery 119
Globe Pottery 119
Gloria .119
Gmundner Keramik 119
Goebel 120, 121
Goedewaagen 121
Goldscheider 122
Gonder Originals 123
Goodwin Pottery 123
Goss, William Henry 123
Gouda, Holland 124
Goumot-Labesse 124, 125
Gray, A. E. Pottery 125
Greber, Charles 125
Green, T. G. 125, 126
Greenwood Pottery 126
Greiner, Frederick Christian 126
Griffen, Smith & Hall 126
Grimwades 127, 128
Grindley 128, 129
Groschel & Stethmann 129
Grosvenor, F. 129
Grosvenor China 130

Grueby Pottery 130, 131
Guernsey Pottery 131
Gustafsberg . . . . .131 – 133
Gutherz, Oscar & Edgar 133

H

Haas & Czjzek 133, 134
Hache, Alfred 134
Hache & Pepin 134
Hackefors Porcelain 134
Hadley, James 134
Hadley, M. A. 134
Haeger 135, 136
Hall, Ralph & Son 136
Hall China . . . . .136 – 138
Hammersley 138
Hampshire Pottery 138, 139
Hanke, Robert 139
Harker Pottery . . . . .139 – 142
Harrison & Shaw 142
Hautin & Boulanger 142
Haviland, Johann 143
Haynes, Bennett 143
Haynes, D. F. 143
Heath, J. .143
Heath Ceramics 143
Heinrich .144
Heinrich, Franz 144
Henneberg Porcelain 145
Herculaneum 145
Herend 145
Heron, Robert 145
Hertel, Jacob 145
Heubach & Koppelsdorf 145
Heubach Bros. 146
Hewitt & Leadbeater 146
Hibel Studio 146, 147
Hicks, Meigh & Johnson 147
Hochst 147
Hoganas Ceramics 147
Holland, John 147
Hollinshead & Kirkham 147
Honition Pottery 147, 148
Hopper, Robin 148
Horn Bros. 148, 149
Hornsea .149
Howard Pottery 149
Hubbe Brothers 149
Hudson, William 149, 150
Hughes, E. 150
Hughes, Thomas 150
Hughes & Sons 150
Hull Pottery 150, 151
Hull, A. E. 151
Hulme, William 151
Hutschenreuther . . . . .152 – 155
Hyalyn 155

I

Iden Pottery 155
Ilmenau Porcelain 156
Imperial China 156

International Pottery 156
Interpace Corporation 156
Iron Mountain 156
Iroquois China 157
Isle of Wight 157

J

Jackson China 157
Jackson Vitrified China 158
Jaeger 158
Jersey City 159
Johnson, Samuel 159
Johnson Bros. 159, 160
Jones, A. B. 160
Jones, A. G. Harley 161
Jones, George 161, 162
Jonroth Studios 162
Josef Originals 162
Jugtown .163

K

Kaestner, Friedrich 163
Kahla Porcelain 163
Kaiser Porcelain 163
Kalk Porcelain 164
Kammer, Rudolf 164
Karlskrona 164
Keeling & Co. 164, 165
Keller & Guerin 165, 166
Kensington 166
Kent, James 166, 167
Kerafina .168
Keramos .168
Kern Collectibles 168
Kestner, J. D. 169
Kirkham .169
Kister, A. W. 169
Kister, Fr. 169
Klemm, Richard 169
Knowles, Edwin 169, 170
Knowles, Taylor Knowles 170
Kokura 171
Kranichfeld Porcelain Factory 171
Krautheim 171
Krautheim & Adelberg 171
Krister 171
Krister Porcelain Manufactory 172
Kronester 172
Kuba 172
Kunst 172
Kuznetsov 172

L

Laeuger, Max 173
Lancaster 173
Lang, Anton 173
Langenthal 174
Late Mayers 174
Laughlin, Homer . . . . .174 – 177
Lawrence, Thomas 177
Leach, Bernard 177, 178
Leach, David 178

Lebeau Porcelain 178
Lefton 178, 179
Leigh Potters 179
Lenox 179
Leonard, P. H. 179
Levy, Ch. 180
Lietzke Porcelains 180
Limbach .180
Limoges, A. Lanternier 180, 181
Limoges, Bawo & Dotter 181
Limoges, Beaux-Arts 181
Limoges, Bernardaud & Co. 182
Limoges, Blakeman
        & Henderson 182
Limoges, Camille Tharaud 182, 183
Limoges, Castel 183
Limoges, Charles
        Ahrenfeldt 183, 184
Limoges, Charles Field
        Haviland 184, 185
Limoges, Coiffe 185
Limoges, Comte D'Artois 185
Limoges, Delinieres
        & Bernardaud 185
Limoges, Delinieres & Co 185
Limoges, Flambeau China 186
Limoges, F. Legrand 186
Limoges, Fontanille & Marraud . . .186
Limoges, Frank Haviland 186
Limoges, G. Demartine 186
Limoges, George Bassett 186
Limoges, George Borgfeldt 187
Limoges; Gerard, Dufraisseix,
        & Abbot 187
Limoges, Haviland & Co. 187, 188
Limoges, Jean Pouyat 188
Limoges, Klingenberg
        & Dwenger 188
Limoges, Latrille Freres 189
Limoges, Laviolette 189
Limoges; Lazeyras, Rosenfeld
        & Lehman 189
Limoges, Leon Sazerat 189
Limoges, L. W. Levy 189
Limoges, Martial Redon 189, 190
Limoges, Mavaleix & Granger 190
Limoges, P. M. Mavaleix 190
Limoges, Pallas 190
Limoges, Paroutaud Freres 190
Limoges, Porcelaine Limousine . . .190
Limoges, Raynaud & Co. 190
Limoges, Ribes 190
Limoges, Robert Haviland 191
Limoges, Tharaud 191
Limoges, Theodore
        Haviland 191, 192
Limoges, Tressemanes & Vogt 192
Limoges, Union Ceramique 193
Limoges, Vignaud Freres 193
Limoges, Wannamakers 193
Limoges, William Guerin 193, 194
Lindner 194

Linthorpe Pottery 195
Lladro 195
L. Lourioux 196
Locke & Co. 196
Lomonosov Porcelain Factory 196
Longwy Faience . . . . .196 – 198
Lord Nelson Pottery 198, 199
Los Angeles Potteries 199
Lovatts Potteries 199
Low Art Tile 199, 200
Ludwigsburg 200
Lyman, Fenton & Co. 200

M
MacIntosh, Harrison 200
MacIntyre, James 200, 201
Maddock, John 201, 202
Maddock Pottery 202
Maddux .202
Mafra & Son 203
Maling, C. T. 203, 204
Manka, Franz 204
Manzoni, Carlo 204
Marblehead Pottery 204
Maria Pottery 204
Mark & Gutherz 204
Marseille, Armand 205
Martin Bros. 205, 206
Masons 206
Massier, Clement 206, 207
Matsumura 207
Matthews & Clark 207
Mayer, T. J. & J. 207, 208
Mayer China 208
McCoy . . . . .208 – 210
McNicol, D. E. . . . . .210 – 212
McNicol, T. A. 212
McNicol-Smith 212
Meakin, Alfred . . . . .212 – 214
Meakin, Charles 214
Meakin, J.&G. 214, 215
Mehlem, Franz Anton 216
Meigh, Charles 217
Meir, John 217
Mercer Pottery 218
Meredith, Roper 218
Merkelbach, Reinhold 218, 219
Merkelbach & Wick 219, 220
Merrimac Pottery 220
Metenier, Gilbert 220
Metlox Pottery 220
Metthey, Andre 220
Metzler & Ortloff 220
Middleton, J. H. 221
Midwinter 221
Mikasa 221
Minton . . . . .222 – 226
Minton, Hollins & Co. 226
Miramar .226
Mitterteich 226, 227
Moira Pottery 227
Moorcroft 227, 228

Moore 228
Moravian 228
Morgan, William De 228, 229
Morimura Bros. 229
Morley, Francis 229
Morley & Co. 229
Morris, Thomas 230
Mortlock, John 230
Mosa Maastricht 230
Mosaic Tile Co. 230, 231
Mountainside Art Pottery 231
Muller, Carl 231
Muller, E.&A. 231
Muller, Paul 231
Muller & Co. 231
Muncie Pottery 231
Musterschutz 232
Myott 232, 233

N
National Potteries 233
Natzler 233
Naudot, Camille 233
Nautilus Porcelain 234
Neuerer, Hans 234
Neukirchner, Franz 234
Neu-Tettau 234
New Chelsea 234
Newcomb Pottery 235
New Devon 235
New England Pottery 235
New Hall Pottery 235
New Porcelain Factory 235, 236
Newport Pottery 236
New Wharf 236
New York & Rudolstadt 236
Nicodemus, Chester 236, 237
Niloak Pottery 237
Nippon 237, 238
Nittsjo Earthenware 238
Nonne, Christian 239
Noritake China 239, 240
Norman Rockwell Museum 240
Norse Pottery 240
North Carolina 240
North Staffordshire Pottery 240
Northwestern Terra Cotta 241
Norton Pottery 241
Nove 241
Nymolle .241
Nymphenburg 241

O
Occupied Japan 242
Ohme, Hermann 242, 243
Ohr, George 243
Onondaga Pottery 243, 244
Ott & Brewer 244, 245
Owens Pottery 245

P
Paden City Pottery 246

Palissy Pottery 246, 247
Pankhurst, J. W. 248
Paragon China 248, 249
Pauline Pottery 249
Pearl China 249
Pech, R.&E. 249
Pennsbury Pottery 249, 250
Peoria Pottery 250
Petit, Jacob 250
Pewabic Pottery 250
Pfaltzgraff 250, 251
Pfeffer Bros. 251
Pfeiffer & Lowenstein 251
Philadelphia City Pottery 251
Phillips, G. 251
Picasso 252
Pick, Albert 252
Pickard China 252
Pierce, Howard 252, 253
Pigeon Forge 253
Pilkingtons 253
Pillin Pottery 253
Pillivuyt, Charles 253
Pinder Bourne 254
Pioneer Pottery 254
Pisgah Forest 254, 255
Plankenhammer 255
Plant, R. H. & S. L. 255
Plaue Porcelain 256
Podmore, Walker 256
Poole, Thomas 257
Poole Pottery 257, 258
Pope-Gosser 258
Porcelain Factory
    Konigszelt 259
Porcelain Fles 259
Porcelain Union 259
Porcelier .259
Porquier, Adolphe 260
Porquier Beau 260
Porsgrund 260
Portheim & Son 260
Portmeirion Pottery 260, 261
Potters Co-Operative 261
Pottery Guild 261
Pountney 262
Pouplard-Beatrix 262
Powell, Bishop & Stonier 262, 263
Pratt 263
Precious Moments . . . . .263 – 265
Price & Kensington 265
Prospect Hill Pottery 265
Purinton Pottery 265

Q
Quarry Tile 265
Quimper . . . . .265 – 266

R
Radford, E. 266
Radford, Samuel 266, 267
Radford Pottery 267

R.J. Ernst Enterprises 267
Rappsilber, A. 267
Rathbone, T. 267
Rauschert, Paul 267, 268
Redware .268
Red Wing 268, 269
Regal China 269, 270
Regency China 270
Registry mark 270
Regout, Petrus 270, 271
Reichenbach 271
Reutter 271
Revere, Paul Pottery 271, 272
Rhead, Charlotte 272
Rhead, Frederick 272
Rhead Pottery 272
Rhodes, Daniel 272
Richardson, A. G. 272, 273
Richter, Fenkl
    & Hahn 273
Ridgewood China 273
Ridgway Pottery . . . . .273 – 276
River Shore 276
Robertson Pottery 276
Robinson, W. H. 276
Robinson Ransbottom 276, 277
Robj 277
Rockingham Works 277
Roman Ceramic
    Corporation 278
Rookwood 278
Rorstrand 278, 279
Roselane 279, 280
Rosemeade 280
Rose Medallion 280
Rosenthal . . . . .280 – 282
Roseville Pottery . . . . .282 – 284
Rosina 284
Rowland & Marsellus 284
Royal Bayreuth 285, 286
Royal China 286, 287
Royal Copely 289
Royal Copenhagen 287, 288
Royal Kendal 289
Royal Porcelain
    Manufactory 289, 290
Royal Windsor 291
Rozenberg 291
Ruskin Pottery 291
Russian 291, 292
Russian Imperial Porcelain Factory
   292
Rye Pottery 292, 293

S

Sabin Industries 293
Sadler, James 293, 394
Salem China 294, 295
Salt & Nixon 295
Sampson Bridgwood 295, 296
Sampson Hancock 296
Samson 296, 297

Sandizell .297
Santa Anita Pottery 297
Schachtel, Joseph 297
Schafer & Vater 297
Schaller, Oscar 297, 298
Schau Bach Kunst 298
Scheibe-Alsbach 298
Scheier 298
Schierholz, Von 299
Schiller, W. & Son 299, 300
Schiller & Gerbing 300
Schirnding 300
Schlegelmilch, Erdmann 300
Schlegelmilch, Oscar 301
Schlegelmilch, Reinhold 301, 302
Schmid 302, 303
Schmider, Georg 303
Schmidt 303
Schmidt, Hugo 303
Schnabel & Sons 304
Schneider, Carl 304
Schoenau & Hoffmeister 304
Schonwald Porcelain 304, 305
Schoonhoven 305
Schramberger Majolica Factory . . .305
Schumann, Carl 305, 306
Schutzmeister & Quendt 306
Schwarzburg 306
Sebring Pottery 306, 307
Seltmann, Christian 307
Seltmann, Johann 307, 308
Sevres 308, 309
Sevres China 309
Sewell 310
Shaw, Anthony 310
Shawnee .310
Shearwater 310, 311
Shelley 311
Shenango Pottery 311, 312
Shorter & Son 312
Silver Springs 312
Simpson, T. A. 312, 313
Sitzendorf 313
Smith, W. T. H. 313
Smith Phillips 313, 314
Societa Ceramica 314, 315
Societe Ceramique 315
Sohn, Ernest 315
Solly, John 315
Solon and Schemmel 315
Southern Potteries 315, 316
Spode . . . . .316 – 320
Springer & Co. 320
Stafford Pottery 320
Standard China 320
Stanforderware 320
Stangl 320
State's Porcelain Manufactory 321
St. Clements 321
Steinmann, K. 321, 322
Stellmacher 322
Sterling China . . . . .322 – 324

Stetson China 324, 325
Steubenville Pottery 325, 326
Stevenson, Ralph 326
Stevenson & Williams 326
Steventon, John 326
Stnact, Josef 326
Stockhardt & Schmidt-Eckert 327
Stockton Art Pottery 327
Straub, Paul 327
Straus, Lewis & Sons 327
Stubbs, Joseph 327
Swasey, E. 327
Swastika Keramos 328
Swift, John 328
Swillington Bridge 328
Swinnertons 328
Syracuse China 328, 329
Szeiler Studio 330

T

Takito 330
Tamac 330
Taylor, Tunnicliffe 330
Taylor & Kent 330
Taylor Bros. 331
Taylor Smith & Taylor . . . . .331 – 333
Teichert, C. 333
Teichert, Ernst 334
Terra Nigra 334
Tharaud, Justin 334
Thewalt, Albert Jacob 334
Thieme, Carl 334
Thomas, F. Porcelain 335
Thomas, Mark 335
Thomas & Co. 335
Thomas China 335
Thompson, C. C. 335
Thorley, Palen 336
Tielsch, C. 336
Tiffany Pottery 336, 337
Till, Thomas 337
Tirschenreuth 337
Tomkinson Bros. 337
Tooth & Ault 337
Torquay 338
Trenle Blake China 339
Trenle China 339
Trent Tile .339
Trenton Potteries 339
Triebner, Ens, Eckert 339, 340
Turner, John 340
Turner & Tomkinson 340
Twisted Rope 340

U

Ungemach Pottery 340
Union Porcelain Works 340, 341
United China 341
United States Encaustic Tile 341
United States Pottery 341
Universal Potteries 341, 342
University City Pottery 342

University of North Dakota 342
Unterweissbach 343
Upchurch Pottery 343
Upper Hanley 343
Upsala-Ekeby 343
Utzchneider & Co. 343, 344

V

Van Briggle 344
Vance 345
Variazioni, Tema 345
Veneto Flair 345
Vernon Kilns . . . . .345 – 347
Victoria Porcelain 347
Vienna Art Ceramic 347
Vienna Porcelain 347
Vienna Workshops 348
Viletta .348
Villeroy & Boch . . . . .348 – 350
Vodrey & Brothers 350
Vohann of California 351
Volkmar Ceramic 351
Volkstedt 351

W

Wachter, R. 351
Wachtersbach 351, 352
Waco 352
Wade 352
Wade, George 352
Wade, Heath 352, 353
Wagner & Apel 353

Wahliss, Ernst 353
Wain, H. A. 353
Waldsassen Porcelain 354
Walker China 354
Walkure 354
Wallace & Chetwynd 354, 355
Wallace China 355
Wallendorf 355
Walley, Edward 355
Walley Pottery 355
Walrath, Frederick 355
Walrich Pottery 355
Walton .356
Wannopee Pottery 356
Wardle .356
Warwick China 357
Watt Pottery 357, 358
Weatherby, J. H. 358
Wedge Wood, John 359
Wedgwood . . . . .359 – 361
Wedgwood, Enoch 361
Wedgwood & Bentley 362
Wehinger, H. 362
Weil 362
Weller Pottery . . . . .362 – 365
Wellington China 365
Wellsville China 365
Wessel, Friedrich Wilhelm 365
Wessel, Ludwig 365, 366
West End Pottery 366
West Germany Mark 368
Western Pottery 367

Western Stoneware 367, 368
Wheatley Pottery 368
Wheeling Pottery 369
Whites Pottery 369
Whittaker & Co. 370
Wild, Thomas C. and Sons 370
Wileman 370, 371
Wilkes, V. M. 371
Wilkinson, Arthur 371, 372
Willets 372, 373
Williamson, H. M. & Sons 373
Williamsons, H. W. & Sons 373
Wiltshaw & Robinson 373
Winfield Pottery 373, 374
Winkle, F. 374, 375
Winterling 375
Wolfsohn, Helena 375
Wood, Arthur 376
Wood, Enoch 376
Wood, H. J. 377
Wood & Sons 377, 378
Worcester . . . . .378 – 380
Worcester Royal Porcelain 380
Wranitzky, P. A. 381

Z

Zaneware 381
Zark 381
Zdekauer, Moritz 381
Zeh, Scherzer 381, 382
Zsolnay .382

Date Index

1725 – 1799

Caughley, 1775 – 1778 60
Caughley, 1785 60
Chelsea-Derby, 1756 – 1775 62
Davenport, 1793 – 1810 79
Derby Porcelain Works,
    1760 – 1825 84
Derby Porcelain Works,
    1782 – 1825 84
Derby Porcelain Works,
    1784 – 1795 84
Derby Porcelain Works, 1790 84
Herculaneum, 1796 – 1833 145
Herculaneum, 1790 – 1830 145
Nonne, Christian, 1767 – 1800 . . .239
Nove, 1727 – 1835 241
Royal Porcelain Manufactory,
    1725 – 1763 289
Royal Porcelain Manufactory,
    1740 – 1745 289
Royal Porcelain Manufactory,
    1750 – 1775 289
Royal Porcelain Manufactory,
    1766 – 1780 289
Royal Porcelain Manufactory,
    1770 289
Royal Porcelain Manufactory ,
    1774 – 1817 289
Sevres, 1753 308
Sevres, 1756 308
Sevres, 1765 308
Spode, 1790 – 1827 316
Wedgwood, 1769 – present 359
Wedgwood, 1780 – 1795 359
Wedgwood & Bentley,
    1768 – 1780 362
Worcester, 1755 – 1792 378
Worcester, 1762 – 1785 378
Worcester, 1770 378

1800 – 1839

Adams, William, 1804+ 5
Adams, William, 1804 – 1840 5
Adams, William, 1819 – 1864 5
Adams, William, 1829 – 1861 5
Adams, William, 1836 – 1864 . . . .5, 6
Adams, William, 1839 – 1855 6
Alcock, Samuel, 1828 11
Beadmore & Berks, 1831 – 1843 28
Bloor Derby, 1820 – 1840 35
Boyle, Zachariah, 1823 – 1828 45
Boyle, Zachariah, 1823 – 1850 45
Bristol, Pountney, Goldney, 1836 –
    1849 46
Chamberlains Worcester,
    1811 – 1840 62
Chamberlains Worcester,
    1820 – 1840 62
Chinese Export, 19th century 63
Clementson, J., 1839+ 64

Clementson, J., 1839 – 1864 64
Clews, James & Ralph,
    1810 – 1820 65
Clews, James & Ralph,
    1818 – 1834 65
Coalport, 1820 67
Davenport, 1800 – 1840 80
Davenport, 1800 – 1860 80
Davenport, 1805 – 1820 80
Davenport, 1820 – 1860 80
Davenport, 1830 – 1835 81
Davenport, 1830 – 1880 81
Derby Porcelain Works,
    1800 – 1820 84
Dillion, Francis, 1834 – 1843 87
Dimmock, Thomas, 1828 – 1859 . . .87
Elkin, Knight, Bridgwood, 1827 –
    1840 100
Fischer & Mieg, 1810 – 1846 106
Flight, Barr, Barr Worcester,
    1807 – 1813 . . . . .106, 107
Flight, Barr, Barr Worcester,
    1813 – 1840 107
Ford & Sons, 1839 – 1938 108
Furnivals, 1818 – 1890 111
George Grainger Worcester,
    1810 – 1820 114
Gustafsberg, 1839 – 1860 131
Hall, Ralph & Son, 1825 136
Harrison & Shaw, 1800+ 142
Heath, J., 1802 – 1850 143
Hicks, Meigh & Johnson,
    1822 – 1835 147
Horn Bros., 1830 – 1860 . . . . .148, 149
Maling, C. T., 1817 – 1853 203
Masons, 1813 – 1825 206
Masons, 1820 206
Mayer, T. J. & J., 1830+ 207
Mayer, T. J. & J., 1834 – 1848 207
Meigh, Charles, 1835 – 1849 217
Minton, 1800 – 1830 222
Minton, 1830 – 1860 222
Minton, 1836 – 1841 222
Petit, Jacob, 1830 – 1862 250
Phillips, G., 1834 – 1848 251
Podmore, Walker, 1834 – 1859 256
Porcelain Fles, 1800+ 259
Pratt, 1800+ 263
Redware, 1830 – 1860 268
Ridgway Pottery, 1814 – 1830 . .274, 275
Ridgway Pottery, 1830 – 1854 275
Ridgway Pottery, 1835 – 1845 274
Ridgway Pottery, 1836 – 1842 275
Ridgway Pottery, 1838 – 1848 275
Rockingham Works,
    1826 – 1830 277
Royal Porcelain Manufactory,
    1800 – 1850 290
Royal Porcelain Manufactory,
    1814 – 1860 290

Royal Porcelain Manufactory,
    1832 – present 290
Schiller & Gerbing, 1829 – 1885 . . .300
Sevres, 1814 308
Sevres, 1820 308
Sevres, 1830 – 1848 308
Sewell, 1804 – 1878 310
Spode, 1805 – 1815 316
Spode, 1814 – 1833 316
Spode, 1833+ 319
Spode, 1833 – 1847 319
Stevenson & Williams, 1825 326
Stevenson, Ralph, 1832 – 1835, . . .326
Swillington Bridge, 1820 – 1850 328
Turner, John, 1800 – 1805 340
Villeroy & Boch, 1836 – 1855 348
Walton, 1800 356
Wedgwood, 1834 – present 359

1840 – 1889

Adams, William, 1850 – 1900 6
Adams, William, 1860 – 1880 7
Adams, William, 1870 – 1890 7
Adams, William, 1870s – 1880s 7
Adams, William, 1879 – 1891 7
Adams, William, 1879 – 1900 7
Adderleys, 1876 – 1905 9
Alcock, Henry, 1880 – 1910 10
Alcock, John, 1855 10
Alcock, John, 1857 11
Allerton, Charles, 1870 – 1890 11
American Encaustic Tile Co,
    1875 – 1935 12
Ashworth, G. L. & Bros.,
    1860 – 1880 20
Ashworth, G. L. & Bros.,
    1862 – 1880 . . . . .20, 21
Ashworth, G. L. & Bros.,
    1862 – 1890 21
Ashworth, G. L. & Bros., 1870 21
Ault, 1887 – 1923 . . . . .22, 23
Baker & Chetwynd, 1882 – 1901 24
Baker & Co., 1880 – 1920 24
Bawo & Dotter, 1884 – 1914 28
Beech & Hancock, 1840 – 1860 28
Bell, J&MP, 1850 – 1860 29
Bell, J&MP, 1850 – 1870 29
Bell, J&MP, 1881 – 1928 29
Belleek, 1863 – 1891 29
Belleek, 1863 – present 29
Bennett, Edwin, 1876 – 1936 30
Bennett, Edwin, 1886 30
Boch Freres, 1841+ 36
Bodley, E. F. D., 1887 38
Bodley, E. F. D., 1875 – 1892 38
Bodley, E. J. D., 1875 – 1892 38
Bohne Sons, Ernst, 1878 – 1920 40
Boote, T. & R., 1842 – 1863 40
Boote, T. & R., 1853 40
Boote, T. & R., 1870 40

Booth, Thomas, 1876 – 1883 41
Brianchon, 1864+ 46
Bridgwood & Clarke, 1857 – 1864 ..46
British Anchor Pottery,
    1884 – 1913 47
Brough & Blackhurst,
    1872 – 1895 48
Brownfield, William,
    1850 – 1871 48
Brownfield, William,
    1871 – 1891 ....48, 49
Brownhills Pottery, 1870 – 1890 49
Brown-Westhead, Moore,
    1869 – 1904 49
Brown-Westhead, Moore, 1875 49
Buckau Porcelain, 1850 – 1920 51
Burgess & Goddard, 1840 – 1860 ..52
Burgess & Goddard, 1878 53
Burgess Campbell, 1860 – 1936 ...54
Burmantofts, 1882 – 1904 54
Burroughs & Mountford,
    1879 – 1882 55
Campbellfield, 1850 – 1905 56
Cantagalli, 1878 – 1901 57
Cartwright & Edwards, 1870 – 1890 ..58
Cartwright & Edwards, 1880 59
Cartwright Bros., 1880 – 1927 59
Cartwright Bros., 1887 – 1900 59
Cartwright Bros., 1888 59
Cauldon, 1860 – 1880 60
Cauldon, 1862 – 1890 60
Challinor, E., 1842 – 1867 .....61, 62
Challinor, E., 1853 – 1862 62
Chamberlains Worcester,
    1847 – 1850 62
Chelsea Keramic Art Works,
    1872 – 1889 62
Clark, Edward, 1865 – 1877 63
Clementson Bros., 1870+ 64
Cockson & Seddon, 1875 – 1877 ..67
Coxon Pottery, 1863 – 1884 74
Creil & Montereau, 1880 – 1890 ...74
Creil et Montereau, 1870 74
Crescent Pottery, 1881+ 74
Crosse & Blackwell, 1840 – 1890 75
Cumberlidge & Humphrys,
    1880 – 1890+ 78
Dalpayrat, Adrien, 1876 – 1905 78
Davenport, 1840 – 1867 81
Davenport, 1853+ 81
Davenport, 1860 – 1870 81
Davenport, 1860 – 1873 81
Davenport, 1870 – 1886 82
Davis, John Heath, 1881 – 1891 ...82
Deck, Theodore, 1859 – 1891 82
Delinieres, R., 1879 – 1900 83
Derby Porcelain Works,
    1861 – 1935 84
Derby Porcelain Works, 1865 84
Derby Porcelain Works,
    1878 – 1890 ....84, 85
Desvres, 1870 86

Dimmock, J., 1878 – 1904 87
Doulton, 1853+ 88
Doulton, 1855+ 88
Doulton, 1869 – 1872 89
Doulton, 1873 – 1914 89
Doulton, 1876 89
Doulton, 1877 – 1880 89
Doulton, 1880 89
Doulton, 1880 – 1902 89
Doulton, 1881 – 1912 90
Doulton, 1885 – 1891 90
Doulton, 1885 – 1902 90
Doulton, 1885 – 1910 90
Doulton, 1887 – 1906 90
Dresden, 1883 – 1893 93
Dresden Porcelain, 1869 – 1903 ...93
Dresser, Ch., 1879 – 1889 94
Ducal Brunswick, 1850 – 1894 94
Dunn, Bennett, 1875 – 1907 95
East Trenton Pottery, 1888 – 1905 ..97
Edge, Malkin, 1873+ 98
Edge, Malkin, 1873 – 1903 98
Edwards, James, 1841 – 1851 98
Edwards, James, 1847 98
Edwards, James, 1851 – 1882 99
Edwards, John, 1853 99
Edwards, John, 1880 – 1900 99
Edwards Bros., 1880+ 99
Egersund Pottery, 1880+ 99
Elsmore & Forster, 1860s 101
Elsmore & Sons, T., 1878 101
Elton, Sir Edmund, 1879 – 1930 ...101
Empire Pottery, 1884 – 1892 101
Faience Manufacturing Co.,
    1880 – 1892 104
Faience Manufacturing Co.,
    1884 – 1890 104
Fischer, Christian, 1846 – 1857 106
Fischer, Emil, 1866 – 1908+ 106
Ford & Riley, 1882 – 1964+ 107
Forester, Thomas, 1883+ 108
Fulham Pottery, 1864 – 1869 111
Furnivals, 1868 – 1883 111
Furnivals, 1880+ 111
Galle, 1874 – 1904 112
Gebr. Kuhnlenz, 1884 113
George Grainger Worcester,
    1840 – 1860 114
George Grainger Worcester,
    1850 – 1860 114
George Grainger Worcester,
    1870 – 1879 114
George Grainger Worcester,
    1889 – 1902 114
Gien, 1864+ 116
Glasgow Pottery, 1863+ 118
Goldscheider, 1885 – 1897 122
Goodwin Pottery, 1852 123
Goss, William Henry,
    1862 – 1930 123
Greenwood Pottery,
    1868 – 1933 126

Griffen, Smith & Hall,
    1878 – 1889 126
Gustafsberg, 1860 – 1890 131
Gustafsberg, 1880 – 1925 131
Hache & Pepin, 1845 – 1872 134
Hall & Son, Ralph, 1843 – 1849 136
Hampshire Pottery, 1871+ 138
Hampshire Pottery, 1871 – 1923 ...138
Hampshire Pottery, 1883+ 139
Hanke, Robert, 1882 – 1914 139
Hautin & Boulanger, 1880+ 142
Haynes, Bennett, 1881 – 1895 143
Haynes, D. F., 1882 – 1884 143
Haynes, D. F., 1882 – 1885 143
Heron, Robert, 1883 – 1929 145
Heubach & Koppelsdorf, 1882+ 145
Heubach Bros., 1882+ 146
Holland, John, 1852 – 1854 147
Horn Bros., 1860s 149
Horn Bros., 1870 149
Hubbe Brothers, 1882 – 1898 149
Hudson, William, 1889+ 149
Hughes & Sons, 1850s 150
Hutschenreuther, 1882+ 152
Hutschenreuther, 1884 – 1909 152
Hutschenreuther, 1886 – 1945 152
Hutschenreuther, 1887 152
Imperial China, 1885 – 1896 156
International Pottery,
    1860 – 1940+ 156
Jones, George, 1861 – 1873 161
Jones, George, 1873 161
Kaestner, Friedrich,
    1884 – 1929 163
Keeling & Co., 1886 – 1899 164
Keller & Guerin, 1889+ 165
Kister, Fr., 1887 169
Klemm, Richard, 1886 – 1916 169
Kuznetsov, 1875 – 1900 172
Lang, Anton, 1880 – 1938 173
Late Mayers, 1876 174
Laughlin, Homer, 1873 – 1877 174
Lebeau Porcelain, 1879 – 1910 178
Levy, Ch., 1876 180
Limoges, Charles Field Haviland,
    1882 – 1890 184
Limoges, Delinieres & Co.,
    1870s 185
Limoges; Gerard, Dufraisseix &
    Morel, 1882 – 1890 187
Limoges, Haviland & Co., 1879 –
    1889 187
Limoges, Haviland & Co., 1888 –
    1896 188
Limoges, Klingenberg & Charles
    Dwenger, 1880s – 1890s 188
Linthorpe Pottery, 1879 – 1889 ...195
Longwy Faience, 1875+ 196
Longwy Faience, 1878+ 197
Longwy Faience, 1881 – 1889 197
Low Art Tile, 1877 – 1893 199
Low Art Tile, 1881 – 1885 200

Lyman, Fenton & Co., 1849 200
Macintyre, James, 1868 – 1883 200
Maddock, John, 1842 – present . . .201
Mafra & Son, 1853+ 203
Maling, C. T., 1875 – 1908 205
Martin Bros., 1847 – 1918 205
Martin Bros., 1882 – 1914 . . . .205, 206
Masons, 1845+ 206
Massier, Clement,
　　1883 – 1917 . . . . .206, 207
Mayer China, 1881 – 1891 208
Mayer China, 1881 – 1930+ 208
Mayer, T. J. & J., 1840 – 1860 207
Mayer, T. J. & J., 1847 208
Mayer, T. J. & J., 1851 208
Meakin, Alfred, 1875 – 1897 212
Meakin, Charles, 1883 – 1889 214
Meakin, J.&G., 1870 – 1890 214
Mehlem, Franz Anton,
　　1887 – 1920 216
Mehlem, Franz Anton,
　　1888 – 1920 216
Meir, John, 1848 – 1863 217
Mercer Pottery, 1868 – 1937 218
Merkelbach & Wick,
　　1872 – 1921 . . . . .219, 220
Minton, 1840 – 1860 222
Minton, 1841 – 1873 222
Minton, 1843 222
Minton, 1845 222
Minton, 1845 – 1860 222
Minton, 1850+ 223
Minton, 1853 223
Minton, 1862 223
Minton, 1862 – 1871 223
Minton, 1863 – 1872 223
Minton, 1864 224
Minton, 1865 224
Minton, 1869 224
Minton, 1870 224
Minton, 1871 – 1875 224
Minton, 1873 224
Minton, 1873+ 225
Minton, 1877 225
Minton, 1879 225
Minton, 1881 225
Minton, Hollins & Co., 1870+ 226
Morgan, William De, 1882 – 1888 . .228
Morgan, William De, 1888+ 229
Morgan, William De,
　　1888 – 1897 228
Morley & Co, 1879 – 1884 229
Morley, Francis, 1845 – 1858 229
Mortlock, John, 1877 230
Mosa Maastricht,
　　1883 – present 230
New England Pottery, 1887+ 235
New England Pottery,
　　1889 – 1895 235
New York & Rudolstadt,
　　1887 – 1918 236
Norton Pottery, 1845 – 1847 241

Ohme, Hermann, 1882+ 242, 243
Ohr, George, 1883+ 243
Onondaga Pottery, 1874 – 1893 . . .243
Ott & Brewer, 1863+ 244
Ott & Brewer, 1863 – 1894 244
Ott & Brewer, 1866 244
Ott & Brewer, 1876 245
Ott & Brewer, 1882 245
Ott & Brewer, 1886 245
Owens Pottery, 1885+ 245
Pankhurst, J.W., 1870s 248
Pauline Pottery, 1883+ 249
Peoria Pottery, 1873 – 1902 250
Philadelphia City Pottery, 1868 . . .251
Phillips, G, 1845 251
Pillivuyt, Charles, 1854+ 253
Pinder Bourne, 1862 – 1882 254
Podmore, Walker, 1849 – 1859 256
Porquier Beau, 1875 – 1900 260
Portheim & Son, 1860 – 1870 260
Pountney, 1840s – 1860s 262
Pountney, 1889+ 262
Powell, Bishop & Stonier, 1856 262
Powell, Bishop & Stonier,
　　1876 – 1936 262
Powell, Bishop & Stonier,
　　1878 – 1891 262
Powell, Bishop & Stonier, 1880+ . . .262
Prospect Hill Pottery, 1880+ 265
Radford, Samuel, 1880+ 266
Red Wing, 1878 – 1892 268
Registry mark, 1842 – 1883 270
Regout, Petrus, 1870 270
Ridgway Pottery, 1841+ 274
Ridgway Pottery, 1842 – 1844 275
Rookwood, 1881 – 1892 278
Rookwood, 1882 278
Rookwood, 1886 – 1900 278
Rorstrand, 1884 278
Rorstrand, 1885+ 278
Rose Medallion, 1850 280
Rowland & Marsellus,
　　1860 – 1912+ 284
Royal Bayreuth, 1887 – 1902 285
Royal Copenhagen,
　　1863 – 1920 287
Royal Porcelain Manufactory,
　　1860 – 1924 290
Royal Porcelain Manufactory,
　　1870 – present 290
Royal Porcelain Manufactory,
　　1880+ .290
Samson, 1873 – 1905 296
Samson, 1875 296
Samson, 1885+ 297
Sampson Bridgwood,
　　1853 – 1897+ 295
Sampson Bridgwood, 1870+ 295
Sampson Bridgwood, 1885 295
Sampson Bridgwood, 1885+ 296
Schlegelmilch, Reinhold,
　　1870s – 1880s 301

Schneider, Carl, 1879 – 1954 304
Sevres, 1843 – 1845 309
Shaw, Anthony, 1851+ 310
Shaw, Anthony, 1851 – 1856 310
Shaw, Anthony, 1851 – 1860 310
Simpson, T. A., 1870 – 1880 312
Sitzendorf, 1887 – 1900 313
Societa Ceramica, 1842 – 1860 314
Societa Ceramica, 1856 – present . .314
Societa Ceramica, 1883+ 314
Societe Ceramique, 1887+ 315
Spode, 1848 317
Spode, 1850 317
Spode, 1850 – 1867 319
Spode, 1851 – 1885 317
Spode, 1867+ 317, 318
Spode, 1875 – 1890 318
Spode, 1882 – 1890+ 318
Stafford Pottery, 1840 – 1860 320
Steinmann, K., 1868 – 1938 321
Stellmacher, 1859 – 1897 322
Stellmacher, 1885 – 1897 322
Steventon, John, 1880 326
Stnact, Josef, 1881 – 1932 326
Swasey, E., 1886 – 1891 327
Swift, John, 1843 328
Syracuse China, 1886 – 1898 328
Takito, 1880 – 1948 330
Taylor Bros., 1860 – 1880 331
Taylor, Tunnicliffe, 1875 – 1898 . . .330
Teichert, C., 1882 – 1930 333
Teichert, Ernst, 1884+ 334
Thieme, Carl, 1888 – 1901 334
Tielsch, C., 1875 – 1918 336
Tielsch, C., 1875 – 1934 336
Till, Thomas, 1861+ 337
Tomkinson Bros., 1860 – 1872 337
Tooth & Ault, 1884 – 1887 337
Torquay, 1887 – 1901 338
Trent Tile, 1882+ 339
Triebner, Ens, Eckert,
　　1884 – 1894 339
Triebner, Ens, Eckert,
　　1886 – 1894+ 340
Turner & Tomkinson,
　　1860 – 1872 340
Twisted Rope, 1865 – 1935 340
Union Porcelain Works, 1878+ 340
Union Porcelain Works,
　　1879 . . . . .340, 341
United States Pottery,
　　1852 – 1858 341
Utzchneider & Co.,
　　1850 – 1870 343
Utzchneider & Co.,
　　1890 – 1915+ 343
Villeroy & Boch, 1850 348
Villeroy & Boch,
　　1874 – present 348
Villeroy & Boch, 1880 – 1883 348
Villeroy & Boch,
　　1880s – 1890s 348

Villeroy & Boch, 1883 – 1930s 349
Villeroy & Boch, 1885 349
Villeroy & Boch, 1885 – 1895 349
Villeroy & Boch, 1887 – 1945 349
Vodrey & Brothers, 1876 – 1896 ...350
Wallace & Chetwynd,
    1882 – 1901 ....354, 355
Walley, Edward, 1845 – 1865 355
Wannopee Pottery,
    1886 – 1903 356
Wardle, 1882 – 1909 356
Wedge Wood, John,
    1841 – 1860 359
Wedgwood, 1840 359
Wedgwood, 1861 360
Wedgwood, 1862 – 1890 360
Wedgwood, 1870 – 1880 360
Weller Pottery, 1882+ 362
Wheatley Pottery, 1879 – 1882 368
Wheeling Pottery, 1879 369
Wheeling Pottery, 1888 – 1893 369
Whittaker & Co, 1886 370
Wileman, 1869 – 1892 370
Willets, 1879 – 1884 372
Willets, 1879 – 1912+ 372
Willets, 1879 – 1930+ 372
Willets, 1884 373
Winkle, F., 1885 374
Wolfsohn, Helena, 1850 – 1881 ...375
Wood & Sons, 1886 377
Worcester Royal Porcelain,
    1865 – 1886 380
Worcester, 1852 – 1875 378
Worcester, 1862 – 1875 .....378, 379
Worcester, 1870 – 1887 379
Worcester, 1874 379
Worcester, 1878 379
Worcester, 1887 379
Worcester, 1889 379
Zdekauer, Moritz, 1884 – 1909 381
Zeh, Scherzer, 1880+ 381
Zsolnay, 1862+ 382
Zsolnay, 1862 – 1900 382
Zsolnay, 1865 382

1890 – 1930

Adams, William, 1891+ 7
Adams, William, 1893 – 1917 8
Adams, William, 1896+ 8
Adams, William, 1914 – 1940 8
Adams, William, late 1800s 8
Adderleys, 1912 – 1926 9
Allerton, Charles, 1891 – 1912 11
Allertons Ltd., 1912+ 11
Allertons Ltd., 1915 – 1929 11
Allertons Ltd., 1929 – 1942 11
Altenburg, 1900 – 1915 11
Altrohlau Porcelain, 1918 – 1939 ...12
American China, 1894 – 1910 12
American Chinaware, 1929 – 1931 ...12
American Encaustic Tile Co,
    1893 13

American Encaustic Tile Co,
    1926 13
American Limoges China,
    1900+ 13
American Limoges China, 1910 –
    1930 13
American Limoges China, 1927 –
    1932 13
American Terra Cotta & Ceramic,
    1888 – 1929 14
American Terra Cotta & Ceramic,
    1895 – 1930 14
Amphora, 1892 – 1905 15
Amphora, 1903 – 1918 15
Amphora, 1905 – 1910 ....15, 16
Amphora, 1918 – 1939 16
Anchor Pottery, 1893 – 1927 16
Anchor Pottery, 1894 – 1898 16
Anchor Pottery, 1894 – 1910 16
Anchor Pottery, 1908 – 1927 16
Arabia Porcelain, 1928 – 1932 17
Arabia Porcelain, 1930+ 17
Arcadian China, 1920s 17
Arequipa Pottery, 1911 – 1918 18
Arkinstall & Sons, 1904 – 1924 18
Arkinstall & Sons,
    1905 – 1930 ....18, 19
Arzberg Porcelain, 1927 – 1981 20
Ashtead Potters, 1926 – 1936 20
Ashworth, G.L. & Bros,
    1910 – 1920 21
Augarten Porcelain,
    1923 – present 22
Aultcliff, 1923 – 1937 23
Avon Art Pottery, 1930 – 1939 23
Avon Faience, 1902 – 1905 23
Aynsley, 1891+ 24
Balleroy, Jullien, 1914+ 24, 25
Barker Bros., 1912 – 1930 ......25, 26
Barons Pottery, 1905 – 1938 27
Batchelder, Ernest, 1900 – 1920 27
Bauer Pottery, 1905 – 1958 27
Bauscher Bros., 1910 – 1939 28
Bauscher Bros., 1915 – 1939 28
Bauscher Bros., 1921 – 1939 28
Belford, 1892 – 1918 29
Belleek, 1891 – 1926 30
Belleek, 1927 – 1941 30
Bennett, Edwin, 1890+ 30
Bennett, Edwin, 1895 – 1897 31
Bennett, Edwin, 1897 – 1904 31
Berlin Porcelain Manufactory,
    1904 – 1911 31
Beyer & Bock, 1905 – 1931 32
Beyer & Bock, 1914 32
Bing & Grondahl, 1899+ 33
Bing & Grondahl, 1915+ 33
Birks, Rawlins, 1917 – 1933 34
Bishop & Stonier, 1891 – 1910 34
Bishop & Stonier, 1891 – 1936 34
Bishop & Stonier, 1910 34
Black Knight, 1925 – 1941 34

Blairs, 1914 – 1930 34
Blau, 1880 – 1950 35
Blin, J., 1920 – 1995 35
Bloch, B., 1915 – 1920 35
Blyth Porcelain, 1913 – 1935 36
Boch Freres, 1900 36
Boch Freres, 1900 – 1930+ 36
Boch Freres, 1914+ 36, 37
Boch Freres, 1920 37
Boch Freres, 1920 – 1930 37
Boch Freres, 1924 37
Boch, B., 1923 – 1940 36
Bock, Josef, 1893 – 1933 36
Bodley, E. F. D., 1890 38
Boote, T. & R., 1890 – 1906 ....40, 41
Boote, T. & R., 1900 41
Booths, 1891 – 1912 41
Booths, 1906 – 1912 42
Booths, 1912+ 42
Borgfeldt, George, 1926+ 42
Bourdois & Bloch, 1890 – 1948 43
Bourne & Leigh, 1892 – 1939 43
Bourne & Leigh, 1912+ 44
Brannam, C. H., 1914+ 45
Brian & Co., E., 1905 – 1930s 45
Bridgwood, 1890 – 1920 46
British Anchor Pottery,
    1913 – 1940 47
Brown-Westhead, Moore,
    1891 – 1920 49
Brunt, William Pottery,
    1892 – 1911 50
Buffalo China, 1920s – 1930s 51
Buffalo Pottery, 1905+ 51
Buffalo Pottery, 1907 – 1940s 51
Buffalo Pottery, 1909 – 1925 52
Buffalo Pottery, 1911 52
Buffalo Pottery, 1915 – 1920+ 52
Burford Bros., 1895 52
Burford Bros., 1900 52
Burgess & Leigh, 1891 53
Burgess & Leigh, 1906 – 1912 53
Burgess Bros., 1920s 54
Burgess Bros., 1922 – 1939 54
Burgess Campbell, 1904 54
Burmantofts, 1890 ....54, 55
Bursley Ware, 1920s 55
Bursley Ware, 1930s 55
Bybee, 1900+ 55
Bybee, Selden, 1927 – 1928 55
California Faience, 1920+ 55
Camark Pottery, 1927+ 56
Cambridge Art Pottery,
    1895 – 1903 56
Cambridge Art Pottery,
    1895 – 1909 56
Cambridge Art Pottery, 1904 56
Canonsburg China, 1920s – 1940s ..56
Canonsburg Pottery,
    1900 – 1909 56
Cardew, Michael Ambrose,
    1926+ 57

Cardew, Michael Ambrose,
   1939 – 1942 57
Carlton Ware, 1925 – present 58
Carrollton China, 1910 – 1920 58
Carstens, C. & E., 1918 – 1945 58
Carter, Stabler, Adams, 1921+ 58
Cartwright & Edwards, 1900s 59
Cartwright China, 1896 – 1927 59
Cauldon, 1905 – 1920 61
Chelsea Keramic Art Works,
   1891 – 1895 63
Chikusa, 1905+ 63
Clementson Bros., 1891 – 1910 64
Clementson Bros., 1901 – 1913 65
Clementson Bros., 1913 – 1916 65
Clewell, 1906+ 65
Clews, 1920s – 1930s 66
Cliff, Clarice, 1920+ 66
Clifton, 1905 – 1911 . . . . .66, 67
Clinchfield Pottery, 1920 – 1930 67
Coalport, 1891 – 1920 67
Colclough, 1919 – 1931 67
Colclough, 1928 – 1937 67
Cook & Hancock, 1894 – 1929 69
Cook Pottery, 1893 – 1926 69
Cook Pottery, 1894 69
Cook Pottery, 1900 69
Coors, 1900 – 1930 71
Coors, 1920 – present 72
Corn, W & E, 1900 – 1904 72
Count Thun, 1918 – 1939 73
Cowan Pottery, 1912 – 1931 73
Cowan Pottery, 1913 – 1917 73
Cox, Paul, 1900+ 73
Coxon Pottery, 1926 – 1930 74
Cranston Pottery, 1910 74
Crescent Pottery,
   1899 – 1902 . . . . .74, 75
Crown Ducal, 1915+ 76
Crown Ducal, 1916 – 1970+ 76
Crown Ducal, 1925+ 76
Crown Potteries, 1891 77
Crown Potteries, 1902 – 1962 77
Dachsel, Paul, 1904 78
Dahl Jensen, 1928 – present 78
Dalpayrat, Adrien, 1900 78
Dartmouth Pottery, 1920 79
Dean, S. W., 1904 – 1910 82
Decoeur, Emile, 1907+ 82
Dedham Pottery, 1891+ 82
Dedham Pottery, 1895 – 1932 82
Delaherche, Auguste,
   1894 – 1940 83
Denver, 1893 – 1960 83
Derby Porcelain Works,
   1890 – 1940 85
Derby Porcelain Works, 1906 85
Devonmoor, 1922+ 87
Distel, 1897 – 1901 87
Distel, 1897 – 1923+ 87
Donath & Company,
   1893 – 1916 88

Donath, P., 1896 – 1922 88
Donath, P., 1910 – 1916 88
Doulton, 1891 – 1910 91
Doulton, 1900 91
Doulton, 1900+ 91
Doulton, 1900 – 1935 91
Doulton, 1902+ 91
Doulton, 1902 – 1922 91
Doulton, 1902 – present 92
Doulton, 1905 92
Doulton, 1912 – 1956 92
Doulton, 1920 – 1936 92
Doulton, 1922 – 1927 93
Doulton, 1922 – 1956 93
Dresden Pottery Co., 1900 94
Dresden Pottery Co., 1900 – 1927 . .93
Dresden, 1900 93
Dressel, Kister, 1907 – 1922 94
Dressler, Julius, 1900 94
Dressler, Julius, 1900 – 1945 94
Dudson, Wilcox & Till,
   1902 – 1926 . . . . .94, 95
Durant Kilns, 1911 – 1929 95
Dux porcelain, 1900 – 1918 95
Dux porcelain, 1912 – 1918 96
Dux porcelain, 1918 – 1945 96
East End Pottery, 1894 – 1901 96
East End Pottery, 1903 – 1907 96
East End Pottery, 1894 – 1908 96
East Liverpool Potteries, 1896+ 96
East Liverpool Potteries,
   1896 – 1901 96
East Liverpool Potteries,
   1901 – 1907 96
East Liverpool Potteries,
   1907 – 1925 . . . . .96, 97
Eckert, Richard, 1894 – 1918 97
Edge, Malkin, 1890+ 98
Elbogen, 1900+ 100
Empire Crockery, 1920+ 101
Empire Pottery, 1892 101
Ens Porcelain, 1915 – 1981+ 102
Ens Porcelain, Karl, 1919 – 1972 . .102
Epiag, 1910 – 1945 102
Epiag, 1920 – 1939 . . . . .102, 103
Epiag, 1920 – 1945+ 103
Exeter Art Pottery, 1891 – 1895 . . .104
Fasold & Stauch, 1914 – 1972 104
Fielding, S., 1891 – 1913 . . . . .104, 105
Fielding, S., 1913 105
Fielding, S., 1913 – 1930s 105
Fishley, William, 1900+ 106
Forester, Thomas, 1891 – 1912 108
Forrester & Son, Rembrandt,
   1890 – 1910 108
Fraureuther, 1898 – 1928 108
Fraureuther, 1898 – 1935 109
French China, 1900 – 1916 109
French China, 1916 – 1929 109
Frie Onnaing, 1890+ 110
Fritsch & Weidermann,
   1921 – 1939 110

Fulper Pottery, 1910 – 1929 111
Furnivals, 1890 112
Furnivals, 1890 – 1910 111
Furnivals, 1900 – 1915+ 112
Furnivals, 1905 – 1913 112
Furnivals, 1913 112
Furstenberg, 1922 – present 112
Galluba & Hoffman,
   1895 – 1927 . . . . .112, 113
Gater Hall, 1895 – 1907 113
Gater Hall, 1900 113
Gater Hall, 1914+ 113
Georgia Art Pottery,
   20th century 115
Gerz, Simon Peter, 1910+ 115
Gesetzlitch Geschutzt,
   1897 – 1900 115
Gibson & Sons, 1896 – 1920 115
Gibson & Sons, 1912+ 115
Gibson & Sons, 1928+ 115
Gladding, McBean, 1923+ 116
Glasgow Pottery, 1899 118
Glasgow Pottery, 1904+ 118
Globe Pottery, 1900 – 1912 119
Globe Pottery, 1914 119
Gmundner Keramik,
   1909 – 1922 119
Goebel, 1914 – 1920 120
Goebel, 1919 120
Goebel, 1923 – 1949 120
Goedewaagen, 1902 121
Goodwin Pottery, 1893 – 1906 123
Greber, Charles, 1899 – 1933 125
Green, T. G., 1892+ 125
Greenwood Pottery, 1904 126
Greiner, Frederick Christian,
   1894 – 1936 126
Grimwades, 1900+ 127
Grimwades, 1906+ 127
Grimwades, 1906 – 1910 127
Grindley, 1891 – 1914 128
Grindley, 1908+ 128
Grindley, 1925 . . . . .128, 129
Groschel & Stethmann,
   1892 – 1915 129
Grueby Pottery, 1897 – 1911 130
Grueby Pottery, 1904 130
Grueby Pottery, 1910+ 130, 131
Gustafsberg, 1895 – 1900 131
Gustafsberg, 1895 – 1930 132
Gustafsberg, 1900 – 1929 132
Gustafsberg, 1900 – 1929+ 132
Gustafsberg, 1902 132
Gustafsberg, 1903 132
Gustafsberg, 1910 – 1940 132
Gutherz, Oscar & Edgar,
   1899 – 1918 133
Haas & Czjzek, 1918+ 133
Hache, Alfred, 1903 134
Hackefors Porcelain,
   1929 – 1957 134
Hadley, James, 1896 – 1897 134

Hadley, James, 1902 – 1905 134
Haeger, 1915 – present 135
Haeger, 1930 – present 135
Hall China, 1916 – 1930 136
Hammersley, 1912 – 1939 138
Hampshire Pottery,
    1900 – 1920 139
Harker Pottery, 1890 139
Harker Pottery, 1890 – 1900 140
Harker Pottery, 1929 140
Haynes, D. F., 1900+ 143
Heinrich, 1896 – present 144
Heinrich, 1900 144
Heinrich, Franz, 1911+ 144
Heubach Bros., 1904+ 146
Heubach Bros., 1915 146
Hewitt & Leadbeater, 1907 – 1926 . .146
Hollinshead & Kirkham,
    1900 – 1924 147
Howard Pottery, 1925 – 1964+ 149
Hudson, William, 1892 – 1912 150
Hughes, E., 1908 – 1912 150
Hughes, Thomas, 1895+ 150
Hughes, Thomas, 1910 – 1930 150
Hull Pottery, 1910 – 1935 150
Hulme, William, 1891 – 1936 151
Hutschenreuther, 1910 152
Hutschenreuther, 1914+ 152
Hutschenreuther, 1920 – 1945 152
Hutschenreuther,
    1928 – 1963 . . . . .152, 153
Ilmenau Porcelain,
    1905 – 1938 156
International Pottery, 1903+ 156
Jackson China, 1923 – 1946 157
Jackson Vitrified China, 1930s 158
Jaeger, 1900 – 1978 158
Jaeger, 1902+ 158
Johnson Bros., 1890 159
Johnson Bros., 1900+ 159
Johnson Bros., 1904+ 159
Johnson Bros., 1913+ 159
Johnson, Samuel, 1916 – 1931 159
Jones, A. B., 1900 – 1913 160
Jones, A. B., 1905 – 1935 160
Jones, George, 1891 – 1924 161
Jones, George,
    1924 – 1951 . . . . .161, 162
Jonroth Studios, 1900 162
Jugtown, 1920s – 1930s 163
Kalk Porcelain, 1904+ 164
Karlskrona, 1924 – 1933 164
Keeling & Co., 1912 – 1936 164
Keller & Guerin, 1890+ 165
Keller & Guerin, 1891+ 165
Keller & Guerin, 1900+ 166
Kensington, 1900+ 166
Kent, James, 1897 – 1901 166
Kent, James, 1901+ 166
Kent, James, 1901 – 1910 166
Kent, James, 1913+ 167
Keramos, 1920+ 168

Kestner, 1900+ 169
Kister, A. W., 1900 – 1972 169
Knowles, Edwin, 1900 – 1948 169
Knowles, Edwin, 1910 – 1948 169
Knowles, Taylor & Knowles,
    1890 170
Knowles, Taylor & Knowles,
    1890 – 1905 170
Knowles, Taylor & Knowles,
    1890 – 1907 170
Knowles, Taylor & Knowles,
    1891 – 1898 170
Knowles, Taylor & Knowles, 1925 . .170
Kokura, 1921 – 1940 171
Kranichfeld Porcelain Factory,
    1903+ .171
Krautheim & Adelberg,
    1922 – 1945 171
Krister Porcelain Manufactory,
    1904 – 1927 172
Laeuger, Max, 1920 173
Lancaster, 1906+ 173
Laughlin, Homer, 1900 174
Laughlin, Homer, 1901 – 1915 174
Laughlin, Homer, 1907 174
Laughlin, Homer, 1912 175
Leach, Bernard, 1921 – 1964+ . .177,178
Leigh Potters, 1926 – 1931 179
Lenox, 1906 – 1924 179
Lenox, 1906 – present 179
Leonard, P. H., 1890 – 1908 179
Limbach, 1919 – 1944 180
Limoges, A. Lanternier, 1890s 180
Limoges, A. Lanternier,
    1891 – 1914 180
Limoges, A. Lanternier, 1900 180
Limoges, A. Lanternier, 1915+ 181
Limoges, Bawo & Dotter,
    1891 – 1900 181
Limoges, Bawo & Dotter, 1900+ . . .181
Limoges, Bawo & Dotter,
    1900 – 1914 181
Limoges, Beaux-Arts, 1900 181
Limoges, Bernardaud & Co.,
    1914 – 1930+ 182
Limoges, Bernardaud, 1900 – 1929 . .182
Limoges, Blakeman & Henderson,
    1900 – 1910 182
Limoges, Camille Tharaud, 1920s . .182
Limoges, Camille Tharaud, 1922+ . .183
Limoges, Charles Ahrenfeldt,
    1886 – 1910 183
Limoges, Charles Ahrenfeldt,
    1893+ .183
Limoges, Charles Ahrenfeldt,
    1894 – 1930s 183, 184
Limoges, Charles Ahrenfeldt,
    1918 184
Limoges, Charles Field Haviland,
    1900 . . . . .184, 185
Limoges, Charles Field Haviland,
    1900 – 1941 185

Limoges, Coiffe, 1891 – 1914 185
Limoges, Delinieres & Bernardaud,
    1900 185
Limoges, Delinieres & Co.,
    1894 – 1900 185
Limoges, F. Legrand, 1924 – 1944 . .186
Limoges, F. Legrand,
    1924 – 1962+ 186
Limoges, Flambeau China,
    1890s – 1900s 186
Limoges, Flambeau China,
    1900 – 1914 186
Limoges, Frank Haviland,
    1910 – 1914 186
Limoges, G. Demartine,
    1891 – 1910 186
Limoges, George Bassett,
    1890 – 1914 186
Limoges, George Borgfeldt,
    1906 – 1920 187
Limoges, Haviland & Co.,
    1893 – 1930 188
Limoges, Jean Pouyat, 1900 – 1906 . .188
Limoges, Jean Pouyat, 1906 – 1932 . .188
Limoges, Jean Pouyat, 1908 188
Limoges, Klingenberg & Charles
    Dwenger, 1900 – 1910 188
Limoges, L. W. Levy, 1915 – 1920+ . .189
Limoges, Latrille Freres,
    1908 – 1913 189
Limoges, Laviolette, 1896 – 1905 . .189
Limoges; Lazeyras, Rosenfeld &
    Lehman, 1920s 189
Limoges, Leon Sazerat,
    1891 – 1900 189
Limoges, Martial Redon,
    1891 – 1896 189
Limoges, Martial Redon,
    1905 – 1939 190
Limoges, Mavaleix & Granger,
    1922 – 1938 190
Limoges, P. M. Mavaleix,
    1908 – 1914 190
Limoges, Paroutaud Freres,
    1903 – 1917 190
Limoges, Porcelaine Limousine,
    1930 190
Limoges, Ribes, 1891+ 190
Limoges, Robert Haviland,
    1924+ .191
Limoges, Theodore Haviland,
    1893+ .191
Limoges, Theodore Haviland,
    1904 – 1925 191
Limoges, Theodore Haviland,
    1920 – 1936 192
Limoges, Theodore Haviland,
    1925+ .192
Limoges, Theodore Haviland,
    1925 – 1945 192
Limoges, Tressemanes & Vogt,
    1891 – 1907 192

Limoges, Tressemanes & Vogt, 1892 – 1907 192
Limoges, Tressemanes & Vogt, 1905 – 1910 192
Limoges, Union Ceramique, 1909 – 1938 193
Limoges, Vignaud Freres, 1911 – 1938 193
Limoges, Wannamakers, 1906 – 1932 193
Limoges, William Guerin, 1900 – 1932 . . . . .193, 194
Limoges, William Guerin, 1908 . . .194
Limoges, William Guerin, 1920 – 1932 194
Locke & Co., 1895 – 1900 196
Lomonosov Porcelain Factory, 1917 – present 196
Longwy Faience, 1890s 197
Longwy Faience, 1891+ 197
Longwy Faience, 1910 197
Longwy Faience, 1920 – 1940 . . . . .197, 198
Lovatts Potteries, 1895+ 199
Ludwigsburg, 1918+ 200
MacIntyre, James, 1894 – 1928 200
Maddock, John, 1891 – 1912 201
Maddock, John, 1896+ 201
Maddock, John, 1900+ 201
Maddock, John, 1907+ 201
Maddock Pottery, 1900 – 1929 202
Maddock Pottery, 1904+ 202
Maling, C. T., 1890+ 203
Maling, C. T., 1900 203
Manzoni, Carlo, 1895 – 1898 204
Marblehead Pottery, 1908 – 1936 . .204
Mark & Gutherz, 1890 – 1900 204
Marseille, Armand, 1900 – 1930 . . .205
Martin Bros., 1900+ 206
Massier, Clement, 1917+ 207
Matthews & Clark, 1890 – 1920 . . .207
McCoy, 1906+ 208
McCoy, 1920s – 1930s 208
McCoy, 1925 – 1929 . . . . .208, 209
McNicol, D. E., 1892 – 1910 210
McNicol, D. E., 1897 – 1915 211
McNicol, D. E., 1915 – 1929 211
McNicol, T. A., 1924 212
McNicol-Smith, 1901 212
Meakin, Alfred, 1891 . . . . . . .212, 213
Meakin, Alfred, 1891 – 1930 213
Meakin, Alfred, 1897+ 213
Meakin, Alfred, 1900 213
Meakin, Alfred, 1907+ 213
Meakin, J.&G., 1890 . . . . . . .214, 215
Meakin, J.&G., 1907+ 215
Meakin, J.&G., 1912+ 215
Mehlem, Franz Anton, 1890 – 1920 216
Mercer Pottery, 1900+ 218
Mercer Pottery, 1900 – 1937 218
Mercer Pottery, 1902 218

Meredith, Roper, 1913 – 1924 218
Merkelbach, Reinhold, 1895+ 218
Merkelbach, Reinhold, 1910 219
Merkelbach, Reinhold, 1925 – 1945 219
Merrimac Pottery, 1902 – 1908 220
Metenier, Gilbert, 1896 – 1939 220
Metthey, Andre, 1901 220
Midwinter, 1910 – present 221
Minton, 1890+ 225
Minton, 1900 – 1908 225
Minton, 1908 226
Minton, 1912 – 1950 226
Mitterteich, 1918+ 226
Moira Pottery, 1922+ 227
Moorcroft, 1919+ 227, 228
Moorcroft, 1919 – 1945 . . . . . .227, 228
Moore, 1891+ 228
Moravian, 1899 – 1918 228
Morgan, William De, 1898+ 229
Morimura Bros., 1891+ 229
Morris, Thomas, 1912+ 230
Mosa Maastricht, 1930s+ 230
Mosaic Tile Co., 1894+ 230
Mosaic Tile Co., 1894 – 1964 230
Muller, Carl, 1920 231
Muller, E.&A., 1890+ 231
Muller, Paul, 1920 – 1928 231
Muller & Co., 1907 – present 231
Muncie Pottery, 1922+ 231
Naudot, Camille, 1904 – 1919 233
Nautilus Porcelain, 1896 – 1913 . . .234
Nautilus Porcelain, 1903 – 1913 . . .234
Neukirchner, Franz, 1916 – 1977 . .234
Neu – Tettau, 1904 – 1935 234
New Chelsea, 1919+ 234
New Wharf Pottery, 1890 – 1894 236
New York & Rudolstadt, 1904 – 1924+ 236
Newcomb Pottery, 1896 – 1945 235
Newport Pottery, 1920+ 236
Niloak Pottery, 1909 – 1944 237
Nippon, 1890 – 1921 . . . . . . .237, 238
Nippon, 1891 – present 238
Nippon, 1894 – 1921 238
Nippon, 1911+ 238
Nippon, 1921 – 1965 238
Noritake, 1890 – 1921 239
Noritake, 1906+ 239
Noritake, 1911+ 239
Noritake, 1925 – 1935 239
Norse Pottery, 1903 – 1913 240
Northwestern Terra Cotta, 1920 . . .241
Nymphenburg, 1895+ 241
Ohr, George, 1899 – 1906 243
Onondaga Pottery, 1900 – 1966 . . .244
Owens Pottery, 1891 – 1907 245
Owens Pottery, 1901+ 245
Owens Pottery, 1906+ 245
Palissy Pottery, 1908 – 1936 . . .246, 247
Paragon China, 1893 – 1920+ 248

Paragon China, 1904 – 1919 248
Paragon China, 1915 248
Paragon China, 1915 – 1919 248
Pewabic Pottery, 1903 – present . . .250
Pewabic Pottery, 1920 250
Pfeffer Bros., 1900+ 251
Pfeiffer & Lowenstein, 1914 – 1918 251
Pickard China, 1895 – 1898 252
Pickard China, 1919 – 1922 252
Pickard China, 1925 – 1938 252
Pilkingtons, 1900 253
Pilkingtons, 1904 – 1914 253
Pilkingtons, 1914 – 1938 253
Pioneer Pottery, 1894 – 1900 254
Pisgah Forest, 1920 – 1961 . . .254, 255
Plankenhammer, 1920 – 1978 255
Poole Pottery, 1921 – 1925 257
Poole, Thomas, 1912+ 257
Pope-Gosser, 1900 258
Pope-Gosser, 1902 258
Pope-Gosser, 1902 – 1958 258
Porcelain Factory Konigszelt, 1912 – 1928 259
Porcelain Fles, 1900+ 259
Porcelain Union, 1921 – 1927 259
Porcelier, 1928 – 1949 259
Porquier, Adolphe, 1897 – 1904 . . .260
Potters Co-Operative, 1896 261
Potters Co-Operative, 1915 261
Potters Co-Operative, 1920+ 261
Pountney, 1900 – 1930s+ 262
Pouplard-Beatrix, 1890 – 1898 262
Powell, Bishop & Stonier, 1899 – 1936 263
Quarry Tile, 1892 – 1908 265
Quimper, 1922 – 1968 . . . . . . .265, 266
Radford, Samuel, 1891+ 267
Radford, Samuel, 1928+ 267
Radford Pottery, 1896+ 267
Radford Pottery, 1903 – 1912 267
Rappsilber, A., 1900 – 1912 267
Rathbone, T., 1912 267
Red Wing, 1906 – 1936 268
Regout, Petrus, 1891+ 270
Regout, Petrus, 1929 – 1931+ 270
Revere, Paul Pottery, 1906 – 1942 . .271
Rhead, Charlotte, 1920s – 1930s . . .272
Rhead, Frederick, 1920s – 1930s . . .272
Rhead Pottery, 1913 272
Richardson, A. G., 1916 – 1970+ 272, 273
Richter, Fenkl & Hahn, 1900+ 273
Ridgway Pottery, 1891+ 276
Ridgway Pottery, 1912+ 276
Robinson, W. H., 1901 – 1904 276
Robinson Ransbottom, 1920 – present 277
Robj, 1920 277
Rookwood, 1901 – 1967 278
Rorstrand, 1890 279
Rorstrand, 1910+ 279

Rosenthal, 1897 – 1939 280
Rosenthal, 1900+ 280, 281
Rosenthal, 1901 – 1956 281
Rosenthal, 1907 – 1956 281
Roseville Pottery, 1892 – 1904 282
Roseville Pottery, 1904 . . . . . .282, 283
Roseville Pottery, 1905 283
Roseville Pottery, 1914 – 1930 283
Roseville Pottery, 1915+ 283
Roseville Pottery, 1930 283
Roseville Pottery, 1930+ 283
Royal Bayreuth, 1902+ 285
Royal Bayreuth, 1919 285
Royal Copenhagen, 1889+ 287
Royal Copenhagen, 1894 – 1900 . .287
Royal Copenhagen, 1897 – 1922 . .288
Royal Copenhagen,
    1903 – present 288
Royal Copenhagen, 1919 288
Royal Copenhagen, 1921 288
Royal Copenhagen, 1922 – present . .288
Rozenberg, 1890 – 1914 291
Ruskin Pottery, 1904 – 1930+ 291
Russian Imperial Porcelain Factory,
    1894 – 1917 292
Russian, 1900 291
Russian, 1903 291
Russian, 1920s 292
Salem China, 1918+ 294
Salt & Nixon, 1921 – 1934 295
Sampson Hancock, 1906 – 1912 . . .296
Sampson Hancock, 1910 296
Schachtel, Joseph, 1896 – 1919 297
Schafer & Vater, 1896 – 1962 297
Schaller, Oscar, 1892 – 1918 297
Schaller, Oscar, 1918+ 297, 298
Schaller, Oscar, 1921+ 298
Schierholz, Von, 1907+ 299
Schiller, W. & Sons, 1895+ 299, 300
Schlegelmilch, Erdmann,
    1891+ 300
Schlegelmilch, Erdmann,
    1900 – 1938 300
Schlegelmilch, Erdmann,
    1902 – 1938 300
Schlegelmilch, Oscar, 1892+ 301
Schlegelmilch, Oscar, 1904+ 301
Schlegelmilch, Reinhold,
    1904 – 1938 . . . . .301, 302
Schlegelmilch, Reinhold,
    1919 – 1921 302
Schmider, Georg, 1907+ 303
Schmider, Georg, 1907 – 1928 303
Schmider, Georg, 1930+ 303
Schmidt, 1918 – 1939 303
Schmidt, Hugo, 1911 – 1945 303
Schnabel & Sons, 1900 – 1931 304
Schoenau & Hoffmeister,
    1909 – 1952 304
Schonwald Porcelain, 1911 – 1945 . .304
Schonwald Porcelain, 1920 – 1927 . .304
Schoonhoven, 1900 305

Schramberger Majolica Factory,
    1918+ .305
Schumann, Carl, 1918+ 305, 306
Schutzmeister & Quendt,
    1899 – 1927 306
Schwarzburg, 1908 – 1938 306
Sebring Pottery, 1890 – 1905 306
Sebring Pottery, 1895 306
Sebring Pottery, 1925 – 1942 .306, 307
Seltmann, Johann, 1901+ 307
Sevres China, 1900 – 1908 309
Sevres, 1897+ 309
Sevres, 1900 309
Sevres, 1910 309
Sevres, 1917 309
Sevres, 1928 – 1940 309
Shearwater, 1920s+ 310, 311
Shelley, 1925 – 1940 311
Shenango Pottery, 1901+ 311
Shenango Pottery, 1905 – 1912 . . .311
Silver Springs, 1924+ 312
Simpson, T.A., 1900 313
Sitzendorf, 1902 – 1972 313
Smith Phillips, 1901 – 1929 . . .313, 314
Smith, W.T.H., 1898 – 1905 313
Smith – Phillips, 1901 – 1929 314
Societa Ceramica, 1920 – 1931 314
Solon and Schemmel, 1920 315
Southern Potteries, 1920+ 315
Southern Potteries, 1930 316
Spode, 1890 – 1920 318
Spode, 1900 318
Spode, 1928+ 318
Springer & Co., 1891 – 1918 320
State's Porcelain Manufactory,
    1924 – 1934 321
Steinmann, K., 1900 – 1938 321
Steinmann, K., 1914 – 1932 322
Stellmacher, 1895 – 1905 322
Stellmacher, 1904 – 1912 322
Sterling China, 1917+ 322, 232
Sterling China, 1920+ 323
Stetson China, 1919 – 1965 324
Steubenville Pottery, 1920 – 1930s . .325
Steventon, John, 1923 – 1936 326
Stockhardt & Schmidt-Eckert,
    1912 – present 327
Stockton Art Pottery,
    1895 – 1902 327
Straus, Lewis & Sons,
    1895 – 1917 327
Swasey, E., 1890+ 327
Swastika Keramos, 1904+ 328
Syracuse China, 1893 – 1898 329
Taylor & Kent, 1912+ 330
Taylor Smith & Taylor,
    1901 – 1930 331
Taylor Smith & Taylor,
    1908 – 1915 331
Taylor Smith & Taylor, 1925 331
Taylor Smith & Taylor,
    1928 – 1945 331

Teichert, C., 1890 – 1914 333
Teichert, C., 1892 – 1914 333
Thewalt, Albert Jacob,
    1920 – 1930 334
Thieme, Carl, 1902+ 334
Thomas China, 1902 – 1905 335
Thomas, F. Porcelain, 1908+ 335
Thompson, C.C., 1890 – 1910 335
Thompson, C.C., 1916 – 1938 335
Thompson, C.C., 1927 – 1938 335
Tielsch, C., 1895 – 1918 336
Tiffany Pottery, 1904+ 336
Till, Thomas, 1919 337
Tirschenreuth, 1903 – 1981+ 337
Tirschenreuth, 1927+ 337
Torquay, 1904 – 1918 338
Trenle China, 1909 – 1917 339
Union Porcelain Works,
    1891 – 1904 341
United States Encaustic Tile, 1893 . .341
University City Pottery,
    1910 – 1915 342
University of North Dakota,
    1892 – 1963 342
Upchurch Pottery, 1913 – 1961 . . .343
Upper Hanley, 1895 – 1910 343
Upsala-Ekeby, 1918 – 1942 343
Utzchneider & Co, 1900 343
Van Briggle, 1900 – 1920 344
Van Briggle, 1901 – 1949 344
Van Briggle, 1902 344
Vance, 1900 345
Victoria Porcelain, 1891 – 1918 . . .347
Vienna Art Ceramic, 1899 – 1940 . .347
Vienna Porcelain, 1923 – 1981+ . . .347
Vienna Workshops, 1913 – 1923+ . .348
Villeroy & Boch, 1890 . . . . . . .349, 350
Villeroy & Boch, 1890 – 1920 349
Villeroy & Boch, 1895 – 1912 350
Villeroy & Boch, 1897 350
Vodrey Brothers, 1896 – 1920 350
Volkmar Ceramic, 1895 351
Volkstedt, 1915+ 351
Volkstedt, 1915 – 1981+ 351
Wachter, R., 1927+ 351
Wachtersbach,
    1914 – present 351, 352
Waco, 1900 – 1930 352
Wahliss, Ernest, 1894 – 1921 353
Wahliss, Ernest, 1897 – 1906 353
Wahliss, Ernest, 1899 – 1918 353
Walker China, 1923 – present 354
Walkure, 1920+ 354
Walley Pottery, 1898 – 1919 355
Walrath, Frederick, 1900 – 1920 355
Walrich Pottery, 1922 355
Wannopee Pottery, 1900 356
Wannopee Pottery, 1901+ 356
Wardle, 1900 356
Wardle, 1930 356
Warwick China, 1893 – 1898 357
Weatherby, J. H., 1892 – present . . .358

Wedgwood, 1890+ 360
Wedgwood, 1900+ 360
Wedgwood, 1906+ 360
Wedgwood, 1908+ 360
Wedgwood, 1908 – 1920s 360
Wedgwood, Enoch, 1925+ 361
Wehinger, H., 1905 – 1945 362
Weller Pottery, 1894 – 1895 362
Weller Pottery, 1895 – 1915 362
Weller Pottery,
　　1895 – 1918 . . . . .362, 363
Weller Pottery, 1897 – 1910 363
Weller Pottery, 1900 – 1925 363
Weller Pottery, 1902 – 1907 363
Weller Pottery, 1904 363
Weller Pottery, 1910 364
Weller Pottery, 1920+ 364
Weller Pottery, 1925 364
Weller Pottery, 1925+ 364
Weller Pottery, 1928 364
West End Pottery, 1893 – 1910 366
West End Pottery, 1893 – 1938 366
Western Pottery, 1905 – 1936 367
Western Stoneware, 1892 – 1906 . .367
Western Stoneware, 1906 – 1936 . .367
Western Stoneware, 1921 – 1928 . .367
Wheatley Pottery, 1903 – 1936 368
Wheeling Pottery, 1893 369
Wheeling Pottery, 1893+ 369
Wheeling Pottery, 1894+ 369
Wheeling Pottery, 1900+ 369
Whites Pottery, 1901 369
Wild, Thomas C and Sons,
　　1927 – 1934 370
Wileman, 1892+ 371
Wileman, 1892 – 1925 371
Wilkes, V. M., 1895 – 1922 371
Wilkinson, Arthur, 1891+ 371
Wilkinson, Arthur, 1896+ 371
Wilkinson, Arthur, 1907 371
Williamson,H.M & Sons, 1903+ . . .373
Williamsons, H.W.
　　& Sons, 1928 373
Wilton & Robinson, 1894 373
Wiltshaw & Robinson, 1890+ 373
Wiltshaw & Robinson,
　　1890 – 1957 373
Winkle, F., 1890+ 374
Winkle, F., 1890 – 1920 . . . . . .374, 375
Winkle, F., 1908 – 1925 375
Wood & Sons, 1891 – 1907 377
Wood & Sons, 1917+ 377
Wood & Sons, 1920s – 1930s 377
Wood, Arthur, 1904 – 1928 376
Worcester, 1891+ 379
Worcester, 1891 – 1915 376
Worcester, 1897 380
Wranitzky, P. A., 1900 – 1910 381
Zaneware, 1920 – 1941 381
Zark, 1900+ 381
Zeh, Scherzer, 1899 – 1909 381
Zsolnay, 1904 382

1931 – 1959

Abingdon, 1934 – 1950 5
Abingdon, 1940+ 5
Adams, William, 1950+ 8
Adams, William, 1950 – 1966 8
Adderleys, 1947 – 1950 10
Adderleys, 1950 – 1972 10
Alboth & Kaiser, 1953 – 1970 10
Altenkunstadt, 1933 – 1960 12
American Bisque, 1950 – 1960 12
American Limoges China,
　　1933 – 1936 13
American Limoges China,
　　1935 – 1936 14
American Limoges China,
　　1936 – 1950 14
American Limoges China, 1939 14
American Limoges China,
　　1939 – 1950 14
Amison, Charles, 1931 – 1941 15
Amison, Charles, 1953 – 1962 15
Arabia Porcelain, 1932 – 1949 17
Arabia Porcelain, 1949 – present . . .17
Arcadian China, 1950s 18
Arklow Pottery, 1934 – 1950 19
Arklow Pottery, 1950+ 19
Arklow Pottery, 1959 19
Arnart imports, 1957 – 1981 19
Ashworth, G. L. & Bros., 1932+ 22
Ashworth, G. L. & Bros., 1957+ 22
Ashworth, G. L. & Bros.,
　　1957 – 1964 22
Avon Art Pottery, 1939 – 1947 23
Avon Art Pottery, 1947 – 1964 23
Axe Vale Pottery, 1959 – present . . .23
Aynsley, 1940 – 1960 24
Aynsley, 1955+ 24
Baggaley, E., 1947 – present 24
Balsham, Leah, 1933 25
Banko Pottery, 1930s – 1940s 25
Banko Pottery, 1930s – 1960s 25
Bareuther, 1931 – 1950 25
Barker Bros, 1937+ 26
Bauer Pottery, 1931 – 1950 27
Bauer Pottery, 1932+ 27
Bauer Pottery, 1934 – 1942 27
Bauer Pottery, 1945 28
Belleek, 1946 – 1955 30
Belleek, 1956 – 1965 30
Bennington Potters, 1949 – present . .31
Beswick, John, 1936 31
Beswick, John, 1940+ 31
Beswick, John, 1946+ 31
Beswick, John, 1949+ 31
Beyer & Bock, 1931 – present 32
Biltons, 1950 – present 32
Bing & Grondahl, 1948+ 33
Bing & Grondahl, 1952 – 1958 33
Black, Harding, 1957 34
Blake, Trenle, 1940 – 1966 . . . . .34, 35
Bloch, R., 1954+ 35
Boch Freres, 1930s – 1940s 37

Boehm, 1954 – current 38
Bohemia Ceramic, 1941 – 1945 40
Booths & Colcloughs, 1948 – 1954 . .42
Booths & Colcloughs,
　　1950 – present 42
Borgfeldt, George, 1936 – 1976 . .42, 43
Bourne & Leigh, 1930s 44
Bourne, 1930+ 43
Bourne, 1948 – 1964 43
Bourne, 1950s 43
Bourne, 1950s – 1960s 43
Bovey Pottery, 1937 – 1949 44
Bovey Pottery, 1949 – 1956 44
Bowker, Arthur, 1950 – 1958 44
Boyer, Georges, 1936 – 1953 45
Brentleigh, 1950s 45
Brian, E. & Co., 1945 – 1963 46
Brian, E. & Co., 1953 46
Bristol Pountney, 1938 47
Bristol, 1950s 46
British Anchor Pottery, 1945+ 47
British Anchor Pottery, 1950s 47
Broadhurst, 1950s 48
Brock, 1950 – 1955 48
Brusche Ceramics, 1950s 50
Brush McCoy, 1930s 50
Brush McCoy, 1938 – 1965 50
Brush McCoy, 1950s 50
Buchan, A. W., 1949+ 50, 51
Buckfast Abbey Pottery,
　　1952 – 1964 51
Burgess & Leigh, 1930+ 53
Canonsburg Pottery,
　　1940s – 1960s 57
Canonsburg Pottery, 1950s – 1970s . .57
Canonsburg Pottery, 1952 – 1954 . . .57
Carstens, C.&E., 1933 – 1975 58
Carstens, C.&E., 1940+ 58
Castleton China, 1940+ 60
Castleton China, 1940 – present 59
Catalina Pottery, 1935+ 60
Century House, 1950 61
Century Services Corporation,
　　1950+ 61
Ceramic Arts Studio, 1940 – 1955 . .61
Chelsea Art Pottery, 1952+ 62
Chelsea pottery, 1952+ 63
Chugai China, 1945 – 1952 63
Clews, George, 1947 – 1961 65
Cliff, Clarice, 1938+ 66
Cliff, Clarice, 1938 – 1966 66
Colclough, 1937 – 1954 68
Colclough, 1937 – present 68
Colclough, 1939 – 1954 68
Colclough, 1945 – 1948 68
Colclough, 1955 – present 68
Continental Kilns, 1944 – 1954 69
Cooper, Susie, 1930+ 69
Cooper, Susie, 1932 70
Cooper, Susie, 1932+ 70
Cooper, Susie, 1938 70
Cooper, Susie, 1950+ 70, 71

Co-Operative Wholesale Society,
    1946 – 1964 71
Co-Operative Wholesale Society,
    1950 – 1960 71
Co-Operative Wholesale Society,
    1952 71
Cordey, 1942 – 1955 72
Coronado, 1939 – 1944 72
Coronation Ware, 1940s 73
Count Thun, 1947+ 73
Cronin China, 1934 – 1956 75
Crooksville China, 1940 75
Crown Clarence, 1946+ 75
Crown Clarence, 1950 – 1962+ 75
Crown Ducal, 1950+ 76
Crown Lynn pottery, 1950 – 1960 . . .77
Crown Potteries, 1940 – 1962 77
Crown Staffordshire, 1930+ 77
Crownford, 1930s 76
Cybis, 1952 – 1966 78
Dartmouth Pottery, 1947 – present . .79
Denbac, 1930s+ 83
Derby Porcelain Works,
    1940 – present 85
Derby Porcelain Works, 1959 85
Desert Sands Pottery, 1940 – 1978 . .86
Dorchester, 1940 – 1970+ 88
Dorchester, 1950s – 1960s 88
Doulton, 1959 93
Dunn, Bennett, 1937 – 1964+ 95
Ebeling & Reuss, 1955 – present . . .97
Edelstein, 1931+ 97
Efchenbach, 1931+ 99
Egersund Pottery, 1954+ 99, 100
Eichwald, 1931+ 100
Elfinware, 1940s+ 100
Empire Pottery, 1930s 101
Empire Pottery, 1940s – 1960s 102
Epiag, 1941 – 1945 103
Eschenbach, 1945 – present . .103, 104
Ewenny Pottery, 1956 104
Finch, Kay, 1939 – 1963 105
Fischer, Bruce, 1933 – 1940 106
Fischer, Bruce, 1949 – present 106
Fishley, George, 1955+ 106
Flintridge China, 1945 – present . .107
Florence Ceramics, 1940s – 1950s . .107
Forester, Thomas, 1930+ 108
Frankoma, 1931 108
French Saxon China,
    1935 – 1964 . . . . .109, 110
French Saxon China, 1940 – 1958 . .110
Fryer, J., 1954 – present 110
Fukagawa, 1950 – present 110
Gefle, 1931 – 1950+ 113
George, W. S., 1932+ 113
George, W. S., 1934+ 113
George, W. S., 1950s 114
George, W. S., 1954 114
Gibson & Sons, 1940+ 116
Gibsons, 1930+ 116
Gladding, McBean, 1934 – 1962 . . .116

Gladding, McBean, 1937 – 1942 . . .117
Gladding, McBean, 1939+ 117
Gladding, McBean, 1939 – 1947 . . .117
Gladding, McBean, 1947 – 1953 . . .118
Glidden Pottery, 1947 – 1957 119
Globe Pottery, 1930 – 1934 119
Gloria, 1947 – 1981+ 119
Goebel, 1940 – 1955 120
Goebel, 1950 – 1955 . . . . .120, 121
Goebel, 1956 121
Goebel, 1957 121
Goldscheider, 1937 – 1941 122
Goldscheider, 1946 – 1959+ 123
Gonder Originals, 1941 – 1957 123
Goumot – Labesse,
    1955 – 1977 . . . . .124, 125
Gray, A. E. Pottery, 1934 – 1961 . . .125
Green, T. G., 1930 – present . .125, 126
Grimwades, 1930+ 127
Grimwades, 1931 127
Grimwades, 1934 – 1950 127
Grimwades, 1951+ 128
Grindley, 1950s – 1960s 129
Grindley, 1954 – 1960+ 129
Grosvenor China,1930s – 1964+ . . .130
Grosvenor China, 1934 130
Gustafsberg, 1931+ 132
Gustafsberg, 1932+ 132, 133
Gustafsberg, 1937 – 1978 133
Gustafsberg, 1950s – 1960s 133
Haas & Czjzek, 1939 – 1945 134
Hackefors Porcelain,
    1957 – present 134
Hadley, M. A., 1939 – present 134
Haeger, 1940 – present 135, 136
Hall China, 1930 – 1972 136
Hall China, 1932 – 1963 136
Hall China, 1933 – 1976 137
Hall China, 1937 – present 137
Hall China, 1938 – 1953 137
Hall China, 1950+ 137
Hall China, 1950 – 1955 137
Hammersley, 1939 – present 138
Harker Pottery, 1930 – 1935 140
Harker Pottery, 1935 – 1950 140
Harker Pottery, 1936 – 1948 140
Harker Pottery, 1939 – 1947 140
Harker Pottery, 1940 – 1948 141
Harker Pottery, 1948 – 1955 141
Harker Pottery, 1948 – 1963 141
Harker Pottery, 1950 141
Harker Pottery, 1950s 141
Harker Pottery, 1954 – 1965 141
Harker Pottery, 1955 – 1960 142
Hautin & Boulanger, 1930s 142
Haviland, Johann, 1946 143
Heath Ceramics, 1941+ 143
Honiton Pottery,
    1947 – 1956+ 147, 148
Honiton Pottery, 1956+ 148
Hornsea, 1951+ 149
Howard Pottery, 1950+ 149

Hudson, William, 1936 – 1941+ . . .150
Hughes, Thomas, 1930 – 1935 150
Hull Pottery, 1930+ 151
Hull Pottery, 1950+ 151
Hull Pottery, 1958+ 151
Hutschenreuther, 1930 153
Hutschenreuther, 1934 153
Hutschenreuther, 1938 153
Hutschenreuther, 1939 153
Hutschenreuther, 1940 153
Hutschenreuther, 1948+ 153
Hutschenreuther, 1950 – 1963 154
Hutschenreuther, 1955 154
Hutschenreuther, 1955 – 1969 154
Hyalyn, 1940s – present 155
Hyalyn, 1950s 155
Iroquois China, 1946+ 157
Iroquois China, 1950+ 157
Isle of Wight, 1950s 157
Jackson Vitrified China,
    1939 – 1960 158
Jersey Pottery, 1946+ 159
Johnson Bros., 1950s 159
Jones, A. B., 1935+ 160
Jones, A. B., 1949+ 160
Jones, A. B., 1957 – present 160
Jones, A. G. Harley, 1907+ 161
Jones, A. G. Harley, 1923 – 1934 . . .161
Josef Originals, 1945 – 1960 162
Kahla Porcelain, 1957 – 1964 163
Karlskrona, 1933 – 1968 164
Keller & Guerin, 1940s – 1950s 166
Kent, James, 1930+ 167
Kent, James, 1950 – present 167
Kerafina, 1950+ 168
Kerafina, 1950 – 1958 168
Keramos, 1945+ 168
Kirkham, 1946 – 1961 169
Knowles, Edwin, 1956 170
Knowles, Edwin, 1953+ 170
Krautheim & Adelberg,
    1945 – present 171
Krautheim, 1945+ 171
Krister Porcelain Manufactory,
    1930+ .172
Krister, 1939 – 1945 171
Kuba, 1947 – present 172
Lancaster, 1930 – 1964+ 173
Lancaster, 1954 173
Langenthal, 1930+ 174
Laughlin, Homer, 1934 175
Laughlin, Homer, 1935 175
Laughlin, Homer, 1935 – 1941 175
Laughlin, Homer, 1939 175
Laughlin, Homer,
    1940 – 1965 . . . . .175, 176
Laughlin, Homer, 1941 – 1945 176
Laughlin, Homer, 1946 – 1960 176
Laughlin, Homer, 1950 – 1960 176
Laughlin, Homer, 1953 176
Laughlin, Homer, 1954 176
Laughlin, Homer, 1955 176

Lawrence, Thomas, 1936+ 177
Leach, David, 1956+ 178
Lefton, 1940 – present 178, 179
Lietzke Porcelains, 1950s 180
Limoges, Charles Ahrenfeldt,
    1946 – 1969 184
Limoges, Charles Field Haviland,
    1941+ 185
Limoges, Comte D'Artois, 1930s+ ..185
Limoges, Fontanille & Marraud,
    1935+ 186
Limoges; Gerard, Dufraisseix, &
    Abbot, 1937+ 187
Limoges, Haviland & Co.,
    1941 – present 188
Limoges, Robert Haviland, 1949+ ..191
Limoges, Theodore Haviland,
    1937 – present 192
Limoges, Vignaud Freres, 1938+ ..193
Lindner, 1948 – 1981+ 194
Longwy Faience, 1940+ 198
Lord Nelson Pottery,
    1940 – 1960+ 198, 199
Los Angeles Potteries,
    1948 – 1954 199
Lovatts Potteries, 1931 – 1962 199
Ludwigsburg, 1948 – present 200
MacIntosh, Harrison, 1950 – 1955 ..200
Maddock, John, 1940s – 1950s 202
Maddux, 1935 – 1964+ 202
Maling, C. T., 1930 – 1955 ....203, 204
Maling, C. T., 1949 – 1963 204
Manka, Franz, 1936 – 1945 204
Maria Pottery, 1956 – 1958 204
McCoy, 1930+ 209
McCoy, 1935 208
McCoy, 1940 – 1966 209
McCoy, 1940s 209
McCoy, 1940s – 1960s 209
McNicol, D. E., 1930 – 1954 211
McNicol, D. E., 1933 – 1950 211
McNicol, D. E., 1935+ 211
McNicol, D. E., 1935 – 1950 211
McNicol, D. E., 1950s 212
Meakin, Alfred, 1930s 214
Metlox Pottery, 1958 – 1978+ 220
Middleton, J. H., 1930 – 1941+ 221
Midwinter, 1940s – 1960s 221
Minton, 1951 – present 226
Miramar, 1935 – 1964 226
Mitterteich, 1938+ 227
Mitterteich, 1946+ 227
Moorcroft, 1930 – 1949 228
Moorcroft, 1945+ 228
Mosaic Tile Co., 1930 – 1964 231
Mountainside Art Pottery, 1938 ...231
Musterschutz, 1930s+ 232
Myott, 1930+ 232
Myott, 1936+ 232
Myott, 1940s – 1960s 232, 233
National Potteries, 1938+ 233
National Potteries, 1938 – present ..233

Natzler, 1930s+ 233
Neuerer, Hans, 1943+ 234
New Chelsea, 1943+ 234
New Devon, 1957+ 235
New Hall Pottery, 1930 – 1951 ...235
New Porcelain Factory,
    1935 – 1948 235
New Porcelain Factory,
    1948 – 1981+ 236
Niloak Pottery, 1930 – 1942 237
Nittsjo Earthenware, 1934+ 238
Nittsjo Earthenware, 1947+ 238
Noritake China, 1945 – 1952 240
North Carolina, 1930s – 1940s 240
North Staffordshire Pottery,
    1940 – present 240
North Staffordshire Pottery,
    1944+ 240
Nymolle, 1942+ 241
Occupied Japan, 1945 – 1952 242
Paden City Pottery, 1930 – 1956 ...246
Paden City Pottery, 1940 246
Paden City Pottery, 1940+ 246
Palissy Pottery, 1937 – 1946+ 247
Palissy Pottery, 1940s – 1960s 247
Paragon China, 1932+ 248
Paragon China, 1939 – 1949 248
Paragon China, 1940 – present 249
Pearl China, 1930 – present 249
Pech, R.&E., 1945+ 249
Pennsbury Pottery,
    1951 – 1971 ....249, 250
Pfaltzgraff, 1940+ 250
Pfaltzgraff, 1950 – present 250
Picasso, 1946+ 252
Pick, Albert, 1935 252
Pickard China, 1938 – present 252
Pierce, Howard, 1941+ 252
Pigeon Forge, 1946+ 253
Pillin Pottery, 1950s – 1980s 253
Pioneer Pottery, 1935 – 1958 254
Plant, R. H. & S. L.,
    1947 – present 255
Poole Pottery, 1952 – present 257
Poole Pottery, 1956 – 1966 257
Pope-Gosser, 1930s 258
Pope-Gosser, 1950 258
Potters Co-Operative, 1959 261
Pottery Guild, 1937 – 1946 261
Purinton Pottery, 1941+ 265
Radford, E, 1930s+ 266
Red Wing, 1930+ 268
Red Wing, 1933 – 1938 ......268, 269
Red Wing, 1935+ 269
Red Wing, 1936 – 1967 269
Red Wing, 1946+ 269
Regal China, 1938 – 1990 ...269, 270
Regency China, 1953+ 270
Reichenbach, 1949 – 1968 271
Reutter, 1948 – present 271
Ridgewood China, 1948 – 1971 ...273
Ridgway Pottery, 1940 – 1960 ...273

Ridgway Pottery, 1950s 273
Ridgway Pottery, 1950s – 1960s 273
Robertson Pottery, 1934 – 1952 ...276
Robertson Pottery, 1940 276
Roman Ceramic Corporation,
    1940 – 1982 278
Rorstrand, 1930s – 1940s 279
Rorstrand, 1938+ 279
Rorstrand, 1940+ 279
Roselane, 1938 – 1977 .....279, 280
Rosemeade, 1940 – 1961 280
Roseville Pottery,
    1935 – 1954 ....283, 384
Roseville Pottery, 1939 – 1953 284
Roseville Pottery, 1950s 284
Rosina, 1946+ 284
Royal Bayreuth, 1957+ 285
Royal China, 1933 – present 286
Royal China, 1934 – 1955 286
Royal China, 1934 – 1960 286
Royal China, 1940 – 1950 286
Royal China, 1949 – 1960 286
Royal China, 1950 – 1960 286
Royal China, 1951 – 1960 287
Royal Copenhagen, 1950s 288
Royal Copenhagen, 1955+ 288
Royal Copley, 1942 – 1957 289
Russian, 1940s – 1960s 292
Rye Pottery, 1947 – 1953 292
Rye Pottery, 1947 – 1956 292
Rye Pottery, 1955 – 1956 292
Sadler, James, 1947 – present 293
Salem China, 1940 – 1967 ....294, 295
Sampson Bridgwood, 1950+ 296
Sandizell, 1951 – present 297
Santa Anita Pottery, 1948+ 297
Schaller, Oscar, 1950 – 1981+ 298
Schau Bach Kunst, 1950 – present ..298
Schlegelmilch, Erdmann, 1938 300
Schlegelmilch, Oscar,
    1950 – 1972 301
Schlegelmilch, Reinhold,
    1932 – 1938 302
Seltmann, Christian, 1946 – 1975 ..307
Shawnee, 1936 – 1961 310
Shenango Pottery, 1930 – present ..311
Shenango Pottery, 1935+ 312
Shenango Pottery, 1940+ 312
Shenango Pottery, 1940 – 1960 ...312
Shorter & Son, 1930s 312
Silver Springs, 1938 312
Sohn, Ernest, 1950 – 1955 315
Solly, John, 1953 – 1986 315
Southern Potteries, 1950s 316
Spode, 1930s 319
Spode, 1940 – 1956 316
Spode, 1950 – 1960+ 316
Standard China, 1930 – 1949 320
Stanfordware, 1945 – 1961 320
Stangl, 1930 320
State's Porcelain Manufactory,
    1934 – present 321

State's Porcelain Manufactory,
    1943 – 1957 321
St. Clements, 1930s+ 321
Sterling China, 1940 323
Sterling China, 1946 – present 323
Sterling China, 1947 – 1948 323
Sterling China, 1949 . . . . . . .323, 324
Stetson China, 1940s – 1950s 324
Stetson China, 1946+ 324
Stetson China, 1950+ 324
Stetson China, 1958 325
Steubenville Pottery, 1930 – 1959 . .325
Steubenville Pottery, 1930 – 1960 . .325
Steubenville Pottery, 1939+ 325
Steubenville Pottery, 1940 – 1960 . .325
Straub, Paul, 1948 – 1970 327
Swinnertons, 1946+ 328
Syracuse China, 1930+ 329
Syracuse China, 1935+ 329
Syracuse China, 1940s – 1960s 329
Tamac, 1950s – 1960s 330
Taylor Smith & Taylor,
    1935 – 1955 331
Taylor Smith & Taylor,
    1935 – 1981 . . . . .331, 332
Taylor Smith & Taylor,
    1938 – 1945 332
Taylor Smith & Taylor,
    1940s – 1960s 332
Terra Nigra, 1930s 334
Tharaud, Justin, 1948 – 1953 334
Thomas & Co., 1937 – 1957 335
Thomas, Mark, 1950s 335
Trenton Potteries, 1930s 339
Ungemach Pottery, 1937 – 1966+ . .340
United China, 1953 – present 341
Universal Potteries,
    1934 – 1956 . . . . .341, 342
Universal Potteries, 1947 – 1956 . . .342
Unterweissbach, 1959 – present . . .343
Utzchneider & Co, 1935+ 344
Utzchneider & Co, 1940+ 344
Van Briggle, 1955 – 1968 344
Variazioni, Tema, 1950 – 1955 345
Vernon Kilns, 1930s 345
Vernon Kilns, 1931+ 345
Vernon Kilns, 1938 – 1940 346
Vernon Kilns, 1942 – 1947 346
Vernon Kilns, 1947 – 1956 346
Vernon Kilns, 1950 346
Vernon Kilns, 1950 – 1954 346
Vernon Kilns, 1953 – 1954 347
Vernon Kilns, 1955 347
Vernon Kilns, 1956+ 347
Vernon Kilns, 1956 – 1960+ 347
Vohann of California, 1950+ 351
Wade, George, 1936+ 352
Wade, Heath, 1934 – 1945 352
Wade, Heath, 1953 . . . . .352, 353
Wagner & Apel, 1954 353
Wain, H.A., 1946 – present 353
Wallace China, 1931 – 1964 355

Warwick China, 1930s – 1940s 357
Warwick China, 1940s 357
Warwick China, 1944 357
Watt Pottery, 1936 – 1965 . . . .357, 358
Wedgwood, 1930s+ 361
Wedgwood, 1940 – present 361
Wedgwood, 1940s – 1960s 361
Weil, 1950+ 362
Weller Pottery, 1930+ 364
Weller Pottery, 1935+ 365
Wellington China, 1930s 365
Wellsville China, 1933 – 1960 365
Wellsville China, 1940 – 1950 365
Wessel, Friedrich Wilhelm,
    1949 – 1964 365
West Germany, 1949 – 1990 368
Western Stoneware, 1930+ . . .367, 368
Western Stoneware, 1930 – 1935 . .367
Western Stoneware, 1950s 368
Wild, Thomas C. and Sons, 1934 . .370
Wild, Thomas C. and Sons,
    1935 – 1945 370
Wilkinson, Arthur, 1930+ 372
Winfield Pottery,
    1937 – 1960 . . . . .373, 374
Wood, Arthur, 1930s 376
Wood & Sons, 1930+ 378
Wood & Sons, 1931+ 378
Zeh, Scherzer, 1930s 382

1960 – 1979

Abbeydale, 1962+ 5
Adams, William, 1962+ 9
Adams, William, 1972 9
Alboth & Kaiser, 1960s – 1980s 10
Altenkunstadt, 1960 to present 12
Anna Perenna, 1977 – present 17
Arklow Pottery, 1978+ 19
Artists of the World, 1977 – present . .20
Arzberg Porcelain, 1970 – present . .20
Arzberg Porcelain, 1974 – present . .20
Bareuther, 1966 – 1981+ 25
Barker Bros., 1960+ 26
Biltons, 1970 – current 32
Bing & Grondahl, 1962+ 33
Bing & Grondahl, 1970+ 33
Block China, 1960 – present 35
Boehm, 1971+ 38, 39
Boehm, 1973 39
Boehm, 1976 39
Borgfeldt, George, 1978 43
British Anchor Pottery, 1960s 47
Canonsburg Pottery,1960 – 1978 . . .57
Canonsburg Pottery, 1970+ 57
Castleton China, 1968 – 1979 60
Chessell Pottery, 1978 – present 63
Coalport, 1960 – present 67
Colclough, 1962+ 68
Colclough, 1964 – present 68
Cone, Thomas, 1960 – present 68
Corning Glass Works, 1962+ 72
Crown Devon, 1972+ 75, 76

Crown Staffordshire, 1970+ 78
Crownford, 1960+ 77
D'Arceau Limoges, 1973 – 1979 79
Derby Porcelain Works, 1964 85
Derby Porcelain Works,
    1964 – 1975 85
Derby Porcelain Works, 1975+ 86
Desiree Denmark, 1970 86
Doulton, 1974+ 93
Fasold & Stauch, 1972 104
Finney, A. T., 1961 – present 105
Frankoma, 1972+ 108
Gien, 1970+ 116
Gladding, McBean, 1963 – 1964 . . .118
Goebel, 1968 – 1979 121
Goebel, 1972 – 1979 121
Guernsey Pottery, 1964+ 131
Gustafsberg, 1970+ 133
Hall China, 1969 – 1980+ 138
Harker Pottery, 1960 – 1972 142
Harker Pottery, 1965 142
Haviland, Johann, 1972 143
Heinrich, 1976 – present 144
Henneberg Porcelain,
    1973 – present 145
Hertel, Jacob, 1969+ 145
Hibel Studio, 1979+ 146, 147
Hochst, 1965 – present 147
Hoganas Ceramics, 1976+ 147
Hull Pottery, 1960+ 151
Hull, A. E., 1960+ 151
Hutschenreuther, 1963 – present . .154
Hutschenreuther, 1970 154
Hutschenreuther, 1975 . . . . . .154, 155
Iden Pottery, 1961 – present 155
Interpace Corporation,
    1974 – 1979 156
Iron Mountain, 1968+ 156
Josef Originals, 1960 – 1985 162
Jugtown, 1978 163
Kaiser Porcelain, 1970 – present . . .163
Kammer, Rudolf, 1961 – 1972 164
Karlskrona, 1961 – 1970s 164
Knowles, Edwin, 1974 – present . . .170
Kronester, 1969 – present 172
Laughlin, Homer, 1960 . . . . . .176, 177
Laughlin, Homer, 1970 – 1980+ . . .177
Laughlin, Homer,
    1970 – present 177
Lenox, 1970+ 179
Limoges, Castel, 1979+ 183
Limoges, Tharaud, 1977+ 191
Lladro, 1965+ 195
Lladro, 1965 – present 195
L. Lourioux, 1971+ 196
Lovatts Potteries, 1960 – present . . .199
Maddock, John, 1960+ 202
Matsumura, 1960s+ 207
McCoy, 1960s – 1970s 209, 210
McCoy, 1967 – 1974 210
McCoy, 1970s – 1980s 210
Meakin, J.&G., 1962 215

Merkelbach, Reinhold,
   1964 – 1968 219
Metzler & Ortloff, 1970+ 220
National Potteries, 1970+ 233
Nicodemis, Chester, 1965+ . .236, 237
Norman Rockwell Museum,
   1976 – current 240
Palissy Pottery, 1970 – present 247
Plaue Porcelain, 1974 – present . . .256
Poole Pottery, 1960s – 1970s 257
Poole Pottery, 1972+ 257
Poole Pottery, 1973+ 258
Portmeirion Pottery, 1962+ 260
Portmeirion Pottery,
   1962 – present 260
Portmeirion Pottery, 1972 – 1977 . .261
Portmeirion Pottery,
   1972 – present 261
Precious Moments, 1977 263
Precious Moments, 1978 264
Price & Kensington,
   1963 – present 265
Quimper, 1968 – 1983 266
R. J. Ernst Enterprises,
   1976 – present 267
Rauschert, Paul,
   1971 – 1981+ 267, 268
Red Wing, 1967 269
Regout, Petrus, 1970+ 270, 271
Ridgway Pottery, 1960 274
Ridgway Pottery, 1962 274
Ridgway Pottery,
   1964 – present 274
River Shore, 1975 – present 276
Rosenthal, 1962 – present 281
Rosenthal, 1969 – 1981+ 282
Rosenthal, 1969 – present 282
Royal Bayreuth, 1968 – present . . .285
Royal Bayreuth, 1972+ 285
Royal China, 1965 287
Royal China, 1968 287
Royal China, 1970 287
Sabin Industries, 1970+ 293
Scheibe – Alsbach, 1972+ 298
Schierholz, Von, 1967 – 1972 299
Schirnding, 1974 – present 300
Schonwald Porcelain,
   1968 – present 304, 305
Sohn, Ernest, 1963+ 315
Spode, 1970 – present 317
Stangl, 1972+ 320
Steubenville Pottery,
   1960 – 1978 326
Steubenville Pottery, 1966 326
Syracuse China, 1966+ 329
Syracuse China, 1972 329
Taylor Smith & Taylor, 1960 332

Taylor Smith & Taylor,
   1963 – 1968 . . . . .332, 333
Taylor Smith & Taylor, 1970 333
Taylor Smith & Taylor, 1972 333
Tirschenreuth, 1970s 337
Utzchneider & Co, 1965+ 344
Waldsassen Porcelain,
   1960 – 1970 354
Waldsassen Porcelain, 1970+ 354
Wallendorf, 1964+ 355
Wedgwood, Enoch,
   1965 – present 361
Winterling, 1970 – present 375
Wood, H. J., 1960 377
Worcester, 1960 – present 380

1980 – current

Adams, William, current 9
Arklow Pottery, current 19
Arnart Imports, 1982 20
Belleek, 2000 30
Block China, 1997 35
Boch Freres, 1980 – present 38
Boehm, 1980+ 39
Boehm, 1989+ 39
Bopla, 1980 – present 42
Brannam, C. H., 1980+ 45
Broadhurst, current 48
Buffalo China, 1985 – present 51
Buffalo Pottery, 1980 52
Burgess & Leigh, current 53
Burleigh, 1980+ 54
Ceralene, present 61
Coors, 1980+ 72
Dartmouth Pottery, current 79
Dedham Pottery, 1980s – present . . .83
Denby Tableware, 1980+ 83
Ebeling & Reuss, current 97
Elizabethan, 1980 – present 100
Ephraim, 1990s+ 102
Fitz and Floyd, 1985+ 106
Goebel, 1980 – present 121
Green, T. G., 1980+ 126
Grindley Hotelware,
   1980 – present 129
Herend, 1980s 145
Honiton Pottery, current 148
Hopper, Robin, 1980+ 148
Hutschenreuther, 1985 155
Johnson Bros., current 160
Kent, James, current 167
Kern Collectibles, current 168
Kunst, current 172
Lenox, current 179
Limoges, Camille Tharaud,
   1980 – present 183
Limoges, Castel, 1980s – 1990s 183

Limoges, Gerard, Dufraisseix, &
   Abbot, 1980 – present 187
Limoges, Pallas, 1980 – present . . .190
Limoges, Raynaud & Co,
   1980 – present 190
Lladro, 1987 – 1991 195
Maddock, John, 1980+ 202
Meakin, J.&G., 1980 – present 215
Metlox Pottery, 1980 220
Midwinter, current 221
Mikasa, 1980 – present 221
Myott, 1980 – present 233
Noritake, 1980 – present 239, 240
Pfaltzgraff, current 251
Pierce, Howard, 1993 253
Porsgrund, current 260
Precious Moments, 1987 264
Precious Moments, 1989 263
Precious Moments, 1993 263
Precious Moments, 1986 263
Precious Moments, 1984 263
Precious Moments, 1983 263
Precious Moments, 1994 265
Precious Moments, 1988 264
Precious Moments, 1992 264
Precious Moments, 1981 264
Quimper, 1984+ 266
Rorstrand, 1980 – present 279
Rosenthal, 1980 – present 282
Rye Pottery, 1980 – present 293
Sadler, James, 1980 – present 293
Sadler, James, 2002 294
Scheier, 1980s+ 298
Schmid, 1980 – current 302, 303
Schumann, Carl, 1980 – present . . .306
Seltmann, Johann,
   1980 – present 307, 308
Seltmann, Johann, 2002 308
Shenango Pottery, 1980 – present . .312
Societa Ceramica, 1980 – present . .315
Spode, 2000 320
Sterling China, 1980 – 1990+ 324
Sterling China, 1980 – present 324
Syracuse China, 1980 – present . . .329
Szeiler Studio, 1980 – present 330
Tiffany Pottery, 1980+ 337
Veneto Flair, 1980 – present 345
Viletta, current 348
Villeroy & Boch, 1980 – present . . .350
Wade, 1980 – current 352
Weatherby, J.H., 1980+ 358
Wedgwood, 2000 361
Wild, Thomas C and Sons,
   1980 – current 370
Wood, Arthur, 1980 – present 376
Wood & Sons, 1980 – present 378

Sight Index

16 • Watt Pottery 357, 358
1764 • Wallendorf 355
1772 • Limbach 180
1777 • Henneberg Porcelain 145
1849 • Lyman, Fenton 200
1861 • Schegelmilch, Erdmann . . .300
21 • Watt Pottery 357, 358
62 • Watt Pottery 357, 358
88 • Shield Dresden 93
A • Van Briggle 344
A • Wolfsohn, Helena 375
A.E. Tile • American Encaustic
    Tile Co. 12, 13
AA • Schonwald 304, 305
Acorn • Cambridge Art Pottery 56
Acorn • Dux Porcelain 95, 96
Adamantine • Wheeling
    Pottery 369
Adelaide • Willets 372, 373
Albany & Harvey • Gibson
    & Son 115, 116
Albion Pottery • Bourne
    & Leigh 43, 44
Alexandra • Royal
    Copenhagen 287, 288
Aluminia • Royal
    Copenhagen 287, 288
AM • Metthey, Andre 220
American Heritage • Stetson
    China 324, 325
Amphora • Amphora
    Work Reissner 15, 16
Anchor • Anchor Pottery 16
Anchor • Bohne Sons, Ernst 40
Anchor • British
    Anchor Pottery 47
Anchor • Chelsea-Derby 62
Anchor • New Chelsea 234
Anchor • Ridgway . . . . .273 – 276
Anchor • Samson 296, 297
Anchor • Stafford Pottery 320
Anchor • Tielsch, C. 336
Anchor • Vodrey & Brothers 350
Angel • Cartwright
    & Edwards 58, 59
Anova • Mayer, T. J. & J. 207, 208
Antique Subjects • Bristol,
    Poutney, Goldney 46
AP • Ault 22, 23
AP • Porquier, Adolphe 260
Arabian • Dillion, Francis 87
Arcadian China • Arkinstall
    & Sons 18, 19
Archer • Schlegelmilch,
    Reinhold 301, 302
Arm • Epiag 102, 103
Arm • Springer & Co. 320
Arrow • Clifton 66, 67
Arrow • Harker Pottery . . . . .139 – 142
Arrow • Minton . . . . .222 – 226
Arrow • Porquier, Adolphe 260

Arrow • Ridgway . . . . .273 – 276
Arrow • Teichert, C. 336
Arrows • Bloch 35
Arrows • Bourdois & Bloch 43
Arrows • Kalk Porcelain 164
Art Wells • Laughlin . . . . . .174 – 177
Artist's Palette • Lenox 179
Artist's Palette •
    Steubenville 325, 326
Artist's Palette • Sabin
    Industries 293
Asiatic Pheasants •
    Gustafsberg . . . . .131 – 133
Atlas China • Grimwades 127, 128
Aurora • Morley, Francis 229
Avalon • Haynes, D. F. 143
AW • Wood, Arthur 376
Axes • French Saxon
    China 109, 110
B • British Anchor Pottery 47
B • Hautin & Boulanger 142
B & B • Brough & Blackhurst 48
B G • Bing & Grondahl 33
B.F.K. • Boch Freres . . . . .36 – 38
Bakerite • Harker
    Pottery . . . . .139 – 142
Ball • Royal Porcelain
    Manufactory 289, 290
Ballerina • Universal
    Potteries 341, 342
Balt • Haynes, D. F. 143
Balto • Haynes, D. F. 143
Bareuther • Waldsassen 354
Baronet China • Fischer, Bruce . . .106
Beaver • New Devon 235
Bee • Goebel 120, 121
Bee • Goldscheider 122
Beehive • Arnart Imports 19, 20
Beehive • Augarten Porcelain 22
Beehive • Dunn, Bennett 95
Beehive • Ridgway . . . . .273 – 276
Beehive • Schlegelmilch, Oscar . . .301
Beehive • Victoria Porcelain 347
Bell • Bell, J&MP 29
Bell • Manka, Fraz 204
Bell • Limoges, Tressemanes
    & Vogt 192
Bell • Vernon Kilns . . . . . . .345 – 347
Belleek • Lenox 179
Belleek • Ott & Brewer 244, 245
Belleek • Willets 372, 373
Belzoni • Wood, Enoch 376
Ben Owen • Jugtown 163
BF • Burmantofts 54, 55
BFB • Flight, Barr, Barr 106, 107
Bird • Blake, Trenle 34, 35
Bird • Cybis 78
Bird • Jaeger 158
Bird • New York & Rudolstadt 236
Bird • Rathbone, T. 267
Bird • Royal Porcelain 289, 290

Bird • Rozenberg 291
Bird • Schlegelmilch,
    Reinhold 301, 302
Bird • Schlegelmich 301, 302
Bird • Schwarzburg 306
Bird • Tielsch 33
Bird • Union
    Porcelain Works 340, 341
Bird • Williamson &
    Sons, H. M. 373
Bird • Wiltshaw & Robinson 373
Bird • Wood & Sons 377, 378
Bird • Zdekauer, Moritz 381
Bisto • Powell & Bishop 262, 263
Blue Danube • United China 341
Blue Line • Krister Porcelain
    Manufactory 172
Blue Lines • Moorcroft 227, 228
Blue Lines • Muller, E.&A. 231
Blue Lines • Nonne, Christian 239
Blue Ridge • Southern
    Potteries 315, 316
BM de M • Limoges, Mavaleix
    Factory 190
Boehm • Edward
    Marshall Boehm 38, 39
Bologna • Adams . . . . .5 – 9
Bonn • Mehlem, Franz Anton 216
Bonn • Wessel, Ludwig 365, 366
Botanic Garden • Portmeirion
    . . . . .260, 261
Bow • Harker Pottery . . . . . .139 – 142
Bow • Ridgway . . . . .273 – 276
Bow & Arrow • Precious
    Moments . . . . .263 – 265
Brackets • Limoges, Guerin . . .193, 194
Branksome China • Baggaley, E. . . .24
Brendan • Arklow Pottery 19
Brentleigh • Howard Pottery 149
Bretby • Tooth & Ault 337
British Manufacture • Sampson,
    Hancock 296
Brownie • Weatherby 358
Buckle • Cumberlidge
    & Humphry 78
Buckle • Allerton, Charles 11
Buckle • Beadmore & Berks 28
Buckle • Bell, J&MP 29
Buckle • Booth, Thomas 41
Buckle • Campbellfield 56
Buckle • Derby . . . . .84 – 86
Buckle • Mayer, TJ & J 207, 208
Buckle • Minton . . . . .222 – 226
Buckle • Podmore, Walker 256
Buckle • Ridgway . . . . .273 – 276
Buckle • Sewell 310
Buckle • Wallace
    & Chetwynd 354, 355
Building • Gouda 124
Building • Hulme 151
Building • Midwinter 221

Building • Schlegelmich,
  Reinhold 301, 302
Building • Sampson, Hancock 296
Building • Steubenville 325, 326
Building • Zsolnay 382
Burgess • International Pottery . . .156
Butterfly • Precious
  Moments . . . . .263 – 265
C • Ludwigsburg 200
Caledonian • Ridgway . . . . .273 – 276
California • Bell, J&MP 29
California • Knowles,
  Taylor, Knowles 170
California • Metlox Pottery 220
Calypso China • Syracuse
  China 328, 329
Cameo • Harker Pottery . . . .139 – 142
Carefree • Syracuse China . . .328, 329
Caribe • Sterling China . . . .322 – 324
Carmen • Utzchneider 343, 349
Carv-Kraft • Harker
  Pottery . . . . .139 – 142
Cashmere • Morley, Francis 229
Castle • Arabia Pottery 17
Castle • Bing & Grondahl 33
Castle • Exeter Art Pottery 104
Castle • Maling, C. T. 203, 204
Castle • Mehlem, Franz Anton 216
Castle • New Hall 235
Castle • Sampson, Hancock 296
Castle • Seltmann, Johann 307, 308
Castle • Stafford Pottery 320
Castle • Villeroy & Boch . . . .348 – 350
Castle • Wood & Sons 377, 378
Cat • Arcadian China 17, 18
Catalina Pottery • Gladding,
  McBean . . . . .116 – 118
Cattail • Universal Potteries . .341, 342
Catteau • Boch Freres . . . . . . .36 – 38
Cavalier • Laughlin . . . . . . .174 – 177
Celebrate • Borgfeldt, George . . .42, 43
Ceranium • Utzchneider 343, 344
Chantilly • Morley, Francis 229
Characters • Banko 25
Characters • Derby . . . . .84 – 86
Characters • Samson 296, 297
Charlotte • Hutschenreuther
  .152 – 155
Chelsea • Powell & Bishop . . .262, 263
Chicago Crucible • Northwestern
  Terra Cotta 241
Chicken • Henneberg Porcelain . .145
Chinese Man • Powell
  & Bishop 262
Chinese Dragon • Minton . . .222 – 226
Chinese Flora • Boyle,
  Zachariah 45
Chinese Pastime • Davenport
  . . . . .79 – 82
Chodau • Haas & Czjzek 133, 134

Church • Schlegelmich,
  Reinhold 301, 302
Circle • Allerton, Charles 11
Circle • American
  Encaustic Tile Co. 12, 13
Circle • Amphora 15, 16
Circle • Ashworth . . . . .20 – 22
Circle • Beadmore & Berks 28
Circle • Boch Freres . . . . .36 – 38
Circle • Boote, T. & R. 40, 41
Circle • Booth, Thomas 41
Circle • Borgfeldt, George 42, 43
Circle • Brown-Westhead,
  Moore .49
Circle • Campbellfield 56
Circle • Cardew 57
Circle • Clifton 66, 67
Circle • Crown Derby . . . . . . .84 – 86
Circle • Cumberlidge
  & Humphrys 78
Circle • Dresden 93
Circle • East End Pottery 96
Circle • Elfinware 100
Circle • Fraureuther 108, 109
Circle • Gater Hall 113
Circle • Heubach 146
Circle • Hibel Studio 146, 147
Circle • Hochst 147
Circle • Hopper, Robin 148
Circle • Hudson 149, 150
Circle • Hull Pottery 150, 151
Circle • Hutschenreuther . . .152 – 155
Circle • Keller & Guerin 165, 166
Circle • Kronester 172
Circle • Lenox 179
Circle • Longwy . . . . .196 – 198
Circle • Mayer, T.J. & J. 207, 208
Circle • McCoy . . . . .208 – 210
Circle • Meredith, Roper 218
Circle • Metthey, Andre 220
Circle • Minton . . . . .222 – 226
Circle • Pinder Bourne 254
Circle • Robinson, W. H. 276
Cirlce • Worcester . . . . .378 – 380
Circle • Schonwald 304, 305
Circle • Sevres 308, 309
Circle • Stockton 327
Circle • Lewis Straus & Sons 327
Circle • Swasey, E. 327
Circle • Taylor Tunnicliffe 330
Circle • Wallace &
  Chetwynd 354, 355
Circle • Watt Pottery 357, 358
Circle • Whittaker & Co. 370
Circle • Wiltshaw & Robinson 373
Circle • Winkle 374, 375
Circle • Worcester . . . . .378 – 380
Circle • Zsolnay 382
Circle • Gebr. Kuhnlenz 113
CKAW • Chelsea Keramic
  Art Works 62, 63
Cliff • Dimmock, J. 87

Clifton • Haynes, D. F. 143
Clock • Dresden 93
Colonial • Sterling China . . .322 – 324
Colonial Pottery • Winkle, F
  . . . . .374, 375
Compote • Schonwald 304, 305
Continental China • Rosenthal
  .280 – 282
Coral • George Grainger 114, 115
Corinthia • Challinor, E. 61, 62
Cornacopia • Bell, J&MP 29
Corona • Winkle, F. 374, 375
Coronado • Haas & Czjzek . . .133, 134
Coronet • Borgfeldt, George . . .42, 43
Coronet • Hull, A. E. 151
Coronet • Laughlin . . . . .174 – 177
Countess • Minton . . . . .222 – 226
Country Scene • Adams . . . . . . .5 – 9
Craftsman • Laughlin . . . . . .174 – 177
Crescendo • Honiton 147, 148
Crescent • Haynes, D. F. 143
Crescent • Jones, George 161, 162
Crescent • Ott & Brewer 244, 245
Crescent • Worcester . . . . . . .378 – 380
Crest • Anchor Pottery 16
Crest • Ashworth . . . . .20 – 22
Crest • Bourne & Leigh 43, 44
Crest • British Anchor Pottery 47
Crest • East End Pottery 96
Crest • East Trenton Pottery 97
Crest • Furnivals 111, 112
Crest • Glasgow Pottery 118
Crest • Kronester 172
Crest • Mayer China 208
Crest • Meakin, Charles 214
Crest • Meigh, Charles 217
Crest • Onondaga Pottery . . .243, 244
Crest • Ott & Brewer 244, 245
Crest • Prospect Hill Pottery 265
Crest • Ridgway . . . . .273 – 276
Crest • Royal Bayreuth 285, 286
Crest • Swillington Bridge 328
Crest • Taylor Bros. 331
Crest • Villeroy & Boch . . . . .348 – 350
Crest • Vodrey & Brothers 350
Crest • Willets 372, 373
Crest-O-Gold • Sabin Industries . . .293
Cromer • Sampson Hancock 296
Cross • Leach, Bernard 177, 178
Cross • Levy, Ch. 180
Cross • Precious Moments . . .263 – 265
Cross • Thompson, C. C. 335
Crossed Lines • Kister, A. W. 169
Crossed Lines • Kister, Fr. 169
Crossed Lines • Meissen 289, 290
Crossed Swords • Meissen 289, 290
Crown • Amphora 15, 16
Crown • Ashworth . . . . .20 – 22
Crown • Belford 29
Crown • Bennett, Edwin 30, 31
Crown • Beyer & Bock 32
Crown • Bloch, B. 35

Crown • Booth, Thomas 41
Crown • Brown-Westhead,
  Moore 49
Crown • Crown Potteries 77
Crown • Cumberlidge &
  Humphrys 78
Crown • Derby . . . . .84 – 86
Crown • Donath 88
Crown • Dresden 93
Crown • East End Pottery 96
Crown • Ebeling & Reuss 97
Crown • Epiag 102, 103
Crown • Fielding, S 104, 105
Crown • Fischer, Emil 106
Crown • Flight, Barr, Barr
  Worcester 106, 107
Crown • Fraureuther 108, 109
Crown • Galluba
  & Hoffman 112, 113
Crown • Gater Hall 113
Crown • Grimwades 127, 128
Crown • Hanke, Robert 139
Crown • Heinrich 144
Crown • Hicks, Meigh &
  Johnson 147
Crown • Hochst 147
Crown • Hubbe Brothers 149
Crown • Hudson 149, 150
Crown • Hutschenreuther . .152 – 155
Crown • Jensen, Dahl 78
Crown • Kammer 164
Crown • Keller & Guerin . . .165, 166
Crown • Kent, James 166, 167
Crown • Klemm, Richard 169
Crown • Krister 171
Crown • Schlegelmich,
  Reinhold 301, 302
Crown • Kronester 172
Crown • Langenthal 174
Crown • Leonard 179
Crown • Limbach 180
Crown • Longwy . . . . .196 – 198
Crown • Ludwigsburg 200
Crown • Mehlem, Franz Anton . . .216
Crown • Mercer Pottery 218
Crown • Meredith, Roper 218
Crown • Muller & Co. 231
Crown • New England Pottery 235
Crown • New York &
  Rudolstadt 236
Crown • Nymphenburg 241
Crown • Ohme, Hermann . . .242, 243
Crown • Pfeiffer & Lowenstein 251
Crown • Pinder Bourne 254
Crown • Pioneer Pottery 254
Crown • Plant, R. H. & S. L. 255
Crown • Plaue 256
Crown • Porcelain Union 259
Crown • Ridgway . . . . .273 – 279
Crown • Robinson
  Ransbottom 276, 277
Crown • Robinson, W. H. 276

Crown • Rosenthal . . . . .280 – 282
Crown • Royal Worcester 380
Crown • Rozenberg 291
Crown • Donath, P. 88
Crown • Sampson, Hancock 296
Crown • Sandizell 297
Crown • Schafer & Vater 297
Crown • Schaller, Oscar 297, 298
Crown • Schegelmilch,
  Erdmann 300
Crown • Schlegelmich 301
Crown • Schneider, Karl 304
Crown • Schonwald 304, 305
Crown • Schumann 305, 306
Crown • Sevres 308, 309
Crown • Sitzendorf 313
Crown • Smith, W. T. H. 313
Crown • Standard China 320
Crown • Steinmann, K. 321, 322
Crown • Sterling China 322, 324
Crown • Steventon, John 326
Crown • Straub, Paul 327
Crown • Taylor & Kent 330
Crown • Taylor Tunnicliffe 330
Crown • Teplitz 15, 16, 322
Crown • Thomas & Co. 335
Crown • Tirschenreuth 337
Crown • Trenle China 339
Crown • Schierholz, Von 299
Crown • Wachtersbach 351, 352
Crown • Wagner & Apel 352
Crown • Wahliss, Ernst 353
Crown • Walkure 354
Crown • Wallendorf 355
Crown • Wessel, Friedrich
  Wilhelm 365
Crown • Wessel, Ludwig . . .365, 366
Crown • Western
  Stoneware 367, 368
Crown • Wileman 370, 371
Crown • Wilkinson 371, 372
Crown • Wolfsohn, Helena 375
Crown • Worcester . . . . .378 – 380
Crown • Zeh, Scherzer 381, 382
Crown Clarence • Co-Operative
  Wholesale Society 71
Crown Devon • Fielding, S. . . .104, 105
Crown Ducal Ware • Richardson,
  A. G. . . . . .272 – 273
Crown M • Myotts 232, 233
Crown • Utzchneider 343, 344
Crown W • Goebel 120, 121
Cuban • West End Pottery 366
Cup • McCoy . . . . .208 – 210
Cup • Schmider, Georg 303
Currier & Ives • Royal
  China 286, 287
Currier & Ives • Laughlin,
  Homer . . . . .174 – 177
D • Dresden 93
D • Wolfsohn, Helena 375
Dale & Davis • Prospect

Hill Pottery 265
Dale Hall Pottery • Mayer
  China 208
Danesby Ware • Bourne 43
Danmark • Bing & Grondahl 33
Danmark • Royal
  Copenhagen 287, 288
Davis Collamore • Derby . . . . .84 – 86
Dean • Forrester & Son 108
Deer • Wallace
  & Chetwynd 354, 355
Delft • Cook Pottery 69
Delft • Porcelain Fles 259
Delft • Rosenthal . . . . .280 – 282
Delhi • Dimmock, Thomas 87
Delhi • Fielding, S. . . . . . . .104 – 105
Delphine • Middleton, J. H. . . .221
Denby • Bourne 43
Denmark • Bing & Grondahl 33
Denmark • Royal
  Copenhagen 287, 288
Devon Motto Ware • Torquay 338
Diamond • New York
  & Rudolstadt 236
Diamond • Philadelphia
  City Pottery 251
Diamond • Precious
  Moments . . . . .263 – 265
Diamond • Schirnding 300
Diamond • Southern
  Potteries 315, 316
Diamond • Straub, Paul 327
Diamond • Takito 330
Diamond • Western
  Stoneware 367, 368
Diamond China • Blyth
  Porcelain 36
Diana China • Schlegelmilch,
  Reinhold 301, 302
Diana China • Borgfeldt,
  George 42, 43
DJ • Dahl Jensen 78
DM 96 • Morgan,
  William De 228, 229
Dog • Edge, Malkin 98
Dolphin • Poole 257, 258
Donatello • Roseville . . . . . .282 – 284
Donkey • Weil 362
Dove • Precious Moments . .263 – 265
Dragon • Goodwin Pottery 123
Dresden • Klemm, Richard 169
Dresden • Sandizell 297
Dresden • Steinmann, K. 321, 322
Dresden • Thieme, Carl 334
Dress • Vernon Kilns . . . . . .345 – 347
Ducal • Crown Ducal 76
Duchess • Finney, A. T. 105
Dudle • Ford & Riley 107
Dura Print • Laughlin . . . . . .174 – 177
E • Bloch, B. 35
E & R • Ebeling & Reuss 97
Eagle • Tielsch 336

Eagle • Adams ....5 – 9
Eagle • Edwards, James 98, 99
Eagle • Forester, Thomas 108
Eagle • Goss 123
Eagle • Hall, Ralph 136
Eagle • Knowles, Taylor,
    Knowles 170
Eagle • Krautheim 171
Eagle • Kuznetsov 172
Eagle • Laughlin ....174 – 177
Eagle • Moravian 228
Eagle • Onondaga Pottery ..243, 244
Eagle • Podmore, Walker 256
Eagle • Sterling China .....322 – 324
Eagle • Union
    Porcelain Works 340, 341
Eagle • Wheeling Pottery 369
Eagle • Wood, Enoch 376
EE • R. J. Ernst Enterprises 267
Eggshell • Nautilus • Laughlin
.............................174 – 177
EJBD • Bodley, E. J. D. 38
Elephant • Steubenville 325, 326
Elf • Weatherby 358
Elite • Limoges,
    Guerin-Pouyat 93, 99
ELP • East Liverpool Pottery ...96, 97
Elsie • Powell & Bishop 262, 263
EM de M • Limoges,
    Mavaleix Factory 190
Empire Crockery • Maddock,
    John 201, 202
English Porcelain • Minton
.............................222 – 226
ENS • Ens, Karl Porcelain 102
Ernest Sohn • Hall China ....136 – 138
ES • Schegelmilch, Erdmann 300
ES • Sohn, Ernest 315
Eton • Cartwright & Edwards ...58, 59
ETP • East Trenton Pottery 97
Etruria • Ott & Brewer 244, 245
Etruscan • Elkin,
    Knight, Bridgwood 100
Etruscan • Griffen, Smith
    & Hall 126
European Scenery • Wood,
    Enoch 376
Eva Zeisel • Hall China ....136 – 138
EW • Teplitz 15, 16, 322
EW • Wahliss, Ernst 353
EW • Wood, Enoch 376
Eye • Ridgway ....273 – 276
Eye • Variazioni, Tema 345
F • Ducal 94
F • Franciscan ....116 – 118
F • Fraureuther 108, 109
F • Furstenberg 112
F & M • Fischer & Mieg 106
Fairy • L. Lourioux 196
Fairy Villas • Adams ....5 – 9
Falcon Ware • Lawrence,
    Thomas 177

Farsta • Gustavsberg ....131 – 133
FBB • Flight, Bar, Bar 106, 107
FE • Fischer, Emil 106
Ferrell • Desert Sands Pottery 86
FF • Fitz and Floyd 106
FH • Fishley, William 106
Figure • Goldscheider 122
Figure • Limoges,
    Guerin-Pouyat 193, 194
Figure • Paul Revere Pottery
.............................271, 272
Figure • Pisgah Forest 254, 255
Figure • Regency China 270
Figure • Schlegelmilch,
    Reinhold 301, 302
Figure • Schlegelmilch, Oscar 301
Figure • Steventon, John 326
Figure • Terra Nigra 334
Figure • Vernon Kilns ....345 – 347
Figure • Wellington China 365
Figure • Wood & Sons 377, 378
Figures • East Trenton Pottery 97
Figures • Onondaga
    Pottery 243, 244
Finland • Arabia Pottery 17
Fish • Merrimac Pottery 220
Fish • Precious Moments ....263 – 265
Flag • Weatherby, J. H. 358
Flag • Willets 372, 373
Flame • Kranichfeld
    Porcelain Factory 171
Flame • Owens Pottery 245
Flame • Precious
    Moments ....263 – 265
Flame • Rookwood 278
Flame • Royal Porcelain 289, 290
Flammfest • Rosenthal ....280 – 282
Fleur de Lis • French China 109
Fleur de Lis • Lancaster 173
Fleur de Lis • Tielsch, C. 336
Floral • Ford & Riley 107
Floral • Swift, John 328
Floral • Teplitz 15, 16, 322
Floral • Wild, Thomas & Sons 370
Floraline • McCoy ....208 – 210
Florentine • Minton ......222 – 226
Florentine Fountain • Davenport
.............................79 – 82
Floretta • Weller Pottery ....362 – 365
Florian Ware Macintyre 200, 201
Flower • Morgan,
    William De 228, 229
Flower • New England Pottery 235
Flower • Pilkingtons 253
Flower • Powell & Bishop ..262, 263
Flower • Schirnding 300
Flower • Schlegelmilch, Oscar 301
Flower • Stellmacher 322
Flower • Volkstedt 351
Flowers • Ridgway ....273 – 276
Fleur de Lis • Schachtel, Joseph 297
Fleur de Lis • Sevres 308, 309

FM • Manka, Fraz 204
Foley • Brian, E. & Co. 45, 46
Foley China • Wileman 370, 371
Forget Me Not • Ridgway ..273 – 276
Fork • Eckert, Richard 97
Fork • Nonne, Christian 239
Fork • Triebner, Ens,
    Eckert 339, 340
Fort • Steubenville 325, 326
Fox • Schwarzburg 306
FPG • Pfeffer, Fr. 251
Franciscan • Interpace
    Corporation 156
French Saxon China • Royal
    China 286, 287
Funny Design • Rauschert,
    Paul 267, 268
G • Heubach 146
G • Schneider, Carl 304
G K • Gebr. Kuhnlenz 113
Garfield • Cumberlidge
    & Humphrys 78
Geisha • Davenport ....79 – 82
Gem • Meigh, Charles 217
Giraffe • Ridgway ....273 – 276
GJ • Jones, George 161, 162
GL • Lawrence, Thomas 177
Globe • Bennett, Edwin 30, 31
Globe • Burford Bros 54
Globe • Grimwades 127, 128
Globe • Kent, James 166, 167
Globe • Locke 196
Globe • Mortlock, John 230
Globe • Smith, W. T. H. 313
Globe • Syracuse China ...328, 329
Globe • Till & Sons 337
Globe • Veneto Flair 345
Globe • Willets 272, 273
Globe • Wood, Arthur 376
GMcB • Gladding
    McBean ....116 – 118
Golden Crown • Ebeling & Reuss ...97
Golden Wheat • Laughlin,
    Homer ....174 – 177
Grafton • Jones, A. B. 160
Granada • Taylor Smith
    & Taylor ....331 – 333
Granite China • Ridgway ....273 – 276
Grecian • Ridgway ....273 – 276
Grecian • Till & Sons 337
Grecian Scenery • Adams ....5 – 9
Griffin • Donath, P. 88
Griffin • Rockingham Works 277
Griffin • Taylor Smith
    & Taylor ....331 – 333
Griffin • Thompson, C. C. 335
Griffin • Vodrey & Brothers 350
GS • Schmider, Georg 303
GS • Teichert, C. 336
Guernsey • Cambridge
    Art Pottery 56
Gustavsberg • Gustafsberg .131 – 133

H • Gater Hall 113
H • Heinrich 144
H • Hibel Studio 146, 147
H • Hull Pottery 150, 151
H & C • Heinrich 144
Hallcraft • Hall China . . . . .136 – 138
Hammer • Plankenhammer 255
Hammers • Epiag 102, 103
Hammers • Kaestner 163
Hand Drawn • Manzoni, Carlo 204
Harmony House • Hall
    China . . . . .136 – 138
Harvard • McNicol, D. E. . . .210 – 212
HB • Quimper 265, 266
Heathcote China • Williamson, H. M ..
    & Sons 373
Helmet • French
    Saxon China 109, 110
Henriot • Quimper 265, 266
Henry Ford • Iroquois China 157
HM • MacIntosh, Harrison 200
HM • Sutherland China 150
Holborn • Adderleys 9, 10
Holdfast • McNicol, D. E. . .201 – 212
Homemaker • Ridgway . . . . .273 – 276
Hong Kong • Pinder Bourne 254
Horn • Hornsea 149
Horse • Paul
    Revere Pottery 271, 272
Hourglass • Precious
    Moments . . . . .263 – 265
Household Institute • Laughlin,
    Homer . . . . .174 – 177
HR • Hutschenreuther . . . .152 – 155
Imperial • Hull Pottery 150, 151
Imperial • Kuznetsov 172
Imperial • New York
    & Rudolstadt 236
Imperial • Pfeiffer
    & Lowenstein 251
Imperial • Pioneer Pottery 254
Imperial • Ridgway . . . . . . .273 – 276
Imperial • Wessel, Ludwig 365, 366
Impressed • Adams . . . . .5 – 9
Impressed • Amphora 15, 16
Impressed • Boote, T. & R. 40, 41
Impressed • Cardew 57
Impressed • Etruscan Majolica 126
Impressed • Fishley, William 106
Impressed • Goldscheider 122
Impressed • Heinrich 144
Impressed • Heubach 146
India Temple • Ridgway . . . .273 – 276
Indian Curl • Meigh, Charles 217
IONA • Taylor Smith
    & Taylor . . . . .331 – 333
IOW • Isle of Wright 157
IPF • Ilmenau 156
Istanbul • Gustafsberg . . . . .131 – 133
Italy • Edge, Malkin 98
J & C, Flowers • Jaeger 158
J.B. • Balleroy, Julien 24, 25

Japan • Ridgway . . . . .273 – 276
Japonica • Ridgway . . . . . . .273 – 276
JDB • Dressler, Julius 94
JDK • Kestner 169
Jeddo • Adams . . . . .5 – 9
Jeddo • Brown-Westhead,
    Moore 49
JH • Imperial
    Porcelain Factory 292
JP • Petit, Jacob 250
JPS • Seltmann, Johann 307, 308
JS • Schachtel, Joseph 297
JS • Stnact, Josef 326
JST • Hampshire Pottery 138, 139
K • Elfinware 100
K • Kammer 164
K & G • Luneville 165, 166
K.T.K. • Knowles, Taylor,
    Knowles 170
Kaolin • Podmore, Walker 256
Keene • Hampshire Pottery . .138, 139
Keramis • Boch Freres . . . . .36 – 38
KG • Keller & Guerin 165, 166
Kiln • Hulme 151
Knot • Salt & Nixon 295
KPM • Kerafina 168
KPM • Kister, Fr 169
KPM • Krister 171
KPM • Royal Porcelain 172
Kronach • Stockhardt &
    Schmidt-Eckert 327
L • Leach, Bernard 177, 178
L • Lenox 179
L • Lomonosov 196
L • Ludwigsburg 200
L • Sevres 308, 309
L • Sterling China 322, 324
La Francaise • French China 109
LaBelle China • Wheeling
    Pottery 369
Labor And Wait • Co-Operative
    Wholesale Society 71
Lamberton • Maddock 202
Lamberton • Sterling
    China . . . . .322 – 324
Lamp • Swinnertons 328
Lasso • Goodwin Pottery 123
Late Mayers • Keeling 164, 165
Laurel • Bennett, Edwin 30, 31
Laurel • Beyer & Bock 32
Laurel • Gutherz, Oscar & Edgar . .133
Laurel • Porcelain Union 259
Laurel • Schlegelmilch,
    Reinhold 301, 302
Laurel • Schaller, Oscar 297, 298
Laurel • Tirschenreuth 337
Laurel • Utzchneider 343, 344
Laurel • Limoges,
    Wannamakers 193
LCT • Tiffany Pottery 336, 337
LD • Leach, Bernard 177, 178
Leaf • Western Stoneware 367, 368

Leeds • Ashworth . . . . .20 – 22
Leighton Pottery • Bourne
    & Leigh 43, 44
Letter • Longwy Faience . . . .196 – 198
Lettuce Leaf • Wannopee
    Pottery 356
Lewis & Conger • Limoges,
    Charles Ahrenfeldt 183, 184
Lily • Matthews & Clark 207
Lines • Dressel, Kister 94
Lines • Eckert, Richard 97
Lines • Ens, Karl Porcelain 102
Lines • Fasold & Stauch 104
Lines • Greiner, Frederick
    Christian 126
Lines • Levy, Ch. 180
Lines • Minton . . . . .222 – 226
Lines • Rosenthal . . . . .280 – 282
Lines • Royal Copenhagen . .287, 288
Lines • Schaller, Oscar 297, 298
Lines • Scheibe-Alsbach 298
Lines • Seltmann, Johann . . .307, 308
Lines • Sevres 308, 309
Lines • Sitzendorf 313
Lines • Teichert, C. 333
Lines • Teichert, Ernst 334
Lines • Thieme, Carl 334
Lines • Triebner, Ens,
    Eckert 339, 340
Lines • LimogesVignaud 193
Lines & Dots • Leach,
    Bernard 177, 178
Lion • Anchor Pottery 16
Lion • Ashworth . . . . .20 – 22
Lion • Limoges, Bawo
    & Dottter 181
Lion • Bourne & Leigh 43, 44
Lion • British Anchor Pottery 47
Lion • Davenport . . . . .79 – 82
Lion • East End Pottery 96
Lion • Furnivals 111, 112
Lion • Glasgow Pottery 118
Lion • Hutschenreuther . . . .152 – 155
Lion • Kronester 172
Lion • Maddock 201, 202
Lion • Mayer, Thomas 208
Lion • Meakin, Charles 214
Lion • Meigh, Charles 217
Lion • Ott & Brewer 244, 245
Lion • Prospect Hill Pottery 265
Lion • Ridgway . . . . .273 – 276
Lion • Royal Bayreuth 285, 286
Lion • Schumann 305, 306
Lion • Sutherland China 150
Lion • Swillington Bridge 328
Lion • Taylor Bros. 331
Lion • Wade, Heath 352, 353
Lion • Willets 372, 373
Lions • Vodrey & Brothers 350
London Views • Wood, Enoch 376
Lonhuda • Weller
    Pottery . . . . .362 – 365

Lotus • Roseville ....282 – 284
Lotus Ware • Knowles, Taylor
   & Knowles 170
Loy-Nel-Art • McCoy ....208 – 210
LS & S • Straus & Sons, Lewis 327
Luneville • Keller
   & Guerin 165, 166
LuRay • Taylor Smith
   & Taylor ....331 – 333
M • Hopper, Robin 148
M • Manzoni, Carlo 204
M • Minton ....222 – 226
M • Muller, E.&A. 231
M & C • Matthews & Clark 207
M & S • McNicol-Smith 212
Maastricht • Regout,
   Petrus 270, 271
Maddock • Empire 202
Madras • Brownfield, William ...48, 49
Mailbox • Vernon Kilns ....345 – 347
Manhattan • American
   Limoges 13, 14
Marcrest • Western
Stoneware 367, 368
Marine • Phillips, G. 251
Marmorzellan • Galluba
   & Hoffman 112, 113
Mary Wright • Bauer Pottery ...27, 28
Masons • Ashworth ....20 – 22
Meissen • Berlin Porcelain 36
MCP • McCoy ....208 – 210
Meissen • Royal Porcelain ...289, 290
Mehun • Pillivuyt, Charles 253
Meissen • States Porcelain 321
Melba Ware • Wain, H. A. 353
Mellor • Cook Pottery 69
Memory Lane • Royal
China 286, 287
Mettlach • Villeroy
   & Boch ....348 – 350
MF • Mehlem, Franz Anton 216
Mikado • Powell & Bishop ...262, 263
Millenium • Stevenson, Ralph 326
MO • Metzler 220
Monmouth • Western
Stoneware 367, 368
Moon • Bennett, Edwin 30, 31
Moon • Haynes, D. F. 143
Moon • Jones, George 161, 163
Moon • Knowles,
   Taylor, Knowles 170
Moon • Ott & Brewer 244, 245
Moon • Worcester ....378 – 380
Mount Vernon • Hall
 · China ....136 – 138
Mountain • Fukagawa 110
MP • Marblehead Pottery 204
MP • Mountainside Art 231
MPC Co • Mercer 218
MR • Limoges,
   Martial Redon 189, 190
MSC • Minton ....222 – 226

MW&G • Merkelbach 219, 220
MZ • Muller & Co. 231
N • Sandizell 297
N.D. • Rosemeade 280
Nankin • Davenport ....79 – 82
Napco • National Potteries 233
NC • Naudot, Camille 233
NC • Newcomb 235
Neapolitan • Dimmock,
   Thomas 87
NEP • New England Pottery 235
Neutettau • New
   Porcelain Factory 235, 236
New Era • Brunt, William
Pottery 50
New Stone • Brough
   & Blackhurst 48
Newcastle • Maling Pottery 203, 204
Ning Po • Hall, Ralph 136
NM • McCoy ....208 – 210
NMCo • McCoy ....208 – 210
NP • New
   Porcelain Factory 235, 236
NS • Nittsjo Earthenware 238
O & B • Ott & Brewer 244, 245
Oakwood • Cambridge
   Art Pottery 56
OH • Ohme, Hermann 242, 243
Ohio • Leigh Potters 179
Old Curiosity Shop • Royal
   China 286, 287
Old Holland • Universal
Potteries 341, 342
Olive Branch • Precious
Moments ....263 – 265
Opaque China • Sampson,
   Hancock 296
Opaque China • Wallace
   & Chetwynd 354, 355
Opaque Porcelain • Willets ..372, 373
OPCo • Syracuse China 328, 329
Orchids • Bodley, E. J. D. 38
Oriental • Davenport ....79 – 82
Oriental Ivory • Powell
   & Bishop 262, 263
OS • Schlegelmilch, Oscar 301
Oval • Bell, J&MP 29
Oval • Hutschenreuther ....152 – 155
Oval • Langenthal 174
Oval • Metzler 220
Oval • Muller & Co. 231
Oval • Podmore, Walker 256
Oval • Ridgway ....273 – 276
Oval • Schlegelmich,
   Reinhold 301, 302
Oval • Schlegelmilch, Oscar 301
Oval • Schnabel & Sons 304
Oval • Sevres 308, 309
Oval • Sewell 310
Oval • Stellmacher 15, 16, 322
Oval • Stubbs, Joseph 327
Oval • Szeiler Studio 330

Oval • Thomas & Co. 335
Oval • Villeroy & Boch ....348 – 350
Oval • Wedge Wood, James 359
Oven Ware • Watt Pottery ...357, 358
Owensart • Owens Pottery 245
Owl • Bennett, Edwin 30, 31
P • Pilkington 253
P • Plankenhammer 255
P & P • Limoges,
   Paroutaud Freres 190
Palestine • Adams ....5 – 9
Palmyra • Brownfield, William ..48, 49
Panamerican Lei • Vernon
   Kilns ....345 – 347
Papoco • Paden City 246
Paramount • Taylor Smith
   & Taylor ....331 – 333
Pasco • Straub, Paul 327
Pastels • Paden City 246
PB • Porquier Beau 260
PB • Pouplard – Beatrix 262
PD • Dachsel, Paul 78
Peacock China • Brian,
   E. & Co. 45, 46
Peacock • Laughlin ......174 – 177
Pearlstone Ware • Podmore,
   Walker 256
Pelew • Challinor, E. 61, 62
Persia • Adams ....5 – 9
PF • Triebner, Ens, Eckert 339, 340
Pheasant • Winkle, F. 374, 374
Phoenix Ware • Forester,
   Thomas 108
Pitch Fork • Eckert, Richard 97
Pitcher • Taylor Smith
   & Taylor ....331 – 333
Pixie • L. Lourioux 196
Plant • Longwy Faience ....196 – 198
Plus • Leach, Bernard 177, 178
PMP • Plaue 256
Poppy • Universal Potteries ...341, 342
Poppy Trail • Metlox Pottery 220
Porcelaine • Bloch 35
Porcelain of Paris • Bloch, R. 35
Potter • Keeling 164, 165
Pretzel • Brownfield, William 48, 49
Pretzel • Salt & Nixon 295
Prov. Sace • Schegelmilch,
   Erdmann 300
PRP • Paul Revere Pottery ...271, 272
PSL • Pfeiffer & Lowenstein 251
PW&C • Podmore, Walker 256
Q.M.D. • Glasgow Pottery 118
QS • Schutzmeister & Quendt 306
Queen Anne • Ridgway .....273 – 276
Quiver • Ridgway ....273 – 276
R • Rorstrand 278, 279
R • Rosenthal ....280 – 282
R • Roseville ....282 – 284
R • Thomas Porcelain, F. 335
R • Volkstedt 351
R & M • Meredith, Roper 218

R St K • Amphora 15, 16
Rabbit • Dedham Pottery 82, 83
Ram • Gouda 124
Ranchero • Taylor Smith
    & Taylor . . . . .331 – 333
Raven • Trenle Blake 34, 35
RC • Rosenthal . . . . .280 – 282
RF • Watt Pottery 357, 358
RH • Wettina 139
Rhead • Crown Ducal 76
RHR • Robertson 276
Ribbon • Ashworth . . . . .20 – 22
Ribbon • Bell, J&MP 29
Ribbon • Gibson & Son 115, 116
Ribbon • Longwy . . . . .196 – 198
Ribbon • Maddock 202
Ribbon • Minton . . . . .222 – 226
Ribbon • Podmore, Walker 256
Ribbon • Rathbone, T. 267
Ribbon • Ridgway . . . . .273 – 276
Ribbon • Salt & Nixon 295
Ribbon • Stafford Pottery 320
Ribbon • Stevenson & Williams . . .326
Ribbon • Thomas China 335
Ribbon • Till & Sons 337
Ribbon • United China 341
Ribbon • Limoges, Wannamakers . .193
Ribbon • Wheeling Pottery 369
Ribbon • Winkle, F. 374, 375
Ribbon Wedge Wood, James 359
Ringtons • Maling Pottery . . .203, 204
RM • Merkelbach 218. 219
Rockingham • Wedgwood,
    Josiah . . . . .359 – 361
Roloc • McNicol, D. E. . . . .210 – 212
Romany • French China 109
Rooster • Cantagalli 57
Rose • Stellmacher 322
Royal Adderley • Ridgway . . . .273 – 276
Royal Albert • Wild,
    Thomas & Sons 370
Royal Alma • Cone, Thomas 68
Royal Austria • Gutherz, Oscar
    & Edgar 133
Royal Blue • International
    Pottery 156
Royal Cauldon • Brown-Westhead,
    Moore 49
Royal Chelsea • New Chelsea 234
Royal China • International
    Pottery 156
Royal China Works • George
    Grainger Worcester 114, 115
Royal Grafton • Jones, A. B. 160
Royal Lancastrian • Pilkingtons 253
Royal Limoges • Limoges; Gerard,
    Dufraissex & Abbot 187
Royal Malvern • Booths
    & Colcloughs 42
Royal Maytime • Royal
    China 286, 287
Royal Porzellan • Kerafina 168

Royal Rudolstadt • Beyer
    & Bock 32
Royal Sphinx • Regout,
    Petrus 270, 271
Royal Stafford • Poole, Thomas . . .257
Royal Stanley Ware • Colclough
    . . . . .67, 68
Royal Steton • Royal China 286, 287
Royal Stone • Royal China . . .286, 287
Royal Swan • Booths
    & Colcloughs 42
Royal Tudor Ware • Barker
Bros 25, 26
Royal Tuscan • Plant,
    R. H. & S. L. 255
Royal Vale • Colclough 67, 68
Royal Windsor • Palissy
    Pottery 246, 247
Royal Winton • Grimwades . . .127, 128
Rozane • Roseville . . . . .282 – 284
RP • Rookwood 278
RRPCo • Robinson
    Ransbottom 276, 277
RS Germany • Schlegelmilch,
    Reinhold 301, 302
RSK • Teplitz 15, 16
RS Prussia • Schlegelmilch,
    Reinhold 301, 302
Ruku • Radford 266
Rum Rill • Red Wing 268, 269
Russel Wright • Knowles, Taylor
    & Knowles 170
Russel Wright • Sterling
    China . . . . .322 – 324
Russel Wright • Steubenville
    .325, 326
Russel Wright • Tharaud, Justin . . .334
Russel Wright • Bauer Pottery 27, 28
Russia • Lomonosov 196
RW • New York & Rudolstadt 236
S • Fasold & Stauch 104
S • Kister, A. W. 169
S • Scheibe-Alsbach 298
S • Sevres 308, 309
S • Sitzendorf 313
S • Steinmann, K. 321, 322
S • Sterling China . . . . .322 – 324
S • Thieme, Carl 334
S & G • Schiller & Gerbing 300
S & S Tiles • Solon and Schemmel . .315
S V China • Knowles,
    Taylor, Knowles 170
S.P.I. • Southern Potteries . . .315, 316
Sailboat • Precious
    Moments . . . . .263 – 265
Salon China • Salt & Nixon 295
Salto • Bing & Grondahl 33
Santa Rosa • Los Angeles
    Potteries 199
Sardinia • Bell, J&MP 29
Satyr • L. Lourioux 196
Savoy China • Birks, Rawlins 34

Saxony • Fraureuther 108, 109
Scheve Crump Low • Barluet
    & Cie 26
Schierholz • Schierholz, Von 299
Scotia Lake • Campbellfield 56
Scroll • Wood, Enoch 376
Sebring • French China 109
SEG • Revere, Paul Pottery . . .271, 272
Seville • Thompson, C. C. 335
SH • Schoenau & Hoffmeister 304
Shamrock • Limbach 180
Shamrock • Porquier Beau 260
Sheep • Dresden 93
Sheild • Keller & Guerin 165, 166
Sheild • Keramos 168
Shell • Ashworth . . . . .20 – 22
Shell • Pearl China 249
Shell Krest • Paden City 246
Shell Pink • Sterling
    China . . . . .322 – 324
Shelledge • Syracuse
    China 328, 329
Shenandoah • Paden City 246
Sheppards Hook • Dressel, Kister . . .94
Shield • Teplitz 15, 16
Shield • Limoges Ahrenfeldt,
    Charles 183, 184
Shield • Bawo & Dotter 28
Shield • Beyer & Bock 32
Shield • Bloch, B. 35
Shield • Bourne & Leigh 43, 44
Shield • Bovey Pottery 44
Shield • Brown – Westhead,
    Moore 49
Shield • Carstens, C.&E. 58
Shield • East Liverpool
    Pottery 96, 67
Shield • Fielding, S. 104, 105
Shield • Galluba
    & Hoffman 112, 113
Shield • George Grainger . . .114, 115
Shield • LimogesGuerin –
    Pouyat 193, 194
Shield • Hanke, Robert 139
Shield • Hutschenreuther . . .152 – 155
Shield • Kent, James 166, 167
Shield • Lancaster 173
Shield • Laughlin . . . . .174 – 177
Shield • Leonard 179
Shield • Longwy . . . . .196 – 198
Shield • L Lourioux 196
Shield • Maling Pottery 203, 204
Shield • McCoy . . . . .208 – 210
Shield • Mercer 218
Shield • Nymphenburg 241
Shield • Onondaga • Pottery
    .243, 244
Shield • Pioneer Pottery 254
Shield • Ridgway . . . . .273 – 276
Shield • Salt & Nixon 295
Shield • Sampson,
    Bridgwood 295, 296

Shield • French
    Saxon China 109, 110
Shield • Schonwald 304, 305
Shield • Schramberger 305
Shield • Schumann 305, 306
Shield • Schwarzburg 306
Shield • Springer & Co. 320
Shield • Sterling China . . .322 – 324
Shield • Stnact, Josef 326
Shield • Thomas Porcelain, F. 335
Shield • Tirschenreuth 337
Shield • Utzchneider 343, 344
Shield • Schierholz, Von 299
Shield • Wachtersbach 351, 352
Shield • Wahliss, Ernst 353
Shield • Walkure 354
Shield • Wilkinson, Arthur 371, 372
Shield • Willets 372, 373
Shield • Zeh, Scherzer 381, 382
Ship • Adderleys 9, 10
Ship • Altenkunstadt 12
Ship • Furnivals 111, 112
Ship • Grindley 128, 129
Ship • Knowles, Edwin 169, 170
Ship • Marblehead Pottery 204
Ship • Pope-Gosser 258
Ship • Ridgway . . . . .273 – 276
Ship • Stevenson 326
Sicard • Weller Pottery . . . .362 – 365
Silesia • Ohme, Hermann . . .242, 243
Silesia • Royal Porcelain 289, 290
Silesia • Steinmann, K. 321, 322
Silesian • Clementson, J. 64
SMF • Schramberger 305
Snake • Willets 372, 373
Sophienthal • Thomas & Co. 335
South Seas • Ashworth . . . . . .20 – 22
Spade • Barluet & Cie 26
Spaghetti • Watt Pottery 357, 358
Spartan • Podmore, Walker 256
Sphinx • Regout, Petrus 270, 271
SPM • Walkure 354
Square • Decoeur, Emile 82
Square • Goldscheider 122
Square • Iron Mountain 156
Square • Laeuger, Max 173
Square • McCoy . . . . .208 – 210
Square • Samson 296, 297
ST • Schlegelmilch,
    Reinhold 301, 302
Staff • Powell & Bishop 262, 263
Staffordshire • Adams . . . . . . .5 – 9
Stagecoach • Wedgwood, Enoch . . .361
Stanley China • Amison, Charles 11
Star • Ilmenau 156
Star • Merkelbach 218
Star • Mortlock, John 201, 202
Star • Nove 241
Star • Pilkingtons 253
Star • Schlegelmilch,
    Reinhold 301, 302
Star • Schafer & Vater 297

Star • Schoenau & Hoffmeister . . .304
Star • Thompson, C. C. 335
Star • Trenton Potteries 339
Star • Volkstedt 351
Star • Wannopee Pottery 356
Star • Wileman 370, 371
Statue of Liberty • Harker
    Pottery . . . . .139 – 142
Statue Of Liberty • McNicol,
    D. E. . . . . .210 – 212
Stoke Pottery • Grimwades . . .127, 128
Stripes • Langenthal 174
Suhl • Schlegelmilch,
    Reinhold 301, 302
Sun • Gebr. Kuhnlenz 113
Sun • Heubach 146
Sunburst • Wannopee Pottery 356
Sutherland China • Hudson,
    William 149, 150
Swansea Ware • Rhead, Frederick . .272
Swastica • West End Pottery 366
Sweden • Upsala-Ekeby 343
Swiss Scenery • Swift, John 328
Sword • Bennett, Edwin 30, 31
Sword • West End Pottery 366
Swords • Samson 296, 297
Syracuse China • Onondaga
    Pottery 243, 244
T • Royal Bayreuth 285, 286
T • Taylor, Tunnicliffe 330
T • Thewalt 334
T • Thieme, Carl 334
T • Thompson, C. C. 335
T. F. & S. • Forester, Thomas 108
TAC • Trenton Potteries 339
Tavern • Barker Bros. 25, 26
Taylorton • Taylor Smith
    & Taylor . . . . .331 – 333
Tazza • Schonwald 304, 305
Teapot • Pottery Guild 261
Teco • American Terra Cotta
    & Ceramic 14
Tepco • Trenton Potteries 339
Teplitz • Amphora 15, 16
Teplitz • Stellmacher 322
Tettau • Royal Bayreuth 285, 286
Thomas • Rosenthal . . . . . .280 – 282
Three Balls • Precious
    Moments . . . . .263 – 265
Three Crowns • Rorstrand . .278, 279
Three Dots • Minton . . . . . .222 – 226
Three Dots • Porquier, Adolphe . . .260
Tokay • Hull Pottery 150, 151
Tophat • Regency China 270
Torch • Wheeling Pottery 369
TR • Maling Pottery 203, 204
Treble Clef • Precious
    Moments . . . . .263 – 265
Tree • Ashtead Potters 20
Tree • Ashworth . . . . .20 – 22
Tree • Iron Mountain 156
Tree • Paragon 248, 249

Tree • Precious Moments . . .263 – 265
Tree • Ridgway . . . . .273 – 276
Tree • Schlegelmilch,
    Reinhold 301, 302
Tree • Schnabel & Sons 304
Tree • Schonwald 304, 305
Tree • Swasey, E. 327
Trees • Haas & Czjzek 133, 134
Triangle • Amphora 15, 16
Triangle • Dux Porcelain 95, 96
Triangle • Maling, C. T. 203, 204
Triangle • Plankenhammer 255
Triangle • Precious
    Moments . . . . .263 – 265
Triangle • Sevres 308, 309
Triangle • Simon Peter Gerz 115
Triangle • Thewalt 334
Triangle • Utzchneider 343, 344
Triangle • Van Briggle 344
Trident • Hopper, Robin 148
Trident • Seltmann,
    Johann 307, 308
Trident • Triebner,
    Ens, Eckert 339, 340
Trilby • Glasgow Pottery 118
Tropico • Gladding
    McBean . . . . .116 – 118
Trumpet • Precious
    Moments . . . . .263 – 265
TST • Taylor Smith Taylor . . .331 – 333
TT • Takito 330
Turn Teplitz • Amphora 15, 16
Turn Teplitz • Dachsel, Paul 78
Turn Wien • Wahliss, Ernst 353
Tuscan • Plant, R. H. & S. L. 255
TV • LimogesTressemanes
    & Vogt 192
Twisted Rope • Brownfield,
    William 48, 49
Tyrolean • Ridgway . . . . . . .273 – 276
U & C • Utzchneider 343, 344
U.N.F. • Frankoma 108
UC • University City Pottery 342
UE • Upsala-Ekeby 343
UND • North Dakota 342
Unicorn • Hornberg 148, 149
Unicorn • Pope-Gosser 258
Unicorn • Wedgwood . . . .359 – 361
Union K • Porcelain Union 259
Unique • Beech & Hancock 28
UPCo • Ungemach 340
UPW • Union
    Porcelain Works 340, 341
Urn • Podmore, Walker 256
Urn • Pope Gosser 258
Urn • Ridgway . . . . .273 – 276
Urn • Stellmacher 322
Urn • Szeiler Studio 330
Urn • Wehinger, H. 362
Urn • West End Pottery 366
Urn • Winkle 374, 375
Urn • Wood & Sons 377, 378

Utopian • Owens Pottery 245
Vance • Avon Faience 23
Vale China • Colclough 67, 68
Valencia • Sampson, Hancock 296
Valentine • Wild
   & Sons, Thomas 370
Vase • Altrohlau Porcelain 12
Vase • Creil & Montereau 74
Vase • Dressler, Julius 94
Vase • Knowles, Edwin 169, 170
Vase • Teplitz 15, 16, 322
Vase • West End Pottery 366
Vase • Winkle 374, 375
Vase • Wood & Sons 377, 378
VB • Villeroy & Boch . . . . . .348 – 350
VB&M • Villeroy & Boch . . . .348 – 350
VBS • Villeroy & Boch . . . . . .348 – 350
Victoria • Cartwright
   & Edwards 58, 59
Victoria • Schmidt 303
Vienna • Leonard 179
Vienna • Teplitz 15, 16, 322
Vistosa • Taylor Smith
   & Taylor . . . . .331 – 333
Vogue • Aynsley 24
Vogue • Brush McCoy 50
Vohenstrauss • Seltmann,
   Johann 307, 308
Volkstedt • Beyer & Bock 32
VP • Kunst 172

W • Worcester . . . . .378 – 380
W • Wallendorf 355
W • Limoges, Wannamakers 193
W • Wannopee Pottery 356
W • Wehinger, H. 362
W • Winkle 374, 375
W & C • Wallace
   & Chetwynd 354, 355
W&Co • Wardle 356
W&Co • Whittaker & Co. 370
W.B.P • Brunt, William Pottery 50
W.S. Coleman • Minton . . . .222 – 226
WA • Wagner & Apel 353
Waco China • East
   Liverpool Pottery 96, 97
Wagons • Vernon Kilns . . . . .345 – 347
Warwick • Podmore, Walker 256
Washington Ware • Podmore,
   Walker 256
Watcombe • Torquay 338
Watteau • Doulton . . . . .88 – 93
Waves • Hornsea 149
WC • Roman
   Ceramic Corporation 278
WC • Wileman 370, 371
WC • Willets 372, 373
Welmar • Carstens, C.&E. 58
Wemyss • Heron, Robert 145
WEPCo • West End Pottery 366
Westward Ho • Wallace China 355

Wheel • Hochst 147
Whieldon Ware • Winkle,
   F. 374, 375
Willow Art • Hewitt
   & Leadbeater 146
Wincester • Vernon Kilns . . .345 – 347
Wings • Plant, R. H. & S. L. 255
Wings • Powell & Bishop 262, 263
WJW • Walley Pottery 355
WM • Moorcroft 227, 228
WMCo • Willets 372, 373
Wolf • Boch Freres . . . . .36 – 38
Worcester • George Grainger
   Worcester 114, 115
World • R. J. Ernst Enterprises 267
WP • Wheeling Pottery 369
Wreath • Schlegelmilch,
   Reinhold 301, 302
WSCo • Western Stoneware . . .367, 368
WW • Wilkinson, Arthur 371, 372
X • Hutschenreuther . . . . . . .152 – 155
X • Kister, A. W. 169
X • Levy, Ch. 180
X • Sevres 308, 309
X • Thieme, Carl 334
X • Limoges, Vignaud 193
York P • Pfaltgraff 250, 251
Zell • Schmider, Georg 303
ZS&Co • Zeh, Scherzer 381, 382

DOLLS, FIGURES & TEDDY BEARS

6315 **American Character Dolls**, Izen $24.95
6317 **Arranbee Dolls**, The Dolls that Sell on Sight, DeMillar/Brevik $24.95
2079 **Barbie Doll** Fashion, Volume I, Eames $24.95
4846 **Barbie Doll** Fashion, Volume II, Eames $24.95
6319 **Barbie Doll** Fashion, Volume III, Eames $29.95
6022 The **Barbie Doll** Years, 5th Ed., Olds $19.95
5352 Collector's Ency. of **Barbie** Doll Exclusives & More, 2nd Ed., Augustyniak .$24.95
5904 Collector's Guide to **Celebrity Dolls**, Spurgeon $24.95
5599 Collector's Guide to **Dolls of the 1960s and 1970s**, Sabulis $24.95
6030 Collector's Guide to **Horsman Dolls**, Jensen $29.95
6224 **Doll Values**, Antique to Modern, 7th Ed., Moyer $12.95
6033 **Modern Collectible Dolls**, Volume VI, Moyer $24.95
5689 **Nippon Dolls** & Playthings, Van Patten/Lau $29.95
5365 **Peanuts Collectibles**, Podley/Bang $24.95
6336 Official **Precious Moments** Collector's Guide to Company **Dolls**, Bomm ...$19.95
6026 **Small Dolls** of the 40s & 50s, Stover $29.95
5253 Story of **Barbie**, 2nd Ed., Westenhouser $24.95
5277 **Talking Toys** of the 20th Century, Lewis $15.95
2084 **Teddy Bears**, Annalee's & Steiff Animals, 3rd Series, Mandel $19.95
4880 World of **Raggedy Ann** Collectibles, Avery $24.95

TOYS & MARBLES

2333 Antique & Collectible **Marbles**, 3rd Ed., Grist $9.95
5900 Collector's Guide to **Battery Toys**, 2nd Edition, Hultzman $24.95
4566 Collector's Guide to **Tootsietoys**, 2nd Ed., Richter $19.95
5169 Collector's Guide to **TV Toys** & Memorabilia, 2nd Ed., Davis/Morgan $24.95
5593 Grist's Big Book of **Marbles**, 2nd Ed. $24.95
3970 Grist's Machine-Made & Contemporary **Marbles**, 2nd Ed. $9.95
6128 **Hot Wheels**, The Ultimate Redline Guide, 1968 – 1977, Clark/Wicker $24.95
5830 **McDonald's** Collectibles, 2nd Edition, Henriques/DuVall $24.95
6237 **Rubber Toy Vehicles**, Leopard $19.95
6340 **Schroeder's Collectible Toys**, Antique to Modern Price Guide, 9th Ed. $17.95
5908 **Toy Car** Collector's Guide, Johnson $19.95

FURNITURE

3716 American **Oak** Furniture, Book II, McNerney $12.95
1118 Antique **Oak** Furniture, Hill $7.95
3720 Collector's Encyclopedia of **American** Furniture, Vol. III, Swedberg $24.95
5359 Early **American** Furniture, Obbard $12.95
3906 **Heywood-Wakefield** Modern Furniture, Rouland $18.95
6338 **Roycroft** Furniture & Collectibles, Koon $24.95
6343 **Stickley Brothers** Furniture, Koon $24.95
1885 **Victorian** Furniture, Our American Heritage, McNerney $9.95
3829 **Victorian** Furniture, Our American Heritage, Book II, McNerney $9.95

JEWELRY, HATPINS, WATCHES & PURSES

4704 Antique & Collectible **Buttons**, Wisniewski $19.95
6323 **Christmas Pins**, Past & Present, 2nd Edition, Gallina $19.95
4850 Collectible **Costume Jewelry**, Simonds $24.95
5675 Collectible **Silver Jewelry**, Rezazadeh $24.95
4940 **Costume Jewelry**, A Practical Handbook & Value Guide, Rezazadeh $24.95
5812 Fifty Years of Collectible **Fashion Jewelry**, 1925 – 1975, Baker $24.95

6330 **Handkerchiefs**: A Collector's Guide, Guarnaccia/Guggenheim $24.95
1424 **Hatpins** & Hatpin Holders, Baker $9.95
5695 **Ladies' Vintage Accessories**, Bruton $24.95
1181 100 Years of Collectible **Jewelry**, 1850 – 1950, Baker $9.95
6337 **Purse Masterpieces**, Schwartz $29.95
4729 **Sewing Tools** & Trinkets, Thompson $24.95
6038 **Sewing Tools** & Trinkets, Volume 2, Thompson $24.95
6039 Signed Beauties of **Costume Jewelry**, Brown $24.95
6341 Signed Beauties of **Costume Jewelry**, Volume II, Brown $24.95
5620 Unsigned Beauties of **Costume Jewelry**, Brown $24.95
4878 Vintage & Contemporary **Purse Accessories**, Gerson $24.95
5696 Vintage & Vogue Ladies' **Compacts**, 2nd Edition, Gerson $29.95
5923 **Vintage Jewelry** for Investment & Casual Wear, Edeen $24.95

ARTIFACTS, GUNS, KNIVES, TOOLS, PRIMITIVES

6021 **Arrowheads** of the Central Great Plains, Fox $19.95
1868 Antique **Tools**, Our American Heritage, McNerney $9.95
4943 Field Gde. to Flint **Arrowheads & Knives** of the N. American Indian, Tully ...$9.95
3885 **Indian Artifacts** of the Midwest, Book II, Hothem $16.95
4870 **Indian Artifacts** of the Midwest, Book III, Hothem $18.95
5685 **Indian Artifacts** of the Midwest, Book IV, Hothem $19.95
6132 **Modern Guns**, Identification & Values, 14th Ed., Quertermous $14.95
1759 **Primitives**, Our American Heritage, 2nd Series, McNerney $14.95
6031 Standard **Knife** Collector's Guide, 4th Ed., Ritchie & Stewart $14.95

PAPER COLLECTIBLES & BOOKS

5902 **Boys' & Girls' Book** Series, Jones $19.95
5153 Collector's Guide to **Children's Books**, 1850 to 1950, Volume II, Jones $19.95
1441 Collector's Guide to **Post Cards**, Wood $9.95
2081 Guide to Collecting **Cookbooks**, Allen $14.95
2080 Price Guide to **Cookbooks** & Recipe Leaflets, Dickinson $9.95
3973 **Sheet Music** Reference & Price Guide, 2nd Ed., Pafik & Guiheen $19.95
6041 Vintage **Postcards** for the Holidays, Reed $24.95

GLASSWARE

5602 Anchor Hocking's **Fire-King** & More, 2nd Ed. $24.95
6321 **Carnival Glass**, The Best of the Best, Edwards/Carwile $29.95
5823 Collectible **Glass Shoes**, 2nd Edition, Wheatley $24.95
6325 Coll. **Glassware** from the 40s, 50s & 60s, 7th Ed., Florence $19.95
1810 Collector's Encyclopedia of **American Art Glass**, Shuman $29.95
6327 Collector's Encyclopedia of **Depression Glass**, 16th Ed., Florence $19.95
1961 Collector's Encyclopedia of **Fry Glassware**, Fry Glass Society $24.95
1664 Collector's Encyclopedia of **Heisey Glass**, 1925 – 1938, Bredehoft $24.95
3905 Collector's Encyclopedia of **Milk Glass**, Newbound $24.95
5820 Collector's Guide to **Glass Banks**, Reynolds $24.95
6454 **Crackle Glass** From Around the World, Weitman $24.95
6334 Encyclopedia of **Paden City Glass**, Domitz $24.95
3981 Evers' Standard **Cut Glass** Value Guide $12.95
6462 Florence's **Glass Kitchen Shakers**, 1930 – 1950s $19.95
5042 Florence's **Glassware Pattern Identification** Guide, Vol. I $18.95
5615 Florence's **Glassware Pattern Identification** Guide, Vol. II $19.95
6142 Florence's **Glassware Pattern Identification** Guide, Vol. III $19.95
4719 **Fostoria**, Etched, Carved & Cut Designs, Vol. II, Kerr $24.95

~26	**Fostoria** Value Guide, Long/Seate $19.95
399	**Glass & Ceramic Baskets**, White $19.95
160	**Glass Animals**, Second Edition, Spencer $24.95
27	The **Glass Candlestick** Book, Volume 1, Akro Agate to Fenton, Felt/Stoer .$24.95
28	The **Glass Candlestick** Book, Volume 2, Fostoria to Jefferson, Felt/Stoer ..$24.95
161	The **Glass Candlestick** Book, Volume 3, Kanawha to Wright, Felt/Stoer $29.95
29	**Glass Tumblers**, 1860s to 1920s, Bredehoft $29.95
44	**Imperial Carnival Glass**, Burns $18.95
27	**Kitchen Glassware** of the Depression Years, 6th Ed., Florence $24.95
00	Much More Early American **Pattern Glass**, Metz $17.95
33	**Mt. Washington Art Glass**, Sisk $49.95
36	Pocket Guide to **Depression Glass** & More, 13th Ed., Florence $12.95
48	Standard Encyclopedia of **Carnival Glass**, 9th Ed., Edwards/Carwile $29.95
49	Standard **Carnival Glass** Price Guide, 14th Ed., Edwards/Carwile $9.95
035	Standard Encyclopedia of **Opalescent Glass**, 4th Ed., Edwards/Carwile $24.95
41	Treasures of **Very Rare Depression Glass**, Florence $39.95

POTTERY

929	**American Art Pottery**, Sigafoose $24.95
312	**Blue & White Stoneware**, McNerney $9.95
351	Collectible **Cups & Saucers**, Harran $18.95
326	Collectible **Cups & Saucers**, Book III, Harran $24.95
344	Collectible **Vernon Kilns**, 2nd Edition, Nelson $29.95
331	Collecting **Head Vases**, Barron $24.95
373	**Collector's Encyclopedia of American Dinnerware**, Cunningham $24.95
931	**Collector's Encyclopedia of Bauer Pottery**, Chipman $24.95
034	**Collector's Encyclopedia of California Pottery**, 2nd Ed., Chipman $24.95
723	**Collector's Encyclopedia of Cookie Jars**, Book II, Roerig $24.95
939	**Collector's Encyclopedia of Cookie Jars**, Book III, Roerig $24.95
748	**Collector's Encyclopedia of Fiesta**, 9th Ed., Huxford $24.95
961	**Collector's Encyclopedia of Early Noritake**, Alden $24.95
312	**Collector's Encyclopedia of Flow Blue China**, 2nd Ed., Gaston $24.95
431	**Collector's Encyclopedia of Homer Laughlin China**, Jasper $24.95
276	**Collector's Encyclopedia of Hull Pottery**, Roberts $19.95
609	**Collector's Encyclopedia of Limoges Porcelain**, 3rd Ed., Gaston $29.95
334	**Collector's Encyclopedia of Majolica Pottery**, Katz-Marks $19.95
358	**Collector's Encyclopedia of McCoy Pottery**, Huxford $19.95
677	**Collector's Encyclopedia of Niloak**, 2nd Edition, Gifford $29.95
564	**Collector's Encyclopedia of Pickard China**, Reed $29.95
679	**Collector's Encyclopedia of Red Wing Art Pottery**, Dollen $24.95
618	**Collector's Encyclopedia of Rosemeade Pottery**, Dommel $24.95
841	**Collector's Encyclopedia of Roseville Pottery**, Revised, Huxford/Nickel ... $24.95
842	**Collector's Encyclopedia of Roseville Pottery**, 2nd Series, Huxford/Nickel. $24.95
917	**Collector's Encyclopedia of Russel Wright**, 3rd Editon, Kerr $29.95
921	**Collector's Encyclopedia of Stangl Artware**, Lamps, and Birds, Runge ..$29.95
314	**Collector's Encyclopedia of Van Briggle Art Pottery**, Sasicki $24.95
680	**Collector's Guide to Feather Edge Ware**, McAllister $19.95
124	**Collector's Guide to Made in Japan Ceramics**, Book IV, White $24.95
425	**Cookie Jars**, Westfall $9.95
440	**Cookie Jars**, Book II, Westfall $19.95
316	Decorative **American Pottery & Whiteware**, Wilby $29.95
909	**Dresden Porcelain** Studios, Harran $29.95
918	**Florence's Big Book of Salt & Pepper Shakers** $24.95
320	Gaston's **Blue Willow**, 3rd Edition $19.95
379	Lehner's Ency. of **U.S. Marks** on Pottery, Porcelain & China $24.95
722	**McCoy Pottery**, Collector's Reference & Value Guide, Hanson/Nissen $19.95
913	**McCoy Pottery**, Volume III, Hanson & Nissen $24.95
333	**McCoy Pottery Wall Pockets** & Decorations, Nissen $24.95
135	**North Carolina Art Pottery**, 1900 – 1960, James/Leftwich $24.95
335	Pictorial Guide to **Pottery & Porcelain Marks**, Lage $29.95

5691	**Post86 Fiesta**, Identification & Value Guide, Racheter $19.95
1670	**Red Wing Collectibles**, DePasquale $9.95
1440	**Red Wing Stoneware**, DePasquale & Thomas $9.95
6037	**Rookwood Pottery**, Nicholson & Thomas $24.95
6236	**Rookwood Pottery**, 10 Years of Auction Results, 1990 – 2002, Treadway $39.95
1632	**Salt & Pepper Shakers**, Guarnaccia $9.95
5091	**Salt & Pepper Shakers** II, Guarnaccia $18.95
3443	**Salt & Pepper Shakers** IV, Guarnaccia $18.95
3738	**Shawnee Pottery**, Mangus $24.95
4629	Turn of the Century **American Dinnerware**, 1880s–1920s, Jasper $24.95
5924	**Zanesville Stoneware** Company, Rans, Ralston & Russell $24.95

OTHER COLLECTIBLES

5916	Advertising **Paperweights**, Holiner & Kammerman $24.95
5838	Advertising **Thermometers**, Merritt $16.95
5898	Antique & Contemporary **Advertising Memorabilia**, Summers $24.95
5814	Antique **Brass & Copper** Collectibles, Gaston $24.95
1880	Antique **Iron**, McNerney $9.95
3872	Antique **Tins**, Dodge $24.95
4845	Antique **Typewriters & Office Collectibles**, Rehr $19.95
5607	Antiquing and Collecting on the **Internet**, Parry $12.95
1128	**Bottle** Pricing Guide, 3rd Ed., Cleveland $7.95
6345	**Business & Tax Guide** for Antiques & Collectibles, Kelly $14.95
6225	Captain John's **Fishing Tackle** Price Guide, Kolbeck/Lewis $19.95
3718	Collectible **Aluminum**, Grist $16.95
6342	Collectible **Soda Pop** Memorabilia, Summers $24.95
5060	Collectible **Souvenir Spoons**, Bednersh $19.95
5676	Collectible **Souvenir Spoons**, Book II, Bednersh $29.95
5666	**Collector's Encyclopedia of Granite Ware**, Book 2, Greguire $29.95
5836	**Collector's Guide to Antique Radios**, 5th Ed., Bunis $19.95
3966	**Collector's Guide to Inkwells**, Identification & Values, Badders $18.95
4947	**Collector's Guide to Inkwells**, Book II, Badders $19.95
5681	**Collector's Guide to Lunchboxes**, White $19.95
4864	**Collector's Guide to Wallace Nutting Pictures**, Ivankovich $18.95
5683	**Fishing Lure** Collectibles, Vol. 1, Murphy/Edmisten $29.95
6328	**Flea Market Trader**, 14th Ed., Huxford $12.95
6227	**Garage Sale** & Flea Market Annual, 11th Edition, Huxford $19.95
4945	**G-Men and FBI Toys** and Collectibles, Whitworth $18.95
3819	**General Store** Collectibles, Wilson $24.95
5912	The **Heddon** Legacy, A Century of Classic **Lures**, Roberts & Pavey $29.95
2216	**Kitchen Antiques**, 1790–1940, McNerney $14.95
5991	**Lighting Devices** & Accessories of the 17th – 19th Centuries, Hamper $9.95
5686	**Lighting Fixtures** of the Depression Era, Book I, Thomas $24.95
4950	The **Lone Ranger**, Collector's Reference & Value Guide, Felbinger $18.95
6028	Modern **Fishing Lure** Collectibles, Vol. 1, Lewis $24.95
6131	Modern **Fishing Lure** Collectibles, Vol. 2, Lewis $24.95
6322	Pictorial Guide to **Christmas Ornaments** & Collectibles, Johnson $29.95
2026	**Railroad** Collectibles, 4th Ed., Baker $14.95
5619	**Roy Rogers and Dale Evans** Toys & Memorabilia, Coyle $24.95
6339	**Schroeder's Antiques** Price Guide, 22nd Edition $14.95
5007	**Silverplated Flatware**, Revised 4th Edition, Hagan $18.95
6239	**Star Wars** Super Collector's Wish Book, 2nd Ed., Carlton $29.95
6139	Summers' Guide to **Coca-Cola**, 4th Ed. $24.95
6324	Summers' Pocket Guide to **Coca-Cola**, 4th Ed. $12.95
3977	Value Guide to **Gas Station Memorabilia**, Summers & Priddy $24.95
4877	Vintage **Bar Ware**, Visakay $24.95
5925	The Vintage Era of **Golf Club Collectibles**, John $29.95
6010	The Vintage Era of **Golf Club Collectibles** Collector's **Log**, John $9.95
6036	Vintage **Quilts**, Aug, Newman & Roy $24.95
4935	The **W.F. Cody Buffalo Bill** Collector's Guide with Values $24.95

This is only a partial listing of the books on antiques that are available from Collector Books. All books are well illustrated and contain current values. Most of these books are available from your local bookseller, antique dealer, or public library. If you are unable to locate certain titles in your area, you may order by mail from **COLLECTOR BOOKS**, P.O. Box 3009, Paducah, KY 42002-3009. Customers with Visa, Master Card, or Discover may phone in orders from 7:00 a.m. to 5:00 p.m. CT, Monday – Friday, toll free **1-800-626-5420**, or online at **www.collectorbooks.com**. Add 3.00 for postage for the first book ordered and 50¢ for each additional book. Include item number, title, and price when ordering. Allow 14 to 21 days for delivery.

1-800-626-5420   Fax: 1-270-898-8890

www.collectorbooks.com

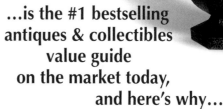